The Tobacco Lords

A Study of the
Tobacco Merchants of Glasgow
and their Trading Activities
c.1740–90

T. M. DEVINE

For my Mother and Father

This edition published in 2024 by
John Donald, an imprint of
Birlinn Ltd
West Newington House
10 Newington Road
Edinburgh
EH9 1QS

www.birlinn.co.uk

ISBN: 978 0 85976 725 5

First published in 1975 by
John Donald Publishers Ltd, Edinburgh

Copyright © T.M. Devine, 1975

The right of T.M. Devine to be identified as the author of
this work has been asserted by him in accordance
with the Copyright, Designs and Patents Act, 1988

All rights reserved. No part of this publication may
be reproduce, stored, or transmitted in any form, or
by any means, electronic, mechanical or photocopying,
recording, or otherwise, without the express written
permission of the publisher.

British Library Cataloguing-in-Publication Data
A catalogue record for this book is available
on request from the British Library

Printed and bound by Ashford Press Ltd, Gosport

Note from the Author

This monograph, my first book, was originally published in 1975, almost half a century ago. I am grateful to Birlinn for their decision to reprint it in their John Donald history series, the imprint under which the study first appeared. The text has not been altered or amended in any way. At first I was tempted to write a revised version which would include material from research undertaken since the 1970s. After consultation with expert colleagues in the field, however, I decided to leave the text as first composed so many years ago. The advice was that my key conclusions of 1975 had not been superseded to date and the volume could therefore be said to have stood the test of time.

The huge expansion of the transatlantic tobacco trade in the eighteenth century depended in the final analysis on chattel slavery. Over the last two decades or so, important work has been done on those connections between Scotland and black slavery between the later seventeenth and mid nineteenth centuries. Indeed, that subject is now a central part of modern Scottish historiography.

The reader will obviously find references to enslaved labour in this book but there is no extensive treatment of the topic. Quite simply (and wrongly), it was not on the research agenda of scholars of modern Scottish history when *The Tobacco Lords* was written nearly fifty years ago. Black slavery as the foundation of the colonial plantation economies was of course well known but did not attract analysis of any depth in Scottish academe. I have explored the reasons for this lack of interest (or amnesia?) in one of the chapters in my edited collection *Recovering Scotland's Slavery Past* (2015).

Moreover, as the title of this present book suggests, it was never intended to be a comprehensive study of the Scottish tobacco trade or the colonial plantation systems in their entirety but was rather designed as a focused examination of the elite Glaswegian merchant community and their associated trading regimes.

Over the last twenty five years, however, I have published widely on Scotland and black slavery. For those readers interested in this new work and how it might help to provide further context for the book, I have appended below a short list of the main contributions.

Scotland's Empire 1600–1815 (2003); 'Did Slavery Make Scotia Great?', *Britain and the World*, 4:1 (2011); *To the Ends of the Earth: Scotland's Global Diaspora 1750–2010* (2011); (ed.) *Recovering Scotland's Slavery Past* (2015), including my chapters on 'Scotland and Transatlantic Slavery', 'Lost to History', 'Did Slavery Make Scotia Great? A Question Revisited', 'History, Scotland and Slavery'.

Tom Devine
Professor Emeritus Sir Thomas Martin Devine
University of Edinburgh

Common Abbreviations

BM	British Museum
CSP	Court of Session Process
EUL	Edinburgh University Library
Econ. Hist. Rev.	Economic History Review
GCA	Glasgow City Archives
GRS	General Register of Sasines
LC	Library of Congress, Washington
ML	Mitchell Library, Glasgow
NLS	National Library of Scotland
PP	Parliamentary Papers
PRO	Public Record Office
PRS	Particular Register of Sasines
SHR	Scottish Historical Review
SL	Signet Library, Edinburgh
SRO	Scottish Record Office
UP	Unextracted Process
UOS	University of Strathclyde

Preface

The rise of Glasgow and its satellite ports to a position of dominance in the American tobacco trade is one of the great success stories of Scottish economic history. Before the eighteenth century Glasgow was already expanding in wealth and population, leaping up the burghal league table, for instance, from a position of eleventh in 1535 to second in 1670. Yet, despite this early growth, the town was still but an important centre of regional activity in an economy widely recognised as more primitive than its neighbour to the south and much inferior to that of such continental states as Holland.[1] In the eighteenth century, however, this old cathedral town and provincial market centre was transformed into an entrepôt of international standing with a sophisticated financial and commercial system and a vigorous urban culture. Several influences coalesced to produce this revolution. Of primary importance, however, was the importation and sale, mainly in European markets, of tobacco grown in the British colonies of North America.

Cold statistics reveal more dramatically than literary generalisation the vital role of this single commodity. In the middle decades of the eighteenth century tobacco formed just less than half of *all* Scottish imports from outside the United Kingdom by value. In the 1760s and 1770s all but two per cent of this total was channelled through the two Clyde ports of Greenock and Port Glasgow. In reality, however, these were simply transhipment points. Financial control lay farther up the unimproved Clyde at Glasgow. As a leading historian of the trade has observed, 'For all practical purposes, Glasgow was Scotland as far as the tobacco trade was concerned'.[2]

In the perspective of Britain as a whole the achievement was, in a sense, even more remarkable. From early beginnings in the later seventeenth century, first by illegally trading with the English colonies or by freighting English (usually Whitehaven) vessels, the Glasgow men soon became a force to be reckoned with in transatlantic commerce.[3] The Treaty of Union of 1707 was the precondition for future development since it permitted the Scots to purchase tobacco for the first time from North American planters on a legal basis. Nevertheless Union in itself was not a sufficient cause of rapid expansion and in subsequent decades, though the secular trend was upwards, the Glasgow colonial trades were punctuated by stagnation, slow growth and periodic crisis.[4] From the 1740s, on the other hand, the importation of tobacco at the Clyde ports began a seemingly irresistible rise. In one year in the 1750s, Scottish imports passed those of both London and the English outports combined! For most of the rest of the period Glasgow struggled with the capital for the position of first tobacco port in the kingdom.

Strangely, however, despite the undoubted importance of the Glasgow tobacco trade in the commercial history of Scotland it has failed, in the main, to attract systematic treatment from scholars. The hagiographers and antiquarians which Victorian Glasgow produced in such rich profusion were indeed fascinated by the story but most of their work was done in a spirit of civic pride rather than in one of historical detachment.[5] In the present century it has been left to American and English historians to describe various facets of the trade's expansion. Professor Jacob Price, in several important works, has explained Glasgow's achievement, examined the structure of eighteenth century demand for tobacco and provided the definitive account of the French market which was so crucial to Glasgow's success.[6] Another American, J. H. Soltow, focused briefly on the commercial activities of the Scots merchants in Virginia[7] and Professor T. C. Barker dealt with the controversial issue of smuggling in the trade in the first few decades of the eighteenth century.[8]

Here it is intended merely to fill some of the many gaps which remain in present knowledge. I have no intention of writing a history of the Scottish tobacco trade, at least not in this volume. Such an undertaking would require a detailed study of the period before the mid-eighteenth century. Here the concentration will be on the 'golden age' after c. 1740. The aim, quite simply, will be to try and answer some pertinent questions about this period.

The focus will be mainly, though not exclusively, on the merchants who prosecuted the trade. Who were they? How many were there? What did they do with the profits they earned? How far were their investments responsible for economic growth in eighteenth century Scotland? A second major area of interest will be trading methods; in particular, an effort will be made to isolate those features, peculiar to the Glasgow trade, which made it successful. Finally, the period of the American War of Independence will be examined in detail. Did the breakdown in political relations with Glasgow's customers destroy merchant fortunes and end the era of the city's supremacy in Atlantic commerce? How far were investments re-deployed in the domestic economy or elsewhere because of the foreign trade crisis?

In trying to answer these questions I have been fortunate to have had the assistance, over the years, of a number of individuals who freely gave of their time and advice. I am indebted for the stimulus provided by my former teachers, now colleagues, in the Department of History, University of

Strathclyde. Three members of that Department, Professor S. G. E. Lythe, Dr. J. H. Treble and Dr. John Butt, have all read parts of the book and have made many useful suggestions for improvement. The last named also gave wise counsel when the research was in its early stages. It need hardly be added that any errors of commission and omission which remain are my own.

I am glad also to be able to make public acknowledgment of the help given by Mr. Stuart Butler, University of St. Andrews (who lent me his transcripts of the important Dunlop Papers), Mrs. Monica Clough and the Directors of James Finlay and Co. Glasgow (for permission to use the Finlay MSS) and Major Crichton-Maitland, Houston, Renfrewshire who gave access to the invaluable Speirs Papers. The staffs of the following institutions were equally generous with their professional advice: the City Archives, the Mitchell Library, Baillie's Institution Library, Glasgow University Library and the Inter-Library Loan Section, Andersonian Library, University of Strathclyde (all in Glasgow); the Scottish Record Office, National Library of Scotland, Signet Library, Edinburgh University Library (Edinburgh); the Public Record Office and British Museum (London).

I am grateful to the editor of the *Journal of Economic History* for permission to use statistical material printed in Professor Richard B. Sheridan's article, 'The British Credit Crisis of 1772 and the American Colonies', XX (1960), 180. I am also indebted to the Council of Scottish History for permission to include Table XXVIII in this volume which formerly appeared in Miss Barbara Crispin's article, 'Clyde Shipping and the American War', *Scottish Historical Review*, 41 (1962). Finally, the editors of *Transport History, Business History* and the *Scottish Historical Review* kindly allowed me to reproduce information taken from my own articles published in their respective journals.

The illustration, an eighteenth century view of Port Glasgow, on which the jacket design is based, was kindly supplied by the Mitchell Library, Glasgow.

Finally, on a more personal note, it must be recorded that my wife and two daughters, by their patience and encouragement, were ultimately responsible for the completion of a project which often seemed elusive.

REFERENCES

1. T. C. Smout, 'The Development and Enterprise of Glasgow, 1556–1707', *Scot. Journ. Pol. Econ.*, VII (1960).
2. Jacob M. Price, 'The Rise of Glasgow in the Chesapeake Tobacco Trade, 1707–1775, reprinted in P. L. Payne (ed.), *Studies in Scottish Business History* (London, 1967), 301.
3. Smout, *loc. cit.;* Theodora Keith, *Commercial Relations of England and Scotland, 1603–1707* (1910), 112–18.
4. H. Hamilton, *An Economic History of Scotland in the Eighteenth Century* (Oxford, 1963), 256–58; Price, *loc. cit.*, 300.

5. The one exception to this criticism is a work, albeit from a later period, by James Gourlay: *A Glasgow Miscellany: the Tobacco Period in Glasgow 1707–75* (privately printed n.d.).
6. See Price *loc. cit.;* 'The Economic Growth of the Chesapeake and the European Market', *Journ. of Econ. Hist.*, XXIV (1964); *France and the Chesapeake*, 2 vols. (Michigan, 1973).
7. 'Scottish Traders in Virginia, 1750–1775', *Econ. Hist. Rev.*, 2nd ser., XII (1959).
8. 'Smuggling in the Eighteenth Century: the Evidence of the Scottish Tobacco Trade', *The Virginia Magazine of History and Biography* (October, 1954).

1975
T. M. Devine

Tables

		Page
I:	Burgess Enrolment in Burgh of Glasgow by Tobacco Merchants, c. 1730–89	5
II:	Occupation of Fathers of Eighteenth Century Glasgow Tobacco Merchants	6
III:	The Investments of Some Glasgow Tobacco Merchants	14
IV:	Location of Estates owned by Glasgow Tobacco and West India Merchants, c. 1770–1815	20
V:	Land Purchases of Alexander Speirs, 1766–80	21
VI:	Glasgow Tobacco Merchants and the Leather Industry	35
VII:	Colonial Merchants and the West of Scotland Sugar Industry	36
VIII:	Tobacco Merchants and the West of Scotland Linen Industry	39
IX:	Scottish Pig Iron Firms, 1779–1810	41
X:	Scottish Cotton Firms and Colonial Merchant Investment, c. 1795	45
XI:	Gross Total of Scottish Industrial Units with some element of colonial merchant capital in stock, c. 1700–1815	47
XII:	Scheme of Goods ordered from London, 27 May, 1760 by Lawson, Semple and Co.	63
XIII:	Tobacco Exports from Greenock and Port Glasgow, April–July, 1775	65
XIV:	Capital Stock of a Sample of Glasgow Tobacco Partnerships, c. 1740–83	75
XV:	Number of Partners in Glasgow Tobacco Firms, c. 1764–83	76
XVI:	William Cunninghame and Company's Shipping Estimates, 1772–3	86
XVII:	Sums borrowed on bond by Bogle, Somervell and Co. at 5 July, 1768	93
XVIII:	Abstract of Sums Owed by Buchanan, Hastie and Co. to 1777 with interest calculated to 1783	94

TABLES

XIX:	Sample of Sums borrowed on bond by Buchanan, Hastie and Co., 1768–72	94
XX:	Bonded Debts of Robert Robertson and James Robertson, 29 September, 1740	95
XXI:	Scottish Imports of Tobacco, 1771–5	108
XXII:	Frequency Distribution of Virginia Debts claimed by selected Merchants in England and Scotland in 1766 (pounds sterling)	113
XXIII:	Estimates of Glasgow's Debts in North America, 1778	114
XXIV:	Clyde Tobacco Imports, 1778–82	128
XXV:	Source of Tobacco Imports, 1778–83, Greenock and Port Glasgow	129
XXVI:	Armament of A. Houston and Co.'s Ships, 1778–83	141
XXVII:	Scottish Tobacco Imports, 1770–1800	161
XXVIII:	Ships Inwards and Outwards, North America—Port Glasgow—Greenock, 1772 and 1791	163

APPENDICES

I:	The Tobacco Merchants of Glasgow, c. 1740–90	177
II:	Partnerships in the Glasgow Tobacco Trade	187

FIGURE

I:	Marital Relationships of leading Glasgow Merchant Families	12

Contents

		Page
Preface		v

PART I: The Nature of the Glasgow Merchant Community
1	The Tobacco Merchants of Glasgow	3
2	Merchant Investments: I Land	18
3	Merchant Investments: II Industry	34

PART II: Trading Methods and Organisation in the Glasgow Tobacco Trade
4	The Organisation of the Glasgow Tobacco Trade, c. 1740–90	55
5(A)	The Emergence of the Tobacco Companies	72
(B)	The Tobacco Firm in Virginia, William Cunninghame and Co., 1768–75	82
6	Sources of Capital for the Glasgow Tobacco Trade	89

PART III: Glasgow Tobacco Merchants and the American War of Independence
7	Merchant Reaction to the American War	103
8	The Opportunities of Trade during the American War	124
9	The Difficulties of Trade during the American War	138

PART IV: The Aftermath of the American War of Independence
10	The Problem of Glasgow's pre-War Debts	153
11	The Renewal of Trade with North America after 1783	161

CONCLUSION	171
APPENDICES	177
BIBLIOGRAPHY	191
INDEX	201

Part I
THE MERCHANT COMMUNITY

1

The Tobacco Merchants of Glasgow

IN the eighteenth century, transatlantic trade was not a sector in which the *arriviste* adventurer whose only assets were cool nerves and business skill could easily or quickly prosper. Tobacco commerce, like most other areas of colonial trade, was dependent on personal relationships developed over several years between members of the international merchant community. Only by long acquaintance (commonly strengthened by marriage or kinship ties)[1] could the necessary trust evolve between individual traders without which progress, in an often hazardous business, was impossible. Above all, the tobacco trade was hungry for capital and this inevitably restricted merchant recruitment to that minority who possessed, or could obtain, the required level of investment funds.

Traders had, for instance, to be able to pay duty on imported tobacco. From the later seventeenth century a succession of governments, conscious of the importance of tobacco exports in Britain's balance of trade, had cut back and ameliorated customs payments.[2] Yet, throughout our period, one penny on each pound of tobacco imported was still payable in ready money while the remainder of the duty was bondable. The 'old subsidy', as this cash duty was called, put a strain on the liquidity of even the richest merchants. In 1729, for instance, George Bogle confided in one of his correspondents how he was 'pretty much straitened at present being to pay the old subsidy of some tobo'.[3] In addition, however, traders were faced with a series of other responsibilities. The record of the voyage of the *Blandford* trading to America and Europe in 1770–1 gives some indication of the perennial costs of overseas commerce. A ship her size, carrying just over 330 hogsheads of tobacco, would probably cost around £500.[4] On entering Port Glasgow in July, 1770, from Virginia, £168.13.7 was expended in port charges and repairs. Her owner had to make a further outlay of £262.4 when she landed tobacco at Rotterdam the following year.[5] This meant that expenses for port charges, customs payments and necessary repairs approximated, in that two year period, to the initial cost of the vessel itself. Yet this was not all. As will be discussed in more detail below, the system of trade developed between the Clyde ports and the tobacco colonies depended on fruitful sources of long-term credit.[6] It was only possible to build up a satisfactory clientele among American planters by providing them with the investment capital which was the vital precondition for expansion in tobacco cultivation.

Thus, because of the financial demands of the trade tobacco merchants formed only a minority among the business community of Glasgow. It has been possible to trace only 163 merchant burgesses of the city who were directly and regularly involved in tobacco importation between 1740–90. Closer study over shorter periods reveals how few the tobacco traders were in relation to their fellow merchants. Between 1740–49, 174 individuals were registered as burgesses and guild brethren of Glasgow. Only nineteen of these were involved in American commerce. A similar picture emerged in subsequent decades. In 1751–5, the figures were 148 and 14 respectively; in 1766–70, 158 and 16 and between 1776–80, 236 and 21. Clearly in these years there was a marked increase in the number of tobacco traders—a reflection of the significant expansion in importation from c.1740. But this rise was more than counter-balanced by a still greater extension in recruitment among other merchant groups which was an indication of the developing complexity of Glasgow's economic structure in the later eighteenth century.

Within the tobacco merchant group itself power and economic control was highly concentrated. Inter-linked partnerships and massive expansion among certain firms left the web of control in the hands of a few great mercantile families and their associates. In the few years of peak importation before 1775, the syndicates headed by William Cunninghame, Alexander Speirs and John Glassford controlled over half the Clyde tobacco trade and their predominant role in American commerce was reflected at a somewhat lower level by the success of the Donalds, Oswalds, Dunlops, Murdochs and Ritchies. The import figures for the two years before the American War suggest that about half the firms handled over five-sevenths of tobacco landed in 1774 and over four-fifths in 1775.[7]

The backgrounds of the men who made up this élite were varied although, as a broad generalisation, it can be said that all of them came from the 'middling' elements in Scottish society. Throughout the period 1730–90 the fathers of only four tobacco merchants were craftsmen, while on the other hand not one, as far as is known, was the scion of a noble or aristocratic family. The vast majority were sons of the well-to-do in lowland Scotland below the ranks of the aristocracy. Clearly, as far as the Glasgow tobacco trade is concerned, the 'rags to riches' story was but a comforting myth.

The biggest single source of recruits was established merchant families in Glasgow itself (see Table I). Between 1740–90, 71 tobacco traders of the total of 163 came into this category. Clearly such men would have obvious advantages in financial support, personal association and relevant training. But the tobacco merchant group was no self-perpetuating caste. In four of

TABLE I

Burgess Enrolment in Burgh of Glasgow by Tobacco Merchants, c.1730–90

Decade	Tobacco Merchants Enrolled as Burgesses and Guild Brethren	By Right of Merchant Fathers	By Right of Craftsmen Fathers	As Sons of Merchants in Other Burghs Ministers, Burgess Landowners	By Purchase	By Marriage	By Nomination	By Apprenticeship	Gratis
1730–39	21	10	2	1	1	4	0	1	2
1740–49	19	11	—	5	—	1	—	1	1
1750–59	27	14	1	4	—	2	5	1	—
1760–69	26	13	1	3	5	2	1	1	—
1770–79	27	10	—	3	9	5	—	—	—
1780–89	12	6	—	3	2	1	—	—	—
TOTAL	132	64	4	19	17	15	6	4	3

Sources—SRO, Collector's Quarterly Accounts, Port Glasgow, E.504/28.
SRO, Collector's Quarterly Accounts, Greenock, E.504/15.
GCA, Burgh Court Register of Deeds, B.10.15.
GCA, Matriculation Book of Merchants House of Glasgow.
J. Anderson (ed.), *The Burgesses and Guild Brethren of Glasgow, 1573–1750* (Edinburgh, 1925).
J. Anderson (ed.), *The Burgesses and Guild Brethren of Glasgow, 1751–1846* (Edinburgh, 1935).

the six decades between 1730 and 1790 more recruits came from outside this circle than from within it (see Tables I and II). The community was therefore sufficiently 'open-ended' to allow newcomers to play a significant role in its expansion. Indeed, the great names of the golden years after c.1740 were often not the sons of established merchants in Glasgow. John Glassford's father was a burgess in Paisley;[8] Alexander Speirs was the offspring of an Edinburgh merchant family;[9] William Cunninghame, although it has not

TABLE II

Occupation of Fathers of Eighteenth Century Glasgow Tobacco Merchants

Merchants in Glasgow	71
Merchants in other Scottish Burghs	6
Craftsmen in Glasgow	4
Landowners with no direct interest in Commerce	8
Ministers of Presbyterian or Episcopalian Churches	12
Lawyers, Notaries and Members of the Judiciary	6
Schoolmasters	1
Physicians	2
Occupation of Fathers unknown but not Merchants in Glasgow	53

Source—As in Table I.

been possible to trace his exact parentage, was the scion of a cadet branch of the Cunninghames of Caprington, lairds in Ayrshire;[10] the Oswalds were from clerical stock in Caithness.[11] Some other families, such as the Ritchies, Bogles, Dunlops and Murdochs, could, on the other hand, trace their connections with the tobacco trade back into the seventeenth century.

Two factors possibly help to explain the degree of mobility within the group. In the first place, commerce with the American colonies was expanding so rapidly during our period that openings were always likely to become available for ambitious young men with suitable connections and financial backing. These two latter elements were well nigh essential ingredients for success. The newcomer had to have personal contacts in the community and be prepared to spend perhaps several years accumulating capital. Samuel

McCall, for example, son of a Dumfriesshire laird and founder of a famous merchant dynasty 'was sent when a boy to the care of a friend of his father in Glasgow where he was designed to engage in commercial pursuits'.[12] John and Henry Riddell, prominent in the tobacco trade in the 1780s, were the sons of a Writer to the Signet in Edinburgh. Their mother was the sister of Anne Nisbet who was the second wife of John Glassford, one of the most celebrated of the tobacco lords. The brothers entered Glassford's service in the early 1760s. Henry proceeded via an apprenticeship and a factory in the colonies to the position of leading partner in his uncle-in-law's firms after Glassford's death.[13] William Cunninghame progressed under the watchful eye of his kinsman, Andrew Cochrane, an established colonial trader, but he still had to spend several years in the colonies before he could afford to obtain a major share in the Glasgow partnership.[14] Similarly, Alexander Speirs first founded his fortune as a plantation owner in Virginia before returning to Glasgow in the 1740s and becoming associated with the Buchanans, Hopkirks and Bowmans, eventually marrying the daughter of Archibald Buchanan of Silverbank.[15] Some tobacco importers, notably John Glassford himself, first made their money in domestic trade before extending their interests overseas; others, like Hugh Wylie, were former sea captains and supercargoes who had saved enough to branch into commerce on their own account.[16]

A second factor facilitating entry of newcomers was insolvency among established merchants. Although, because of its distinctive structure and the nature of its market relationships, the Clyde trade was apparently less affected by financial disaster than that of London and some of the English outports,[17] it was nevertheless true that tobacco merchants were still vulnerable to bankruptcy. Tobacco commerce was inherently speculative dependent as it was on the whims of the weather, the London money market and the vicissitudes of demand in continental Europe. In such years of credit crisis as 1762–3, 1772 and 1793 some of the most respected families in Glasgow experienced the collapse of fortunes carefully built up over generations. One contemporary, for instance, observed in December, 1762:

> You cannot imagine the distress people here are in for want of money. Several of our Virginia and West India merchants are lately broke here and several were much suspected which hurts Credit...[18]

The Bogles of Daldowie fell victim to the crisis of 1772 and had their estates put under trust.[19] In subsequent years such figures as Provost Andrew Buchanan, George McCall, William French, Hugh Wylie and Walter Monteath all became bankrupt.[20] When he died in 1783, John Glassford's affairs were thought to be in some disorder and the greatest single financial collapse in the community came in 1793 when James Dunlop had to apply for sequestration with assets totalling over £140,000 and debts of less than

£110,000.[21] In the 1790s too, Peter Murdoch and Robert Dunmore became insolvent—one the descendant of a family famous in the tobacco trade for over a century, the other worth over £60,000 but who, it was alleged had indulged in 'misapplication of the company's funds' over a long period.[22]

Normally most aspiring merchants had gone through some form of educational and training process. In the second half of the eighteenth century there were 'several schools' in Glasgow itself which offered rudimentary instruction in reading and writing while, for the older child, introducing also the mysteries of the classical languages.[23] In the main, however, there was little 'vocational' or 'commercial' education at this level. At the Grammar School, a popular institution for merchants' sons, the curriculum was strictly academic with the teaching geared to Latin and Greek, Classical Antiquities and Geography.[24] In addition, a high proportion of those bent on a mercantile career spent some time at the University of Glasgow where the teachers at this time were men of such international renown as Adam Smith (Professor of Moral Philosophy from 1751 to 1763), Robert Simson, William Cullen and Joseph Black. Alexander Carlyle, a student at Glasgow in the 1740s, noted how 'it was usual for the sons of merchants to attend the College for one or two years', while as late as the 1820s, a government commission confirmed that 'young men not intended for any learned profession . . . are sent for one or more years to College in order to carry their education farther than that of the schools before they engaged in the pursuits of trade or of commerce'.[25] Between 1728 and 1800, indeed, at least sixty-eight tobacco and West India merchants had been students at Glasgow University.[26]

For those fortunate enough to be born of wealthier than average parents there was the opportunity to be educated privately or to be sent to the Continent to acquire experience, language practice and the finer points of European manners. The 'Grand Tour' was not a monopoly of the sons of aristocrats. In the 1720s, George Bogle was sent abroad for his 'improvement'. During this time he travelled through some of the German states, Holland, France and Flanders, acted as a sort of travelling agent for his family's business and occasionally enrolled at colleges along the route for short periods of instruction. His favourite subject was history:

> I prefer studying history before the Civil Law because I suppose it is not so Intricate a study as the Civil Law and therefore does not require so much time to know something of it—

but his library, which included books by French, Greek and Latin authors, indicated a catholic taste in reading.[27] The continental education of Peter Speirs, son of Alexander, lasted for seven years (at an annual cost of over £1000!) and involved training in languages, commercial skills, dancing, riding and fencing.[28] Some merchants had more specific reasons for sending their sons outside Scotland. Like some other leading traders James Somervell was an Episcopalian and placed his son under the care of the Rev. Robert

Hunter of Barton, Dorset so that he would receive the correct religious upbringing which might be denied him in Presbyterian Scotland. In addition, however, to supervising his spiritual needs, the Rev. Hunter had to do 'ample justice to Mr. Somervell in forwarding his Education and Improvement in useful and polite literature'.[29]

Partly because of the liberal education received by some merchants they were able to sustain a vigorous urban culture in Glasgow in the second half of the eighteenth century. Few were completely absorbed in the business of money-making and the nature of eighteenth century trade allowed them considerable scope for leisure activity. One of the Bogles alleged, for instance, that:

> ...all the Merchants in Glasgow (excepting those who deal in Exchange) are quite idle for one half or two thirds of the year which may be one reason why the frequent keeping of company does prevail so much and in Glasgow more than in any place in the World.[30]

Cultural activity sponsored by the tobacco lords flourished in various ways. Clubs, such as the Hodge Podge Club, the Literary Society of Glasgow and another venture founded by Andrew Cochrane, held debates, discussions and invited such eminent speakers as Adam Smith and Thomas Reid to address them.[31] Directors of the Sacred Music Institution 'designed to promote a taste in sacred music', included Henry Riddell, Cunninghame Corbett and Robert Findlay.[32] The opening of the first theatre in Glasgow in 1764 was due to the efforts of another group of American traders.[33] The famous 'Foulis Academy' or the Academy of Fine Arts in Glasgow was first conceived by the bookseller and printer, Robert Foulis. The venture, however, initially encountered hostility and suffered from a lack of finance and its historian admits that its later development was due to the patronage and financial backing of three tobacco merchants, John Glassford, John Coats Campbell and Archibald Ingram.[34] It cannot be denied, on the other hand, that not all traders were solicitous patrons of the arts. Apparently, at least in the early eighteenth century, hard drinking was the preferred recreation for the younger merchants and tavern gossip rather then intellectual debate was their favourite pastime.[35]

Some experience of colonial conditions was deemed vital for the aspiring tobacco merchant. Almost every figure of note in the trade had spent some time in Virginia or Maryland as an apprentice, as a storekeeper or as a factor. James Lawson's son, Robert, followed the conventional route. In 1763 he was almost sixteen and had spent four years at grammar school, two at college and 'about one year at Counting, Book-keeping and French'. He was now to be sent to Maryland under the supervision of his father's partner there.[36] For those who were not sons or close relatives of established merchants the more common form of training was to serve a term as an indentured apprentice with a Virginia house in its colonial stores. Typical of the arrangement was the terms of an indenture drawn up in 1758 between Glassford, Ingram and Co. and Neil Campbell, son of John Campbell, supervisor of excise at Glasgow. By this Campbell bound himself to serve the firm for the space of five years 'honestly and diligently' and 'not neglect his saids Masters Business night nor day Except in the case of Sickness or Leave'. The penalty for breaking this regulation was 1/- per day or service for a further two days at his master's option. Above all the apprentice was specifically enjoined 'not to reveal any of his saids Masters secrets'. For their part the company undertook to instruct him in trade, to give him board and lodging, free passage to Virginia and a salary which would rise from £5 to £25 by annual increments over the five year period.[37]

Doubtless the eventual aim of most young men who undertook these apprenticeships was an eventual major share in a merchant house. One suspects, however, that only a tiny minority of these aspirants eventually reached this goal. After all the average individual share in a Glasgow tobacco company in the years before the American War was between £1000 and £2000.[38] Only trading on one's own account in the colonies, borrowing from wealthy relatives or marrying into established merchant families could accumulate sums of these magnitudes. However, once a major holding in a firm, in ships or in stores was obtained the prospects for gain were indeed considerable. While the paucity of merchant accounts does not allow us to gauge the rate of profit with any degree of precision there are indications in the kind of successes which were achieved. William Cunninghame, who as late as the 1750s was a factor in a Glasgow store in Virginia, was by the 1780s, able to lend more than £150,000 to his brother-in-law, Robert Dunmore, over a ten year period![39] This was an astonishing sum by eighteenth century standards. Similarly, Alexander Speirs, by dint of 'his industry and success at trade' was worth over £153,000 by the time he was fifty-nine.[40] While few approached wealth on this scale, the income of other tobacco lords does justify the view that they were easily the most opulent business group that emerged in Scotland before the nineteenth century. Archibald Ingram might well fit a description of the 'average merchant'. His shares in two tobacco firms were £2100 and £225 respectively. He owned an expensive chaise, a gold watch, an extensive library and his house and warehouses were valued at over £5,300.[41] The developing tastes of merchants like Ingram for consumer goods and conspicuous display sustained the rise of the luxury trades in Glasgow. In the 1740s Alexander Carlyle thought less than half a dozen families had manservants and:

> There were neither post-chaises nor hackney-coaches in the town, and only three or four sedan chairs for carrying midwives about in the night, and old ladies to church, or to the dancing assemblies.[42]

Yet by the 1770s, sedan chairmen, notable by their absence a few decades before, had become so numerous that they petitioned the Town Council to form a benefit society.⁴³ In addition, Glasgow, by the same period, boasted two coach builders, four architects, two marble cutters, fourteen booksellers, fourteen saddlers, three engravers, one carpet warehouse, three jewellers, no less than twenty-six hairdressers (besides eighteen barbers!) and twenty-three cabinetmakers.⁴⁴

Nevertheless, despite the effects of colonial trade in stimulating income and employment in town society only a few families rose to opulence and prominence on profits from it and, as Figure 1 indicates, this élite was inter-related in one massive and extended kinship group.⁴⁵ The material ascendancy of this exclusive minority was indeed overwhelming. It was apparent, for example, in the physical appearance of Glasgow itself. In a 'Plan of the City of Glasgow' in 1778 only churches and some 'manufactories' rivalled the town mansions of the tobacco aristocracy for size and architectural appeal. In the segment of ground bounded by Buchanan Street in the west, Candleriggs in the east and Argyll Street to the south lay the town house of William Cunninghame, built at a cost of £10,000. The portico of this imposing dwelling is now incorporated in Stirling's Library.⁴⁶ In the same area was situated the mansion of Alexander Speirs which cost £3,500 to construct.⁴⁷ The famous 'Virginia Mansion' belonging to James Buchanan, John McCall's 'Black House' and Patrick Colquohoun's residence (later converted into part of the Kelvingrove Museum) were all unmistakable indications of the distinction of this mercantile élite.⁴⁸ Another was their dominance of political and civic life in Glasgow which endured until near the end of the eighteenth century. Almost every provost of the city had interests in colonial trade throughout this period; the majority of merchant councillors were tobacco traders.⁴⁹ The directorate of the Glasgow Chamber of Commerce established 'on the most liberal and equitable foundations' in 1783 was intended, according to its charter, to be representative of 'all merchants, traders and manufacturers from Glasgow, Paisley, Kilbarchan, Greenock, Port Glasgow, Kilmarnock, together with other towns and villages on the banks of Clyde'. Yet despite this commitment to more open representation, colonial traders held as much as half of the seats in the directorate and yet only formed less than a quarter of the total membership of the Chamber.⁵⁰

It would be quite wrong, however, to conclude that the wealth of this group was based only on the importation of tobacco. Probably for most merchants the American trade was indeed the centre and base of their business strategy, but, at the same time, the majority were successful because their other investments allowed them to achieve a series of gains from alternative markets at home and abroad. It is impossible to detect any among them who were only specialist importers of tobacco and who did not dabble in other trades.

Because of its speculative nature tobacco commerce was frequently unprofitable. In the early 1730s, the Bogles could describe it as 'a losing trade' and as a result switched their main interests temporarily to the Caribbean

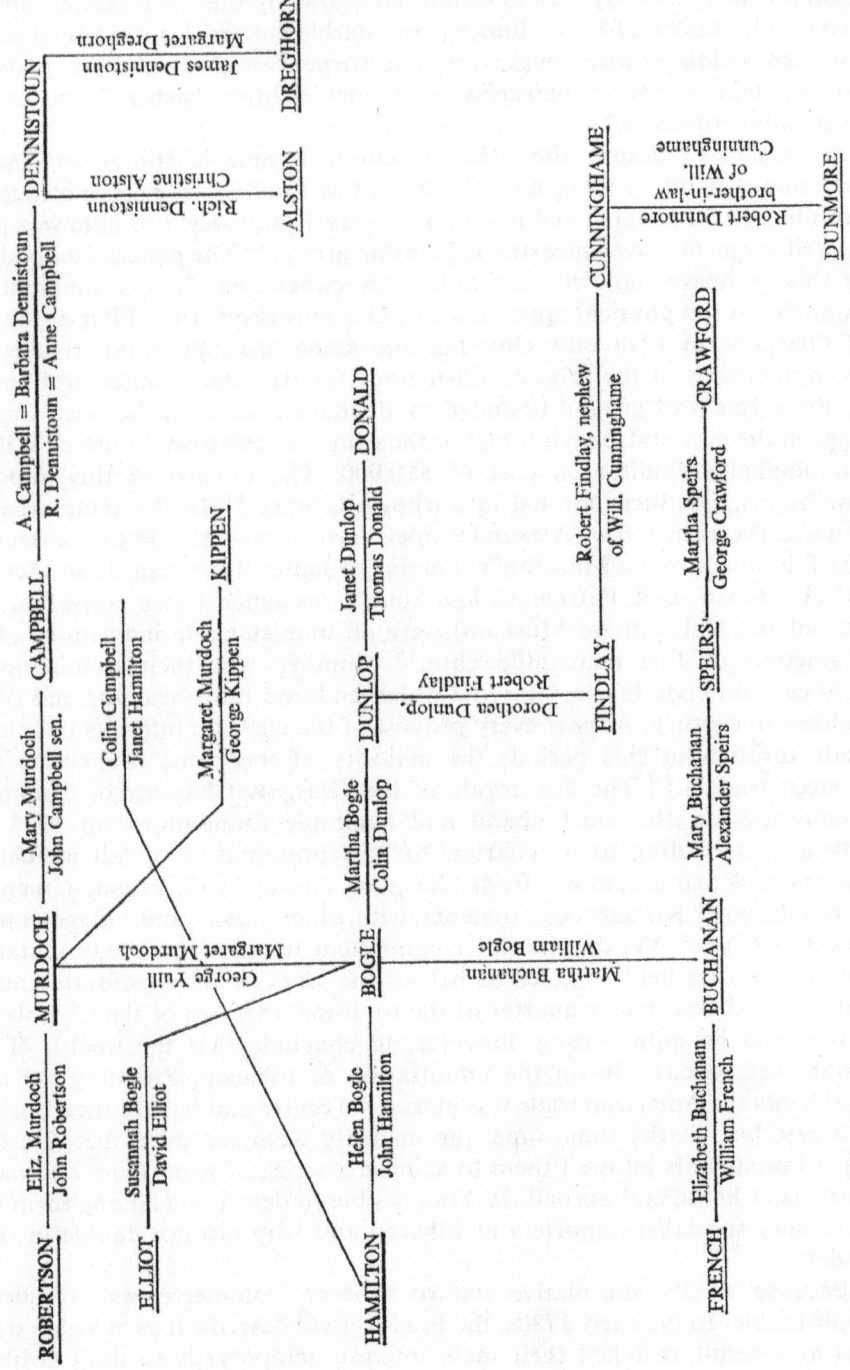

FIGURE 1
Marital Relationships of leading tobacco merchants Families in Glasgow.

Map showing Continental context of Virginia–Maryland–North Carolina area

Virginia, Maryland and North Carolina, 1775.

(to face page 12)

Tobacco being checked and loaded at a Virginia port c. 1775. From the map of Virginia etc. drawn by Joshua Fry and Peter Jefferson in 1775. Courtesy of Colonial Williamsburg Inc.

Glasgow at the Broomielaw. The shallowness of the river at this point meant that ocean-going vessels had to be unloaded farther down the unimproved Clyde at Port Glasgow and Greenock. *Courtesy of the Mitchell Library, Glasgow.*

The Trongate, Glasgow from the east, 1770–71. The area around the Exchange (fronted by the equestrian statue of William III) was the commercial heart of Glasgow. Here the great merchants met socially and talked business. *Courtesy of the Mitchell Library, Glasgow.*

where they dealt in sugar and logwood for several years.[51] Their main problem was the difficulty of gauging the behaviour of disparate European markets for tobacco and relating purchasing strategy in the colonies to these. William Bogle alleged that merchants could expect to make large profits in a single year and hardly break even for several thereafter.[52] In 1759, for example, it was pointed out that 'some companys will lose five or six thousand pounds sterling by this years importation'.[53] There was also a price recession in 1762–3 and one merchant went so far as to claim that a long-term malaise had developed in the trade at this time: 'There is nothing but loss . . . there is too much made for the consumption of Europe at present'.[54]

Because of this perennial uncertainty it was only sensible to spread risk by developing interests in other spheres of overseas commerce and in relevant sectors of the domestic economy. The Oswalds were involved in both American and European trade. Between 1763 and 1764 13 consignments of sugar (195 hogsheads), 890 hogsheads of tobacco and 15 consignments of wine, mainly from Lisbon and Madeira, were entered in their name at Clyde ports.[55] Again, almost every Glasgow merchant house of note with investments in North American commerce, was also involved in the provision trade in wheat and fish between the mainland colonies and the Caribbean islands. Moreover, especially in the second half of the eighteenth century the economy of Virginia and the Carolinas was becoming diversified as the production and export of flaxseed, rice, hemp, cotton, turpentine and planking began to assume significance. Once again Glasgow firms were concerned.[56] Customs house accounts contain notices of licenses granted from the Commissioners at Edinburgh to merchants in Glasgow allowing them to ship rice from South Carolina to Europe, south of Cape Finnisterre.[57] John Glassford and George Kippen, for instance, among several others, were extensively involved too in the importation to Scotland of American flaxseed and barrel staves, which were much in demand by the Scottish textile and fishing industries.[58]

Merchants were not only interested in different sectors of overseas trade but also had a wide spread of assets in the domestic economy. There were several possible investments for those with a surplus and the desire to scatter their risks. The rise of banking in the West of Scotland was a consequence of the re-deployment of capital by tobacco lords. They founded the Glasgow Arms and Ship Banks in the early 1750s and were mainly responsible for financing the Thistle Bank a decade later.[59] Outside Glasgow, such figures as James Dunlop and Archibald Speirs were associated with the Greenock Banking Co. and the Renfrewshire Banking Co. respectively.[60] Lending on bond to other merchants, or more commonly to local landowners in need of extra cash, was also undertaken. George Bogle dealt in this way with Sir John Shaw, Lord Cathcart, John Napier of Napierston, the Earl of Dundonald, and Lady Pollock of Pollock while Richard Oswald, between 1762 and 1780, lent out a total of over £72,000 on bond![61] Somewhat surprisingly, however, the merchants considered here do not appear to have invested to any great extent in government securities. Perhaps this reflected their desire to supervise their loans at close quarters and possibly illustrated also the vigorous nature of the market in personal and heritable bonds in the west of Scotland. B. L. Anderson has commented on a similar trend in Lancashire:

> It was very difficult for provincials to administer satisfactorily investments [in government stock] made through London agents with powers of attorney that would be the envy of a modern stockbroker. By lending on mortgages in one's local region to a borrower who was perhaps a friend or relation it was possible to supervise one's money more carefully and easily.[62]

In addition to this, however, there was probably a more consistently higher rate of return on private bonds in the area around Glasgow than on government stock.[63]

TABLE III
The Investments of some Glasgow Tobacco Merchants

Merchant	Date	Summary of Financial Interests
Alexander Morson	1768	Share in a Boston concern; ⅛ share in the brigantine *Bell*; £503.13 in P. and W. Bogle, tobacco importers; £400 in Jamaica concern with Ebenezer Munro; share in a coal and copper mine; £22.18.5 owed him by Neil Jamieson, merchant in Norfolk, Virginia; £100 in insurance venture; share in a plaiding concern with Ebenezer Munro.
Robert Dunmore	1793	Income in that year; Rent of country lands: £7,531.18.4; produce of Jamaica properties £4,500; stock in different concerns, interest and profit accrual: £2,626; Virginia debts not yet recovered: £15–20,000.
Alexander Speirs	1770	Stocks in concerns: 'Virginia concern': £55,057.4.0; 'Maryland concern': £7,410.19.9; Value of landed property: £49,050; Domestic industry and banks: £18,141.3.7½; 'Occasional transactions' including canal shares: £1,778.9.4¼.
William Cunninghame	1790	Income in that year: John Ferguson and Co. (formerly R. Dunmore and Co.) West India and American merchants: £3,255.6.0; land rentals: £3,696.6.0; East India stock: £436.5.6; government securities: £104.4.5; bills receivable: £13.0.0.
James Somervell	1791	Shares in various concerns: Somervell, Gordon and Co., tobacco and West India merchants: £8,503; David Russell and Co. (West India merchants): £4,936; Money lent on bond to: Findlay, Hopkirks and Co. (tobacco merchants): £1000; Corbett, Russell and Co. (tobacco merchants): £2000; Henry Hardie and Co. (linen merchants and printers): £1000; Muirkirk Iron Co.: £1000; Port Glasgow Ropework Co.: £3000; Tanwork Co.: £3000.

Sources—GCA, Reg. of Deeds, B.10/15/7173, 7174; SRO, GD 237/151/3, Copy, State of Mr. Dunmore's subjects as on 25 October, 1793; GCA, Speirs Papers, TD 131/6/14, States of the Private Affairs of A. Speirs, December, 1770; GCA, Sederunt Book of James Somervell, 1791–97, 13.

Yet, as Table III indicates, the most popular investment outlets for colonial merchants in the domestic economy were in land and industry. Each was complementary to the trader's primary concerns in overseas commerce and land, in particular, could offer the kind of security which most merchants craved. No apology need therefore be made for exploring in detail the nature of these types of investment in the next two chapters.

REFERENCES

1. See Appendix I and Figure I, p. 12.
2. From 1703 duties on tobacco totalled $6\frac{1}{3}$d per lb. Additions made in 1747 and 1758 brought this to $8\frac{1}{3}$d where it remained until the beginning of the American War in 1775. Between 1723 (due to Walpole's initiative) and 1775 duties were re-funded through drawbacks on re-exportation. While, as has been noted in the text, one penny per lb. was payable in ready money, all the remainder was bondable. See L. C. Gray, *History of Agriculture in the Southern United States to 1860* (Washington, 1933), I, 244–5; A. P. Middleton, *Tobacco Coast: a Maritime History of Chesapeake Bay in the Colonial Era* (Newport News, Virginia, 1955), 111.
3. ML, Bogle MSS, George Bogle of Daldowie's Letterbook, to John Govan, 15 October, 1729.
4. GCA, Register of Deeds, B.10/15/5673.
5. GCA, Lockhart Family Papers (on microfilm 612), Master's running accounts for ship *Blandford*, 1768–1771.
6. See below, pp. 76–8.
7. See below, pp. 97–9.
8. James Gourlay, *A Glasgow Miscellany* (privately printed, n.d.), 43.
9. GCA, Register of Deeds, B.10/15/8435, Settlement, Alexander Speirs esq., 16 December, 1782.
10. SRO, GD 247/10, Answers for William Cunninghame, late of Falmouth, 1.
11. W. St. Robinson jun., 'Richard Oswald the Peacemaker', *Ayrshire Collections*, 1950–54, 2nd. ser., III (1955); Robert Reid, *Old Glasgow and its Environs* (Glasgow, 1864).
12. H. B. McCall, *Memoirs of my Ancestors* (Birmingham, 1884), 10.
13. *Glasgow Courier*, 29 May, 1819; PRO, AO 12/9/37; *Glasgow Mercury*, 19 January, 1790; *Scots Magazine*, Vol. 43, 331; SL, Court of Session Process, 438/18, Minutes in Process Henry Riddell versus John Riddell. . . 5.
14. Anon., *Cochran Correspondence regarding the Affairs of Glasgow*, ix–xi; C. A. Oakley, *Connal and Company Ltd. 1722–1946* (Glasgow, 1946), 4; SRO, GD 247/140, Answers for W. Cunninghame, 1, 4, 6, 16.
15. GCA, Register of Deeds, B.10/15/6653, Copartnery, Archibald Buchanan, Speirs etc., registered 8; SL, Court of Session Process 180/7, Answers for Arch. Speirs of Elderslie. . . 1.
16. GCA, TD 200/111, Letterbook of Hugh Wylie.
17. See below.
18. SRO, RH 15/1179, James Lawson Letterbook, Lawson to John Semple, 30 December, 1762.
19. ML, Bogle MSS, Bundle 54, State of debts for which the Lord Justice Clerk and other trustees for Mr. Bogle stand indebted; SRO, Reg. of Deeds, 230/784 MACK.
20. SRO, Currie Dal Seq. B1/1, Buchanan, Hastie and Co. (1777); GCA, Register of Deeds, B.10/15/9250; *Glasgow Mercury*, 25 July, 1787; SRO, UP 1 Currie Dal B5/8; GCA, Register of Deeds, B.10/15/8339; SRO, GD 247/140, Information for R. Bogle of Shettleston. . . 3.

21. GCA, Dunlop Papers, State of the Funds of James Dunlop, 23 March, 1793.
22. GCA, Register of Deeds, B.10/15/9342; SRO, GD 237/151/3, State of Robert Dunmore's subjects, 25 October, 1793.
23. GCA, Council Minute Book, C1/1/35/447, 25 October, 1775.
24. W. M. Wade, *The History of Glasgow, Ancient and Modern* (Paisley, 1821), 288; James Cleland, *Historical Account of the Grammar School of Glasgow* (Glasgow, 1825), 28.
25. Alexander Carlyle, *Autobiography* (Edinburgh, 1861), 74; General Report of the Commissioners appointed to visit the Universities and Colleges of Scotland, October, 1830, 9, quoted in W. H. Mathew, 'The Origin and Occupations of Glasgow Students, 1740–1839', *Past and Present*, 33 (1966), 91.
26. W. J. Addison (ed.), *A Roll of the Graduates of the University of Glasgow* (Glasgow, 1898), 1727–1897. None of them graduated. It may well be, however, that the concept of university attendance necessarily leading to graduation is relatively modern. Students attended 'classes' and the class ticket was a kind of minor degree parchment [I owe this point to Prof. S. G. E. Lythe].
27. ML, Bogle MSS, George Bogle's Letterbook, 1725–1731, *passim*.
28. NLS, Speirs Papers, ACC 3296, Educational expenses for Peter Speirs; GCA, Speirs Papers, TD 131/9, Alexander Speirs to J. G. Martens, 20 May, 1782, to Thomas Eden, 20 June, 1782.
29. GCA, Sederunt Book of James Somervell, Copy letter of Trustees to Rev. Mr. R. Hunter, 13 January, 1792.
30. ML, Bogle MSS, George Bogle's Letterbook, Bogle to Robert Bogle, 5 March, 1726.
31. Carlyle, *op. cit.*, 73; G. Stewart, *Curiosities of Glasgow Citizenship* (Glasgow, 1881), 143; W. R. Scott, *Adam Smith as Student and Professor* (Glasgow, 1937), 81, 86; John Rae, *Life of Adam Smith* (London, 1895), 91; J. F. Bell, 'Adam Smith, Clubman', *Scott. Journ. Pol. Econ.*, VII (1960), 110.
32. *Glasgow Almanack for* 1798, 234.
33. James Muir, *Glasgow Streets and Places* (Glasgow and Edinburgh, 1892), 88.
34. Anon., *Notes and Documents illustrative of the Literary History of Glasgow during the great part of last century* (Glasgow, 1886), 81–90.
35. ML, Bogle MSS, George Bogle's Letterbook, Bogle to Robert Bogle, 10 April, 1726.
36. SRO, RH 15/1179, James Lawson Letterbook, 1762–66, to John Semple, 20 February, 1763.
37. GCA, TD 200/53, Glasgow Southern Parliamentary Debating Association Collection, Indenture between Neil Campbell and Messrs. Archibald Ingram and John Glassford. For another example see GCA, TD 180, Alexander Hamilton Papers, 20.
38. Estimate based on series of contracts of copartnery preserved in burgh deeds (Glasgow City Archives) and national deeds (Scottish Record Office).
39. SRO, GD 247/140, Answers for William Cunninghame...1768, 1; GD 247/141, Scroll of Sederunt of Robert Dunmore and Co. (1792).
40. SL, Court of Session Process 180/7, Answers for Archibald Speirs of Elderslie...1; GCA, Speirs Papers, TD 131/6/3c.
41. Baillie's Institution Library, Sederunt Book of the Trustees of Archibald Ingram.
42. Caryle, *op. cit.*, 75.
43. GCA, Council Minute Book, C1/1/35/473, 19 December, 1775.
44. *A Reprint of Jones's Directory for the year 1789* (Glasgow, 1866), viii.
45. These marital and blood relationships, however, did not inhibit competition between different firms. See below, pp. 60–1.
46. Stewart, *op. cit.*, 194–5.
47. GCA, Speirs Papers, TD 131/5, Ledger C. In addition Speirs had to finance the building and furnishing of his country house in Renfrewshire.
48. Senex (J. M. Reid), *Glasgow Past and Present* (Glasgow, 1884), II, 399, 426; III, 163. Stewart, *op. cit.*, 189.
49. See GCA, Council Minute Book; James Gourlay (ed.), *The Provosts of Glasgow, passim*.
50. University of Strathclyde, Minutes of Glasgow Chamber of Commerce, 1 Jan., 1783 (Xerox copies); ML, Chamber of Commerce MSS, B/15, List of Directors, 1787.
51. ML, Bogle MSS, George Bogle's Letterbook, Bogle to Matthew Bogle, 11 September, 1731.
52. *Ibid.*, William Bogle to George Bogle, 19 November, 1736.

53. SRO, RH 15/1179, James Lawson Letterbook, Lawson to John Semple, 6 July, 1759.
54. *Ibid.*, 24 February, 1762.
55. GCA, TD 188, Oswald Account Book. A hogshead at this time approximated to 1000 lbs.
56. SRO, Customs Accounts, Greenock and Port Glasgow, *passim*.
57. D. I. Fagerstrom, 'The American Revolutionary Movement in Scottish Opinion, 1763 to 1783', Unpublished Ph.D. Thesis, University of Edinburgh, 1951, 28.
58. GCA, TD 132, Records of George Kippen, John Glassford and Co., merchants, Charles Addison to George Kippen, 26 March, 1755.
59. John Buchanan, 'Banking in Glasgow during the Olden Time', in Senex *op. cit.*; Bank of Scotland, Glasgow, Ship Bank Balance Book, 1752–61; GCA, Register of Deeds, B.10/15/8314.
60. SRO, UP 1 Currie Mack, D/6/1(1797), Answers of McBrayne, Stenhouse and Co.; *Glasgow Herald and Advertiser*, 12 June, 1809.
61. ML, Bogle MSS, George Bogle's Letterbook, *passim*; SRO, Register of Deeds, 236/731–47, DUR, Disposition of Richard Oswald to Mary Ramsay.
62. B. L. Anderson, 'Provincial Aspects of the Financial Revolution of the Eighteenth Century', *Business History*, XI (1969), 22.
63. See below, pp. 97–8.

2

Merchant Investments: I Land

I

MOST successful tobacco merchants owned estates at some stage during their life. Examination of the Register of Sasines and other sources reveals, for instance, that between 1760 and 1790 at least fifty-five held land.[1] A proportion of this territory was inherited from fathers or other close relatives who were well-established landowners or, as successful merchants, had themselves acquired property at an earlier period. This generalisation would apply to the Bogles (who had bought Daldowie in Lanarkshire in 1731), the Buchanans (with Mount Vernon and Drumpellier in the same county) and the Ritchies of Craigton, among others.[2] On the other hand, inheritance was not the *most* significant means of accumulating property; only eighteen merchants between 1760–1800 acquired at least part of their estates as heirs of their fathers.[3] In addition, several of those who did so went on to obtain still more territory by purchase. Each generation of a merchant family with roots in the soil was rarely content to rest satisfied with its good fortune. Profits from trade continued to be employed in the service of landed ambition. James Ritchie succeeded to Craigton near Glasgow which his father, John, had purchased in 1746. James added to this by obtaining Busby in Ayrshire in 1763.[4] Similarly James Dunlop inherited Carmyle from his father, Colin. This estate was valued in 1793 at £20,000; Dunlop went on to buy several other properties in Lanarkshire and the barony of Glasgow valued at over £64,000.[5] Another leading merchant, Robert Dunmore, whose interests straddled both the American and Caribbean trades, was owner of Kelvinside by his father's bequest; from 1785 he began a series of land purchases in Stirlingshire and by 1793 had acquired the barony of Ballindalloch and several adjoining areas in that county.[6]

It is conventional to assume too that merchants often came into possession of land, in true romantic fashion, through the marriage bed.[7] Wealthy traders, so the story has it, sought out the daughters of the impoverished gentry in the hope of succeeding to the family estate. In the case of the tobacco merchants in this period, however, matrimony was the route to broad acres for only a tiny minority. Seven merchant-landowners (out of a total of 55) acquired territory in this way and each of them married the daughters of rich traders who were already landowners rather than the offspring of poor lairds.[8]

It follows from what has been said that the vast proportion of property held by the merchant group in the later eighteenth century was obtained by purchase in the market. Such a conclusion requires some explanation because it raises the important question of the availability of estates at this time. In the case of England, for example, some scholars (notably Professors Habbakuk and Mingay) have detected a recognisable decline in the number of lawyers, bankers, merchants and other newcomers entering the landed classes. According to these writers this trend had become established because the land market was narrowing almost to the point of stagnation as a result of the operation of strict settlement and entail procedures.[9] Yet, whatever the relevance of these views to the situation elsewhere in Britain, they obviously have little relationship to the pattern in west-central Scotland in the second half of the eighteenth century. Between 1770 and 1815, sixty-two American and West India merchants were able to achieve landed status with little recognisable difficulty. Again, twenty of this number acquired at least two estates in different counties and ownership was by and large restricted to the environs of Glasgow itself. The number of holdings tended to fall as the distance from the town increased and only six merchants possessed territory outside Lanarkshire, Renfrewshire, Stirlingshire and Ayrshire.[10] Apart from these exceptions Table IV affords an insight into the location of the respective estates.

It is possible to isolate several factors which could account for the availability of desirable properties in the region at this time. For one thing the traditional structure of landownership was peculiarly suited to facilitating the sale of estates. In west-central Scotland large estates owned by aristocratic landlords were uncommon. The typical unit was very small, normally no more than a few hundred acres, in the possession of a 'bonnet laird'.[11] It is possible that this group would be particularly vulnerable to the inflationary pressures of the later eighteenth century and would be less adequately protected from them than their more powerful counterparts by entail and settlement arrangements. The developing consumer tastes of the period—a phenomenon which Professor Smout has described as the 'Revolution in Manners'—encouraged several among this group to live above their means. More varied leisure activities, increasingly elaborate clothing, 'improvement' of estates, more exotic diets all required an augmented income.[12] Indeed such were the pressures of social convention and competitive display that desires were sometimes fulfilled on the narrowest of financial margins. Contemporaries argued that this extravagance encouraged sale of land. Colonel

William Fullarton, the agricultural reporter for Ayrshire, observed that in his county '... a great proportion of the landed estates have changed their owners in consequence of individual extravagance, expensive engagements ...'.[13] He denounced the families of 'very ancient standing' for their 'reigning spirit of conviviality and speculation' which obliged them to sell their property. This he blamed on the 'natural tendency of counting upon imaginary rentals long before they became real ones, including too, the prevailing course of electioneering, show, equipage and the concomitant attacks upon the purse'.[14] John Knox, another knowledgeable writer of the period, agreed with Fullarton's strictures. Although rentals had 'mostly trebled' since 1760, many of the smaller lairds were no wealthier than their forefathers:

> ... on the contrary, the increase of income, though incredibly rapid, hath not amongst the generality of families, corresponded with their taste for the elegancies and luxuries of a more opulent people: insomuch that estates are constantly upon sale, the old families gradually disappear and the landed property falls into new hands, especially in the neighbourhood of Glasgow...[15]

TABLE IV

Location of Estates owned by Glasgow Tobacco and West India Merchants, c. 1770–1815.

Area	No. of Merchant-Landowners	No. of Estates
Barony of Glasgow	34	40
Lanarkshire	22	37
Renfrewshire	19	36
Dunbartonshire	11	11
Stirlingshire	6	10
Ayrshire	8	11

Source—T. M. Devine, 'Glasgow Merchants in Colonial Trade, c. 1770–1815', Unpublished Ph.D. Thesis, University of Strathclyde, 1971, II, 590–608.

Another element influencing the land market was the failure of the Ayr Bank (Douglas, Heron and Co.) in 1772. This was one of the most spectacular bankruptcies in Scottish history and it inevitably had far-reaching consequences at the time.[16] 114 of the 226 partners in the bank became insolvent. Several of them were substantial landowners and the need to pay creditors resulted in the break-up of many estates. One estimate suggests that £750,000 in landed property subsequently changed hands.[17] The sale of so much territory in such a short time depressed prices throughout the western Lowlands. A group of Glasgow merchants observed the fall that the crash had occasioned and how:

> ... the immense losses that have been incurred by the partners in the bank of Douglas, Heron and Co. and the sale of the extensive property of the York Building Co. will bring a much greater proportion of land into the market for many years to come.[18]

Hard on the heels of the failure of the Ayr Bank came the American War of Independence. Traditionally, wartime brought a slump in the land market because many potential buyers preferred to invest in appreciating government stock.[19] To this weakening in demand was added the further complication of increased supply of properties as war taxes and high interest rates produced bankruptcies among landowners especially towards the end of hostilities. For Glasgow merchants eager to purchase land and not too concerned about the comparatively greater profitability of other assets, conditions were certainly attractive at this time. William Cunninghame, for example, enriched with the profits of over three decades in the Virginia trade, bought Lainshaw in his native Ayrshire in 1778 for £20,000, £2100 less than its valuation in 1774. The former owner had realised that 'the debts affecting the estate of Lainshaw appeared so considerable, that a sale was unavoidable'.[20] Several merchants, including James Hopkirk, Robert Dunmore, Robert Findlay, Alexander Houston, James Dunlop, George Crawford and John Alston jun. obtained estates in the last few years of war and the early years of peace.[21] The most dramatic illustration of merchant land buying in this period, however, was provided by Alexander Speirs. By 1773 he had obtained several estates in Renfrewshire valued at over £48,000. In the following ten years until his death, he embarked on a major programme of purchase which included the acquisition of properties in Stirlingshire and Lanarkshire as well as Renfrewshire.[22] Speirs's methods, as revealed in his surviving accounts, indicate that he had bought a series of small adjoining properties and then consolidated them into a major estate (see Table V):

TABLE V
Land Purchases of Alexander Speirs, 1760-80

Property	Value (£)
Neilstonside	14,000
Elderslie	9,000
Kings Inch	8,000
Arkleton	5,600
Deanside	4,000
Deanfield	2,750
Craigenfeoch	2,100
Muirhead	2,000
Bogside	1,500
Fulwood	16,600
Newton	7,750
Culcreuch	15,020
Gauderston	8,400
Kilburn	1,000
Blawarthill and Yoker	7,446
Craigton	400
Overglen	2,025
Provenstone	1,365
	£108,956

Source—GCA, Speirs Papers, TD 131/5, Ledger C.

The availability of purchasable land was also conditioned by the extent to which merchants already owned estates around Glasgow. Long before the eighteenth century the town was ringed by the country seats of successful burgesses.[23] This itself kept the market in land fluid because merchants were often more vulnerable to fluctuation in their fortunes than many a traditional laird whose income through rents, though smaller, was more dependable. Merchant bankruptcies thus sustained the flow of land to market and several traders gained as a result of the misfortune of their fellows. Archibald Smith and Moses Steven both bought part of the estates belonging to the partners of Alexander Houston and Co. after the disastrous collapse of that vast concern.[20] James Hopkirk of Dalbeth further added to his property on the bankruptcy of his neighbour and fellow tobacco merchant, Archibald Smellie, during the American War.[25]

II

Merchants bought land because it brought them social distinction and economic security. Scotland, like most parts of Europe until well into the nineteenth century was dominated by its landlords. Only through ownership of an estate of sufficient size was it possible to participate fully in the life-style of the political and social élite. In a pre-industrial society only slowly beginning to experience the growing pains of change, the landowner's position was unique, affording at once the opportunity for leisure, status, political power and a patriarchal social role. As William Marshall acknowledged in 1804, 'landed property is the basis on which every other species of material property rests; on it alone mankind can be said to live, to move and to have its being'.[26] In their position as heritors, Scottish landowners had virtual control over the selection of parish ministers and village school-teachers, the two most important sources of influence at parochial level. As Commissioners of Supply, Lord Lieutenants (from the 1790s), J.P.s and Members of Parliament, political power, both in national and local terms, was very much their prerogative. Inevitably then most merchants, especially since several of them came from landed stock, wished to see their descendants firmly ensconced in this circle. Coats of arms were acquired, estates consolidated into 'baronies' and entail arrangements carefully formulated to ensure the family's attachment to the chosen property.[27] William Cunninghame was particularly solicitous over the continuation of the family name, insisting that in the case of a female succession, the young lady would be required 'to marry a gentleman of the surname of Cunninghame' or at the very least a husband who would assume the name of Cunninghame immediately after the succession took place.[28] In their eagerness to found a landed family others purchased a series of estates, the largest devolving on the eldest son and the others being divided among younger sons and spinster daughters.[29]

Land was also the most obvious route to a rentier income in the eighteenth century and as such was acquired by wealthy merchants as a sound investment for their families in the event of their deaths. Indeed, on occasion, marriage contracts specified that the spouse should purchase an estate in order to provide his wife with a liferent. For instance, Robert Bogle jun. was married twice and in each case, according to the contracts, he had to buy land. When he wed Jean Carlisle it was deemed desirable that 24,000 merks be spent in this way and after his second marriage, to the daughter of Sir Archibald Stewart of Blackhall, a further 46,000 merks were to be employed in acquiring sufficient property to provide a liferent of 1000 merks per annum for her.[30] When the family estate devolved upon the eldest son, legal settlements ensured that the widow was guaranteed a proportion of the annual rental.[31] For the richest merchants, however, the most effective way to protect the status and independence of their wives and female relatives was to settle one estate among their lands on them. So Alexander Speirs's widow inherited Yoker and Blawarthill and in the 1800s Speirs's trustees were buying land near Bothwell for the tobacco lord's two unmarried daughters.[32] Again, if a husband died without having made due financial provision for his next of kin, it was not uncommon for a close relative to intervene and purchase land for them.[33]

However, ownership of landed property was not based solely on the needs of the family. In the final decades of the century new economic incentives encouraged estate purchase in the vicinity of Glasgow. Land had always had an 'economic' attraction for the merchant. As a safe asset it could be mortgaged to attract loans, and earnings from rentals, though less than income from trade, were probably more dependable. Yet from the second half of the eighteenth century, urban expansion, the spread of industry in the countryside and rapidly changing estate values led to tobacco merchants buying land in order to *exploit* its mineral and industrial resources. Several traders, already owners of substantial estates, purchased smaller pieces of property, not for their amenity or prestige value, but as economic assets. Between the end of the American War of Independence and the turn of the century, Andrew Buchanan of Ardenconnal, William French, John Campbell of Clathic, George Coats and James Hopkirk, among others, all bought up territory in the mineral rich parishes of Old and New Monkland in Lanarkshire. Interestingly enough, purchasing was concentrated in the period after the opening in 1793 of the Monkland Canal, in which several tobacco lords had invested.[34] The Speirs estates were concentrated in Renfrewshire and Stirlingshire yet Archibald, who inherited these in 1782, also began to collect small areas of land in North Lanarkshire. In 1804 he gave a subtack to the Shotts Iron Co. '. . . of the coal, ironstone, limestone, fire clay, and all other metals and minerals' in them.[35] James Dunlop was the outstanding example of a merchant buying up mineral areas in this way. After 1783 his purchases all had three elements in common: proximity to the town of Glasgow, cheap transport there and the availability of extensive resources of coal and iron ore on the territory to be acquired. In ten years he obtained a series of estates valued in 1793 at over £60,000.[36] His confidant and banker, Sir William Forbes of Pitsligo maintained this was the direct result of his client's interest in mining:

> He had embarked deeply in two branches, which had peace continued and money been plenty must have made his fortune, having largely engaged in the working of coal-mines ... he had reduced these two branches of trade to a system by which he proposed every year to accumulate such a sinking fund as would enable him soon to pay off the great debt he was obliged to contract for them, and then leave him in possession of a clear, solid landed property.[37]

In the last two decades of the century the period of relatively low land prices, which had characterised the preceding era, came to an end. To the age-old influx of 'new' landlords had been added the stimulus of an incipient Industrial Revolution boosting mineral rentals and mill-site values. Parallel with this process, the 'improving' movement and its essential base, population and urban growth, had encouraged a farther increase in land prices. They doubled in Lanarkshire, Renfrewshire and the Barony of Glasgow in the 1780s.[38] The Bogle estate at Whitehill, unsaleable in 1778 at a mere £3200 was disposed of in 1809 for £15,000![39] In such a period buying a suitable property and later selling it when the time was ripe could lead to substantial capital gains. As a result, a relatively new type of merchant landowner emerged. Alexander Oswald, for example, became a speculator in land, holding particular areas for brief periods until a profitable sale was possible.[40] Lands adjacent to the main estate, outlying properties or marginal areas were particularly useful for such transactions. They were simply one of the merchant's many investments to be employed judicially to yield maximum returns. Similarly, some merchants who were fortunate enough to own territory in the path of Glasgow's physical expansion ruthlessly subordinated the amenity value of their estates to their function as economic assets. Archibald Smith of Jordanhill and George Oswald of Scotstoun were congratulating one another in 1800 as they realised that leasing land to farmers or mineowners was now much less remunerative than sub-dividing it into plots for villa construction.[41]

III

Possession of an estate was one precondition for entry into the highest political and social circles in the land. It was a route to power and prestige, the conventional method by which the *arriviste* translated his wealth into an asset which conferred not simply secure return but also enduring status and respectability for his family. The evidence indicates that several tobacco merchants did successfully infiltrate that nexus of legal and administrative posts which formed the cornerstone of the authority of the Scottish ruling classes. Andrew Buchanan, James Hopkirk of Dalbeth, James Dunlop of Garnkirk, Robert Bogle, James Ritchie, John Alston and John Wallace were

Justices of the Peace in Lanarkshire in the last two decades of the century.[42] One of these, Robert Bogle, together with four other tobacco lords were appointed Deputy Lieutenants for Lanarkshire and Dumbarton by the wartime government.[43] At the same time, George Oswald, James Dennistoun, Robert Findlay, Cunninghame Corbett and John Alston had been created land and income commissioners for the counties around Glasgow.[44] In addition, some merchants had built up their landed property to such an extent that they were capable of influencing the balance of political power in certain localities. For instance, in Renfrewshire the Speirs and the McDowall families were at once the most important 'interests' and the most bitter political rivals, the latter favouring the Pitt-Dundas grouping of the 1780s, the former loyal to the opposition camp.[45] James Dunlop was one of the important influences in Lanarkshire because he controlled nine votes there and 'had a good deal of interest about Glasgow from his connections with the Houstons and Scott of Aikenhead'. The Oswalds were similarly of much significance in Kirkcudbrightshire politics.[46] Other merchant-landowners played less of a partisan role in county affairs but were nevertheless individuals who had to be reckoned with when political prospects were being assessed. So James Ritchie was described as 'a very independent man' in Ayrshire while William Cunninghame had also no recognisable affiliations. In Dumbartonshire Thomas Buchanan was 'a very independent man' while Henry Glassford had 'an independent fortune'.[47]

The relative ease with which these rich traders were accepted in county society is hardly surprising. Most were scions of well-to-do families which had developed links over generations with the landowning classes. There would be few lairds in the vicinity of Glasgow who did not have some kinsmen 'in trade'. The movement of the tobacco lords into the positions which have been described was not therefore indicative of 'bourgeois' conquest of the landed interest's traditional preserves. Rather, their success was symptomatic of the fluidity which had long characterised the social structure of the region. The life-styles of these men were quite different from those of most of the entrepreneurs who were to be the driving force behind the burgeoning industries of the time. They were wealthy enough to be able to combine business with gentlemanly pleasures—a contemporary print of 'a Meet of the Lanarkshire and Renfrewshire Foxhounds at Crookston Castle, Renfrewshire', depicts a whole array of 'mercantile gentry'—and to ensure that their sons were given an education abroad commensurate with their social standing.[48] Some, such as the Oswalds and the McDowalls, were intimates of the greatest aristocrats in the land; others, as founder members of the Episcopalian Church of St. Andrews-by-the-Green in Glasgow, were co-religionaries of several old county families around the city.[49] As a perceptive writer at the time noted, they were men 'of prodigious wealth, and at the same time highly elevated and enlightened minds, who form a sort of nobility'.[50]

Almost certainly land represented the biggest single investment outside commerce for most of the traders considered here. Yet, by and large they do not seem to have broken their links with business and embraced the life of the country gentry. They aspired rather to create an equilibrium between a series of different but complementary types of investment among which land was very important. The 'haemorrhage of capital' thesis, which proposes that the process of mercantile land-buying resulted in a transfer of funds from more productive sectors (commerce and industry) to a less productive one (agriculture) does therefore require qualification when applied to the tobacco lords.[51] The purchase of land in fact often encouraged rather than discouraged investment in manufacturing, in turnpike road systems and in canals.[52] All these could be seen as integral items of estate exploitation in the same way as enclosures and drainage schemes. The image of the merchant with 'a yird hunger', proposed by Henry Cockburn, who 'if he once gets the acres, a single month of them, with "esquire" changes his nature'[53] is indeed a caricature of the truth. Even the greatest trained their sons in business and, while giving them a gentlemanly education, encouraged them in a commercial career. Alexander Speirs provided his son Peter with an expensive education (including a seven year 'Grand Tour' on the Continent) but his earnest wish was that 'he apply himself to the Counting-House'. When he had reached maturity Alexander intended to purchase for him 'land and an estate and a small firm in trade'.[54] The Glassfords, Ritchies, Somervells, Dunlops and McCalls, among others continued their associations with overseas trade long after their families had first acquired landed property.[55] Occasionally indeed the sons of merchants were only allocated an inheritance on condition that it was invested in commerce.[56] The legal protection afforded in contracts of copartnery to sleeping partners, the seasonal nature of the tobacco trade and the division of labour within the great Glasgow companies allowed time for other pursuits without compromising highly profitable investments. Most traders who owned land had 'town houses' or possessed tenement flats in Glasgow. Some spent half the week there, looking after their business interests in addition to taking part in the social life of the city, and stayed the remainder of the time in their country estates, which as we have seen, were normally situated a short horse-ride from Glasgow.[57]

Commercial interests were retained but these did not seem to conflict with the upward movement of merchant families in the social scale which purchase of land was intended to facilitate. Several of the sons and grandsons of the tobacco lords became successful in politics, law, administration and the military life. Henry Glassford, son of John, was a trained lawyer with a continuing stake in his father's American and Caribbean ventures. At the same time he became a Vice-Lieutenant of Stirlingshire, Member of Parliament for Dumbarton (elected 1806) and Lord Rector of Glasgow University.[58] Francis Dunmore, son of Robert, rose to the position of Commissary-

General in the British Army.⁵⁹ John Coats Campbell's son, Archibald, was nominated to the position of Lord Clerk Registrar for Scotland.⁶⁰ The Dunlops produced a Sheriff of Renfrewshire, the Houstons a Governor of Grenada, the Buchanans of Auchintorlie (of Dennistoun, Buchanan and Co.) an Ambassador to Russia, the Smiths of Jordanhill, one of the most eminent geologists of the nineteenth century.⁶¹ Some, like the Ritchies, Glassfords and Buchanans married into the Scottish aristocracy.⁶²

IV

One of the more important effects of mercantile land-buying was likely to be its economic impact in the counties around Glasgow. It was assumed by some contemporaries and, more recently, by a number of historians, that new landowners with access to plentiful sources of capital and accustomed to evaluating outlay in terms of profit and loss were likely to become very vigorous 'improvers'. Adam Smith, the incumbent of the Chair of Moral Philosophy in the University of Glasgow at this time, saw the merchant landowner as a new breed, disrupting the peace of the countryside:

> Merchants are commonly ambitious of becoming country gentlemen and, when they do, they are generally the best of all improvers. A merchant is accustomed to employ his money chiefly in profitable projects; whereas a mere country gentleman is accustomed to employ it chiefly in expense. The one often sees his money go from him and return to him again with profit; the other, when once he parts with it, very seldom expects to see any more of it. Those different habits naturally affect their temper and disposition in every sort of business. The merchant is commonly a bold, a country gentleman a timid undertaker. The one is not afraid to lay out at once a large capital upon the improvement of his lands, when he has a profitable prospect of raising the value of it in proportion to the expense...⁶³

There is a core of truth in Smith's thesis if applied to the merchants considered here but there is also some distortion. In reality, the distinction between 'merchant' and 'country gentlemen' was less marked than he appreciated; recent scholarly work and even a casual examination of the published agricultural reports of the late eighteenth century indicate that many 'country gentlemen' were not 'timid undertakers' but, on the contrary, were in the van of the 'improving' movement.⁶⁴ It is clear too, that the very fact of their greater wealth permitted some merchants to employ money in wasteful and highly speculative projects which excited the humour of their more canny and less opulent neighbours. The McDowalls, for example, spent over £5000 in attempting to drain the loch of Lochwinnoch in Renfrewshire (despite the advice of their fellow lairds) only to see it fill in again after a few years.⁶⁵ John Glassford, as will be seen, did conduct various 'improvements' on his Dumbartonshire estate of Dougalston, but much of his wealth was also channelled into less productive areas. His country mansion had a facade of 100 feet in length, streams were diverted to form a lake thirty acres in extent and a separate building was constructed, known as the 'Banqueting

Hall'. Apparently, however, this was used for Glassford's main pastime of gambling.[66] There is little here of the rational merchant who 'often sees his money go from him and return to him again with profit'.

A further problem is the difficulty of weighting the contribution of the merchant-landowners as a class to the process of agricultural change.[67] After all even in the counties around Glasgow they represented a minority of estate owners; some were castigated by 'improving' writers for their pedestrian attitude towards the new practices of the time.[68] The paucity of extant evidence compounds the difficulty of overall assessment. Manuscript material on landed estates is often embarrassingly rich yet this author was unable to trace a coherent run of records for any of the properties considered in this analysis. Less fruitful sources had to be employed viz. jottings of estate income, fragments of accounts for short periods, details on landed investment extracted from legal records and evidence from the agricultural compilations of the time. To distinguish the role of merchant-landowners in any precise and balanced fashion would require more material than has been used. The aim here, therefore, will be a modest one and it will merely be the intention to describe briefly the agricultural activities of some merchant families.

In one sense, the extent of land purchase which has been described in the first section of this chapter was likely to effect agricultural change. The buying and selling of estates was one means by which land became an asset, capable of more rational exploitation, as well as the basis of a way of life. The very fact that several of the properties acquired by successful traders belonged formerly to bankrupts would perhaps imply renewed vigour in debt-encumbered estates. William Cunninghame was able to pay all the obligations on Lainshaw in Ayrshire. Within four years, he had achieved 'a small rise in rent' on some farms but to obtain this he had to lay out over £100 in new buildings 'besides other improvements'. Other farms were so exhausted when the property changed hands that Cunninghame was obliged to keep them in his own possession 'under a course of improvement' since 'a great deal of money must be laid out upon the farms, before they can be safely put into the hands of any tenant'.[69] Similarly, a fellow merchant, John Bowman purchased Ashgrove in the same county, 'from the motive of its being the place of his nativity'. The soil of the estate, however, was cold wet clay and 'part of it a sort of morass'. To Bowman such conditions were intolerable at a time when fashionable improvement and the 'desire to be thought good farmers' was a central concern of county society. Thus he embarked on a programme to transform his estate in accordance with the best modern methods. Hollow drains were laid; sand and lime were spread on it 'in abundance' and then mixed into the soil by frequent ploughing and harrowing.[70]

The landowners in the parish of Kirkmichael in Ayrshire included the Marquis of Ailsa, Sir Charles Dalrymple Ferguson and Sir David Hunter

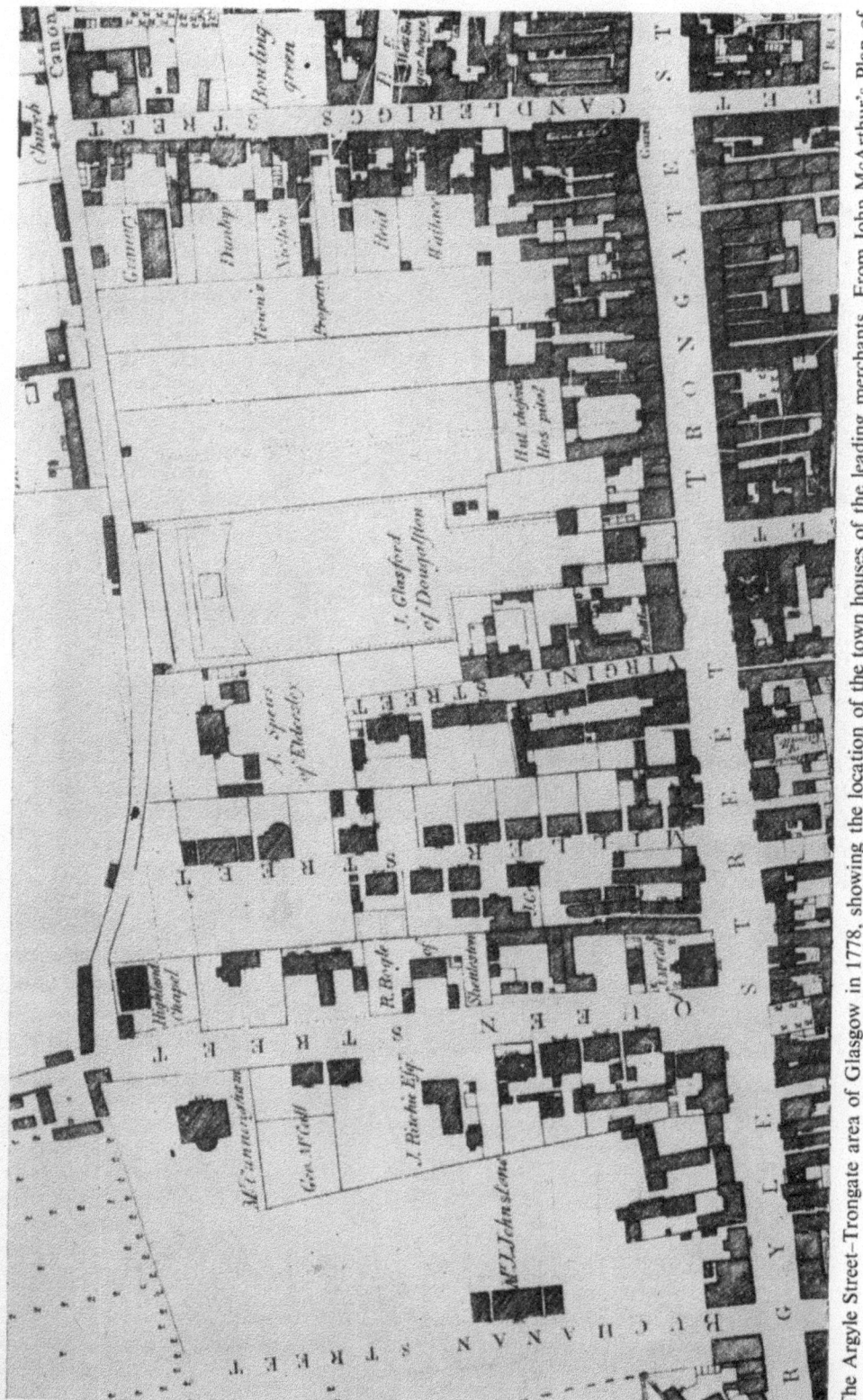

The Argyle Street–Trongate area of Glasgow in 1778, showing the location of the town houses of the leading merchants. From John McArthur's Plan of the City of Glasgow, 1778. *Courtesy of the Trustees of the National Library of Scotland*

John Glassford of Dougalston (1715–83), with his wife and family, by Archibald McLauchlan. Glassford was a subscriber to the Foulis Academy of the Arts, of which McLauchlan was a pupil. The setting is the Shawfield Mansion, the window overlooking the garden, the mirror reflecting part of the Trongate. *Courtesy of Glasgow Art Gallery*.

Alexander Spiers of Elderslie (1714–82), the 'mercantile god of Glasgow' and the most powerful merchant in the years before the American War of Independence. *Courtesy of the Mitchell Library, Glasgow.*

Elderslie House, Renfrewshire. Residence of Alexander Speirs, and typical of the country houses built by successful merchants in the counties around Glasgow. Demolished 1920. *Courtesy of the Royal Commission on the Ancient and Historical Monuments of Scotland.*

Blair of Blairquan; yet the parish minister considered that Henry Ritchie, the great Glasgow tobacco merchant, held 'the first place in this part of the country as an improver of land'. His successful ventures prompted the clergyman to remark piously:

> ... his experience unites with that of other enlightened landowners in establishing the fact that no outlay of capital yields so high and certain a return as what is judiciously applied to the purposes of agricultural improvement.[71]

In Lanarkshire too, the activities of merchant improvers attracted notice. The Monklands area in the pre-industrial era had the reputation of containing some of the most productive land in the West of Scotland: '. . . the stranger is struck with the view: it has the appearance of an immense garden'. This was due, so it was alleged, to the fact that

> ... when a merchant has been successful, he purchases a piece of land, builds an elegant villa and improves his property at the dearest rates. This accounts for the vast number of gentlemen's houses with which this parish is adorned, many of them finished in the greatest taste.[72]

Two of the families concerned in this process of change were the Buchanans and the Dunlops. The former's estate of Drumpellier, containing between 900–1000 acres of fertile land when brought to sale in 1806 was said to contain 'many valuable plantations' and to have been 'immensely improved' during their tenure.[73] When Colin Dunlop came into possession of the lands of Sandyhill in the same area the property was barren and covered with thin grass. He began to plant Scots firs and was imitated by his fellow proprietors. As a result of their efforts '. . . the traveller in a tract of three miles from Cawder Water to the Clyde Ironworks sees a beautiful plantation of firs, pines, larches etc.'. The investment was not intended to produce immediate gain; rather the aim was to increase the amenity and economic value of the estate for subsequent generations of the family.[74]

John Glassford's estate at Netherwood in Dumbartonshire excited the interest of no less a critic than the agricultural commentator Andrew Wight. When the tobacco lord bought it around 1773 the ground was wet and moorish. Glassford drew up an ambitious scheme for improvement because, according to Wight, he was 'accustomed to lay out his money freely on bold adventures in trade'. A cut was made to the Forth and Clyde Canal which brought dung in abundance from Glasgow; expert limeburners from East Lothian were hired and put to work. The highly-critical Wight waxed lyrical over the results, 'Many fields are now like gardens! How delightful the change! If his neighbours be not captivated by it, they deserve not to live'.[75] In correspondence with him, Glassford related how when he first occupied the estate, the ridges were so high that he was out 'a great deal of expense' to reduce them. As he saw it, his was the role of the 'gentleman improver'. He was, for instance, unable to answer some of the more technical questions which Wight put to him. His task was simply to provide the funds for his estate managers—'I know very little myself of the proper management of a farm'. He regarded the operations which were carried out not as valuable for their economic return but as a form of recreation: 'I own I have pleasure to see improvements made'.[76]

Merchant landowners in Renfrewshire were also praised by Wight and others for their exertions. George Oswald of Scotstoun, James Milliken of Kilbarchan, the McDowalls of Castlesemple and, above all the Speirs of Elderslie, had all achieved much.[77] The estate of King's Inch had been one of Alexander Speirs's first purchases, acquired in the 1760s for £8000. Twenty years later it had doubled in value, because of the cash which had been expended on it. Flooding from the Clyde had been stopped by the construction of a massive embankment which required the creation of a canal to facilitate the carriage of hundreds of tons of earth. As his properties were extended in subsequent years, additional sums were spent on building and furnishing a country house (at a cost of £12,300 between 1780–81) in plantations, in enclosures and in aid to tenants.[78]

REFERENCES

1. See Appendix I.
2. GCA, ML, Bogle MSS, Bundle 54, Inventory of Writs of Daldowie, 8 April, 1825; SRO, Reg. of Deeds, 207/2/549 DAL; James Paterson, *History of the Counties of Ayr and Wigton* (Edinburgh, 1866), III, 462; see Appendix I.
3. See Appendix I.
4. Paterson, *op. cit.*, III, 462.
5. SL, CSP, 406/21, Petition of James Dunlop, late of Garnkirk, 14 June, 1799, Appendix 2.
6. SRO, PRS (Stirling), 29/411.
7. T. C. Smout, 'The Glasgow Merchant Community in the Seventeenth Century', *SHR*, XLVII (1968).
8. See Appendix I.
9. H. J. Habbakuk, 'The English Land Market in the Eighteenth Century', in J. S. Bromly and E. H. Kossman (eds.), *Britain and the Netherlands* (London, 1960), 155–65; G. E. Mingay, *English Landed Society in the Eighteenth Century* (London, 1963), 27–8, 39.
10. Significantly most of these were West India merchants who bought land in the early nineteenth century—when the region around Glasgow does seem to have become overcrowded—or had inherited family estates lying at some distance from the city viz. the McDowalls—Garthland in Wigtonshire (Baillie's Library, Glasgow, Alexander Houston and Co. Law Papers, Advertisement of Lands); Alexander Campbell—Kingledoons, Hallyards in Peebleshire (ML, Campbell of Hallyards MSS, Codicil to Settlement by Alex. Campbell, 12 April, 1817); Mungo Nutter Campbell—Ballimore in Argyll (Stewart, *op. cit.*, 184); John Stirling and John Coats Campbell—Kippendavie and Clathick respectively in Perthshire. (Anon., *Old Country Houses of the Old Glasgow Gentry* (Glasgow, 1870), 215).

MERCHANT INVESTMENTS: I LAND

11. L. J. Saunders, *Scottish Democracy 1815–40* (Edinburgh, 1950), 15.
12. T. C. Smout, *A history of the Scottish People, 1560–1830* (London, 1969), 285–290.
13. W. Fullarton, *General View of the Agriculture of the County of Ayr* (1793), 104.
14. *Ibid.*, 137.
15. John Knox, *A View of the British Empire more especially Scotland* 3rd. ed., (London, 1785), I, 97.
16. H. Hamilton, 'The Failure of the Ayr Bank, 1772', *Econ. Hist. Rev.*, VIII, 2nd. ser., 1955–6, 405–18.
17. A. W. Kerr, *History of Banking in Scotland* (4th. ed., Glasgow, 1926), 93.
18. ML, Bogle MSS, Bundle 54, Trustees of Daldowie to George Bogle, 3 March, 1779. Some of the partners' lands were still being advertised in 1781, almost ten years after the failure. See *Edinburgh Evening Courant*, 29 April, 1781.
19. Mingay, *op. cit.*, 38; George Bogle's trustees were keen to sell Daldowie in 1779 but 'the vast demands of government and the high terms they are obliges to offer to procure money occupy all the extensive capital' (ML, Bogle MSS, Bundle 54, Trustees of Daldowie to George Bogle, 3 March, 1779).
20. SL, CSP 162/3; SRO, GD 247/141, Account showing price of the estate of Lainshaw; SRO, GD 247/140, Petition of H. M. Cunninghame and others...
21. SRO, PRS (Renfrew), 25/43, 265; SRO, PRS (Glasgow), 24/202; SRO, GRS, 426/206; SRO, PRS (Glasgow), 25/126.
22. GCA, Speirs Papers, TD 131/4, Ledger B of A. Speirs, 1773–80; TD 131/7, Ledger of the estate of Alexander Speirs, 41–5.
23. Smout, *loc. cit.*, (1968).
24. SRO, PRS (Renfrew), 40/15; GCA, Smith of Jordanhill Papers, TD 1/15, Inventory of the title deeds belonging to Mr. Smith's heirs; SRO, PRS (Renfrew), 61/23.
25. GCA, Reg. of Deeds, B.10/15/8341.
26. Quoted in Harold Perkin, *The Origins of Modern English Society*, (London, 1969), 41.
27. C. G. Thomson, 'An Old Glasgow Family of Thomson', Paper read before members of the Old Glasgow Club, 19 January, 1903; Crawford and Robertson, *op. cit.*, 348.
28. SRO, GD 247/139, Scroll of the Tailzie for the estate of Duchrae and others, 9.
29. See, for instance, the case of Alexander Speirs. His trustees had to expend £8000 for an estate for his second son, Peter, while Archibald, the elder, inherited Elderslie. GCA, Reg. of Deeds, B.10/15/8435, Settlement, Alex. Speirs esq., 16 December, 1782.
30. GCA, Reg. of Deeds, B.10/15/5113, Settlement of Robert Bogle jun. 1736.
31. *Ibid.*, B.10/15/7587, Settlement of James McCall; B.10/15/8814, Disposition and settlement by John Millar of Westertoun in favour of John Alston, 12 May, 1788.
32. *Ibid.*, B.10/15/8435; SRO, GRS 680/238. For similar action by James Dunlop and William Cunninghame see SRO, GRS 411/64, PRS (Barony of Glasgow), 24/404; SRO, GD 247/139, Scroll of the estate of Duchrae...
33. See SRO, PRS (Lanark), 29/189.
34. SRO, PRS (Lanark), 25/138, 164–66; 27/87; 29/189; GRS 415/53.
35. SRO, PRS (Lanark), 32/171; for similar activity by Robert Dunmore in Stirlingshire see *OSA*, XVIII, 239; *Glasgow Mercury*, 19 January, 1796.
36. SL, CSP 406/21, Appendix, 3.
37. Sir William Forbes of Pitsligo, *Memoirs of a Banking House* (London, 1860), 76. Dunlop's coal-mining activities will be considered in more detail in Chapter 3, pp. 56–7.
38. *Scots Magazine*, LIII (1791), 562–3; *OSA*, I, 324; XV, 498; VII, 379; XIII, 117; John Naismith, *General View of the Agriculture of the County of Clydesdale* (Glasgow, 1798), 80.
39. ML, Bogle MSS, Bundles 54, 59, Missive letter upon the sale of Whiteinch, 12 October, 1809.
40. R. Reid, *Old Glasgow and its Environs* (Glasgow, 1864), 28; SRO, GRS 412/223.
41. GCA, Smith of Jordanhill Papers, TD 1/38/27, George Oswald to Archibald Smith, 23 December, 1800. For other merchant estates at Ibrox and Whiteinch being used for this purpose see *Glasgow Courier*, 17 March, 1812; *Glasgow Herald and Advertiser*, 10 June, 1808; 14, 28 August, 1809.
42. *Reprint of Jones's Directory or Useful Pocket Companion for the year 1787, with an introduction and notes of Old Glasgow Celebrities by 'the Rambling Reporter'* (Glasgow, 1868); *Glasgow Journal*, 22 January, 1793.

43. SRO, Buchanan of Auchintorlie Papers, GD 1/512/33, Minutes of the General Meeting of the Lord Lieutenant and his Deputies for the County of Dumbarton, 27 July, 1802; ML, Bogle MSS, Bundle 66, Instructions by his Grace the Duke of Hamilton...
44. *Glasgow Courier*, 17 November, 8 December, 1798; 8, 10 August, 1799.
45. ML, Political State of Scotland in 1788, 213, 279; SL, CSP 608/1-9; 560/41, 47.
46. *Ibid.*, 195, 213.
47. *Ibid.*, 33, 36, 95, 149, 226.
48. Old Glasgow Exhibition Catalogue, 152; for merchant interest in sport and game preservation see *Glasgow Mercury*, 14 September, 1790; *Glasgow Courier*, 1 September, 1792.
49. SRO, Oswald Papers, GD 213/53, George Baird to Richard Oswald, 24 August, 1764; SRO, GD 237/139, McDowall Papers, Summary of work done at Castlesemple, 10 April, 1776.
50. Robert Chambers, *The Picture of Scotland* (Edinburgh, 1827), I, 310.
51. For this view see H. J. Habbakuk, 'Economic Functions of English Landowners in the 17th and 18th Centuries', *Explorations in Entrepreneurial* History (1953).
52. See below, 42-3.
53. *Journal of Henry Cockburn, 1831-1854* (Edinburgh, 1874), II, 170-1.
54. GCA, Speirs Papers, TD 131/9, Alexander Speirs to J. G. Martens, 20 May, 1782; NLS, Speirs Papers, ACC 3296, Educational expenses of Peter Speirs.
55. Paterson, *op. cit.*, III, 462-3; ML, MS Notes on the Family of Dunlop of Garnkirk; GCA, Reg. of Deeds, B.10/15/9961; GCA, Sederunt Book of James Somervell, 1791-97; *Glasgow Mercury*, 19 January, 1790; *Glasgow Courier*, 29 May, 1819.
56. See, for example, SRO, Reg. of Deeds, 231/135 MACK, Disposition by Thomas Hopkirk in favour of James Hopkirk.
57. Strang, *op. cit.*, *passim;* GCA, Speirs Papers, TD 131/10-12, Diary of Alexander Speirs; *Jones's Directory of Glasgow for 1787.*
58. Gourlay, *op. cit.*, 48-9.
59. Glasgow Univ. Matric. Albums, 4955.
60. SRO, CC 9/7/79/623, Testament of John Coats Campbell.
61. Old Glasgow Exhibition Catalogue, Notes and Indexes, 43; SRO, Reg. of Deeds, 271/583, DUR, Commission, Alexander Houston to John Campbell; *Old Country Houses*, XXVI.
62. Paterson, *op. cit.*, 462-3.
James Ritchie in 1758, married the daughter of the 12th Earl of Eglintoun, the biggest landowner in Ayrshire.
63. J. R. McCulloch (ed.), Adam Smith, *An Inquiry into the Nature and Causes of the Wealth of Nations* (Edinburgh, 1863), III, 181. For a similar view from another distinguished contemporary see Sir John Sinclair, *General Report of the Agricultural State and Political Circumstances of Scotland* (Edinburgh, 1814), I, 27.
64. See, for example, the position in Ayrshire: Fullarton, *op. cit.*, 104; W. Aiton, *General View of the Agriculture of the County of Ayr* (Glasgow, 1811), 115-118; J. T. Ward, 'Ayrshire Landed Estates, 19th Century', *Ayrshire Collections*, VIII, 2nd. ser., (1967-9).
65. SRO, GD 237/139, Notebook of work done at Castlesemple, 1770-78; SRO, BCP, I, 75, 756, Dunlop versus McDowall (1801).
66. Gourlay, *op. cit.*, 45-6.
67. Only their agricultural interests in the countryside will be considered here: their establishment of industry will be examined below, pp. 42-3.
68. For example, Andrew Wight criticised Richard Oswald's tenure of Auchencruive in Ayrshire; there was 'no improvement going on so substantial as to bear much additional rent.' See A. Wight, *Present State of Husbandry in Scotland* (Edinburgh, 1778-84), 6 Vols., III, pt. I, 200-2.
69. SRO, GD 247/140, Answers for William Cunninghame to the Petition of H. D. Cunninghame, 4 January, 1785.
70. Wight, *op. cit.*, III, pt. 1, 281-2.
71. *NSA*, V, 502.
72. *OSA*, VII, 377, 379.
73. *Glasgow Herald and Advertiser*, 10 November, 1806.
74. Brown, *op. cit.*, II, 180-2; SL, CSP, 406/21, Petition of James Dunlop... appendix 5.

75. Wight, *op. cit.*, III, 309–14; *Glasgow Mercury*, 19 February, 1784.
76. *Ibid.*, 314–16, John Glassford to Andrew Wight, 12 September, 1778.
77. *Ibid.*, III, 288; *OSA*, XVII, 533; XV, 492; P. A. Ramsay, *Views in Refrewshire with Historical and Descriptive Notices* (Edinburgh, 1839).
78. GCA, Speirs Papers, TD 131/5, Ledger C; TD 131/1, Cash Book, 1760–1778; TD 131/13, Sederunt Book of the Trustees of Alexander Speirs, 20–1; A Martin, *General View of the Agriculture of the County of Renfrew* (London, 1794), 8, 13. Between 1780–1, 20,000 fir, 4000 ash, 2600 oak and 700 beech were planted in various parts. Unfortunately Alexander did not live to see the climax of his improvements. He caught a cold in his expensive new country house and died in 1782.

3

Merchant Investments: II Industry

IN the eighteenth century (and probably later too) the division of economic activity into 'commerce' and 'industry' would have seemed artificial to contemporary businessmen and would have distorted the reality of their investment policies. The period was not one of functional specialisation. It was not easy to distinguish the merchant from the industrialist, the banker from the dealer in grain, the manufacturer of cotton from the coalmaster. Instead businessmen, especially the wealthier, combined a variety of functions, now formally separated into identifiable occupations. Inevitably therefore there were close personal and financial links between trade and industry and in this chapter an attempt will be made to evaluate their importance in eighteenth century Glasgow.

I

In recent years the extent of integration between the colonial trades and domestic manufacturing has been questioned. Several authorities have seen the danger of basing a case on a random series of examples culled in the main from secondary sources.[1] Yet, where modern historical opinion is divided, the viewpoint of an earlier age was virtually unanimous that the investments of the Glasgow tobacco traders had been an important element in the rise of domestic industry. So in 1812, the Merchants House of the city declared how Glasgow was indebted to those who had carried on the American trades not only for 'the extension of commerce' but 'for the establishment and for a considerable time, the support of its manufactures, now so highly advantageous to this Kingdom at large'.[2] The investigations of this author tend to confirm this view. Appendix I outlines the results of an examination of local and national registers of deeds, legal cases, newspapers as well as other sources and lists the number of industrial units at least partly financed by Glasgow colonial merchants.[3] On the basis of these data there would appear to be a fairly close correlation between the rise of tobacco commerce and the foundation of manufactories. The period from 1660–1730 witnessed in effect the infancy of the trade. Before 1707 illicit commerce with England's colonies inevitably operated within narrow limits. After the Treaty of Union, an early phase of rapid advance was followed by an era of stagnation as depression in tobacco markets and more rigorous customs administration combined to keep the rate of development at a stubbornly low level. These years up to c.1730 were apparently reflected in marginal merchant commitment to industry, only nine manufactories being established by colonial traders in the seventy years between 1660 and 1730. Subsequently, however, the pattern altered significantly. In the following period Glasgow rose to a position of prominence in American commerce. Merchants began to accumulate the necessary financial resources to re-direct surpluses into other areas of the economy. At the same time, as economic growth began to gather

TABLE VI
Glasgow Tobacco Merchants and the Leather Industry

Tannery	Merchant Partners	Capital	Merchant Share
Bell's Tannery	John Coats Campbell, John Bowman, Laurence Dinwiddie, James Dunlop, Alexander Speirs.	?	?
Glasgow Tanwork	John Bowman, Alex. Speirs, Robert Bogle, Walter Monteath.	?	90 per cent
Francis Hamilton and Co.	Hugh Wylie, Francis Hamilton	£2400	50 per cent

Sources—Gourlay, *A Glasgow Miscellany*, 97; SRO, Reg. of Deeds, 232/817 MACK; GCA, Reg. of Sasines, 10/30–1, 14 March, 1777; 10/198–202, 6 December, 1793; GCA, Reg. of Deeds, B.10/15/7651.

momentum, returns on industrial investments might well have seemed more attractive. Thus in the decade 1730–40, seven industrial partnerships involving tobacco merchants were established; between 1740–50, eleven and between 1750–60, a further seven.[4]

In the west of Scotland in the second half of the eighteenth century entire industries were dominated by the capital of tobacco lords and West India merchant princes. Each of the three Glasgow companies concerned with the tanning of leather and manufacture of boots and shoes were partly under their control in the 1770s and 1780s.

Furthermore, as befitted their position as centres of the Atlantic trades, the Clyde ports were becoming the focus of a vigorous sugar processing industry

TABLE VII
Glasgow Colonial Merchants and The West of Scotland Sugar Industry

Sugar Houses	Merchant Partners	Capital	Merchant Share
South Sugar House (1740s–1796)	Alexander Houston, William McDowall, George, Alexander and James Oswald.	£8000	5/6
King St. Sugar House (1780s–90s)	James Buchanan, Andrew Buchanan Thomas Wallace	?	90 per cent
Easter Sugar House	George Bogle	?	?
Wester Sugar House (1773)	Alexander Speirs	?	?
Greenock Sugarhouse (1765)	James Hopkirk Arthur Connell	?	?
Greenock Sugarhouse (1788)	John Campbell sen., James Gordon, Henry Riddell	?	80 per cent
Port Glasgow Sugar House	George Crawford, William Crawford, Andrew Buchanan, William Cunninghame, Robert Dunmore	?	?
Sugar House Co. of Port Glasgow (1770s)	John Leitch, Richard Dennistoun John Gordon, David Russell	?	50 per cent
Newark Sugar Refinery (1809–1817)	Robert Dennistoun, Alexander Campbell, James Campbell	?	?

Sources—SRO, Unextracted Process Innes Durie B7/1; SRO, GD237/139, Minutes of meeting of partners of South Sugar House; SRO, GD237/143/4; ML Bogle MSS, Bundle 54; GCA, Speirs Papers, TD131/4–5; SRO, PRS (Renfrew), 25/50, 41/89; *Glasgow Courier*, 29 November, 1798; ML, Campbell of Hallyards Papers, Trustees of R. Dennistoun to trustees of A. Campbell, 15 December, 1823; *Glasgow Mercury*, 29 December, 1789; ML, Campbell of Hallyards Papers, Meeting of trustees of A. Campbell, 27 August, 1817.

in the later eighteenth century. Between 1760 and 1810, for instance, there were four sugar houses in Glasgow, two in Port Glasgow and two in Greenock.[5] As Table VII shows all these units attracted the capital of colonial merchants.

A similar pattern of merchant dominance is apparent in the rope and sailcloth industries of the Clyde. In the 1770s James Corbett and Co., 'the Rope Manufactory of Glasgow', had fifteen partners. Ten of them were involved in the Atlantic trades.[6] George Buchanan jun., James Somervell, James McDowall and James Dennistoun were the principal figures, in the 1780s, in a separate firm, the Glasgow Ropework Co.[7] At Greenock, the two Ritchie brothers, James and Henry, owned seventy-five per cent of the shares in the town's rope manufactory while the Port Glasgow Ropework Co. had Alexander Speirs and Thomas Hopkirk among its partners.[8]

Of the three malleable ironworks in eighteenth century Scotland, the two situated in the Glasgow area—the Smithfield and Dalnottar companies—were financed by tobacco merchants. The first of these was founded in 1734 when a number of traders erected a slitting mill on the banks of the River Kelvin to manufacture nails; this early venture subsequently developed into a major concern producing 'nails, adzes, axes, hoes, spades, shovels, chisels, hammers, bellows and anvils' for the colonial market.[9] Thirty-five years after the Smithfield Company was established, Islay Campbell of Succoth, Advocate and M.P. for Glasgow Burghs, feued parts of the lands of Dalnottar to three wealthy merchants, the brothers Peter and George Murdoch and William Cunninghame all of whom were already fellow partners in a Virginia firm. In this new area they intended to set up works for 'the manufacturing of hoes, bills, axes, spades, raills, hinges, anchors, belts and every other kind or species of ironware also of making of Barr, plate and red iron barr steel of the different kinds and all manner of steelwork'.[10] The initial capital stock was to be £6000, increased in 1787 to £12,000.[11] Throughout its forty-four years of existence until in 1813 it was sold to William Dunn, a leading cottonmaster, the Dalnottar Co. was financed by a series of tobacco merchants who included in addition to those mentioned above, George Kippen, Neil Jamieson and Robert Dunmore.[12]

Once the funding of an industrial venture had occurred commercial prudence often dictated that a secondary involvement should take place because of the need to acquire cheap and reliable sources of power, secure raw material supplies or indeed create foci of demand for the original investment. So, in 1781, the Muirkirk Iron Co. was set up by the merchants who controlled Smithfield and Dalnottar, together with the partners of Cramond Iron Co. in order to maintain a safe supply of cheap bar-iron at a time when Swedish and Russian prices were rising.[13] It was by a similar process of integration that in the last thirty years of the eighteenth century a tight-knit group of tobacco importers obtained control of almost the entire West of Scotland glass industry and a sizeable proportion of its coal extraction developments.

In March, 1786, Peter Murdoch, James Gordon, James Hopkirk, Thomas Donald and Andrew Houston purchased the Glasgow Bottleworks at the Broomielaw.[14] For Murdoch, Gordon and Hopkirk such an acquisition was a logical extension of investment in other manufacturing activity since they were already partners in Murdoch, Warrock and Co., brewers in Glasgow.[15] The other three already had interests in the Dumbarton Glasswork Co.[16] A month after they had absorbed the Bottlework Co., the same group obtained control of the flint glass manufactory at Verreville and a joint concern was set up with an initial capital of £12,000 'for the manufacture of glass in all its branches'.[17] A final stage in the creation of a giant industrial complex was taken in 1793 when the Dumbarton Glasswork Co., in which the combine under discussion had a majority share, purchased the Glasgow Glasswork's premises and later in the 1790s added both the Greenock Bottlework Co. and the Dumbarton Brewery Co. to its series of acquisitions.[18] Several of the investing group, most notably of all, James Dunlop and Andrew Houston, had extensive coal-mining interests. Their stake in the venture can be seen as an attempt to establish secure outlets for their fuel at a time when costs in coal extraction were rising and demand failing to show a similar increase as new pits were opened.[19]

The industrial firms described above have been dismissed by at least one commentator as being 'small-scale' and of only marginal significance.[20] Yet most of them can only be written off in this way by hindsight. Bell's Tannery, described as 'a prodigious large building' in the 1730s, emerged forty years later as the greatest single leather processing plant in Europe apart from one at Cologne. By the latter date it employed over 500 men.[21] The Greenock Ropework Co. had a capital stock of £40,000 in 1785 and that of the Dumbarton Glasswork Co. rose from £20,000 in 1794 to over £84,050 in 1813.[22] Sugarhouses were among the most capital-intensive units in the economy before the era of the Industrial Revolution after c.1780. All in all, the kinds of venture discussed so far in this chapter were typical examples of 'factory' organisation at a time when most production took place in the home or on the farm.

II

Moreover, Glasgow tobacco merchants were also involved in the creation of the foundations of the 'staple' industries of textiles, coal and iron. This is not to say that they were the only or indeed the most important investing group but rather to indicate that their role, especially in the western Lowlands, was a considerable one. Some were associated with several of the pioneering textile firms of the eighteenth century. The manufacture of inkles began in Scotland in 1741 when Alexander Harvie brought knowledge of the process from Haarlem in Holland. From that date until the 1780s the 'Inkle Factory' was supported by a succession of colonial traders.[23] Possibly the most successful concern in the West of Scotland printing and bleaching industry was that of William Stirling and Sons, which had developed out of a cloth-printing manufactory founded on the River Kelvin at Dawsholm in 1750. Initially, however, the family's fortune had been made in the Atlantic trades. John and Walter Stirling were members of 'the great company' which developed 'the trade to Virginia, the Carriby Islands, Barbadoes, New

TABLE VIII

Tobacco Merchants and the Linen Industry in West–Central Scotland, c.1700–1800

Firm	First known Decade of Merchant Involvement
Haarlem Linen and Dye Manufactory	1730–40
Glasgow Inkle Factory Co	1740–50
Shuttlefield Factory Co	,,
Cumberland Factory Co	,,
Pollockshaws Printfield Co	,,
Milngavie Factory Co	,,
Silvercraigs Weaving Factory Co	,,
Holland Manufactory Co	,,
—	1750–60
Brown, Carrick and Co	1760–70
Andrew Buchanan and Co	,,
Cudbear Works Co	,,
Graham, Liddell and Co	1770–80
James McGregor and Co	,,
Joshua Johnston and Co	,,
McBrayne, Stenhouse and Co	1780–90
Coats, Campbell and Co	,,
A. and J. Newbigging and Co	1790–1800
Milton Printworks	,,
Endrick Printfield Co	,,
John Renfrew and Co	,,
Spreul, Somervell and Co	,,
Kilbarchan Bleachfield Co	,,

Sources—GCA, Register of Deeds; SRO, Register of Deeds; Glasgow newspapers; SL, Court of Session Processes.

England, St. Kitts, Monserrat and other colonies in America'.[24] Another outstanding figure in the development of bleaching technology was James McGregor. His firm was the first to use chlorine as a bleaching agent in Scotland and he was backed financially in his activities by such tobacco lords as James and Henry Glassford and John McCall.[25]

The Glassford family also had interests in two other famous manufactories of the period—the Glasgow Cudbear Works, managed by George Mackintosh and the Prestonpans Vitriol Co., the foundation of which in 1749 has been described as '. . . an epoch-making step in the history of bleaching'.[26] In 1779 the first of these was managed by Adam Grant 'dyer in Glasgow' and by Mackintosh himself, but the bulk of the capital was supplied by John Glassford, James Gordon, George Bogle and John Robertson.[27] Over a decade earlier Glassford had become a member of the Prestonpans Vitriol Co. and soon held half the stock together with Patrick Downie (or Downey), 'merchant in Prestonpans'. They 'professed as their business that of making vitriol and aqua forte'.[28] On Glassford's death his son, Henry, took over his share, continued the business and assumed James Gordon, an old associate of his father's in the Virginia trade, into the partnership. Henry Glassford still had a controlling interest, however, and by the end of 1797 had become 'sole Owner and Proprietor of the Oil of Vitriol Works of Prestonpans'.[29]

These companies were pioneers of their type but as Table VIII indicates, tobacco merchants also invested in a wide range of linen manufacturing and bleachfield concerns.

In the last quarter of the eighteenth century there was a marked increase in Scottish investment in coal-mining, pig-iron production and cotton-spinning. Between 1779 and 1815, nine separate pig-iron manufacturing units were developed with a total furnace capacity which rose from 4000 tons in 1780 to 32,000 in 1813. Table IX lists these and where known the origins of the capital of the respective firms.

This information suggests that the extension in pig-iron producing capacity in these years was caused mainly by the movement north of English manufacturers intent on exploiting the cheaper factor costs in Scotland and by the need of domestic iron merchants to gain access to more secure and economic supplies of bar-iron as prices of foreign imports rose. Yet despite the manifest dominance of these groups, colonial traders had interests in two of the nine companies and were almost wholly in control of a third (Muirkirk).

Their role was perhaps more significant in the expansion of coal-mining in west-central Scotland. Most tobacco merchants owned estates and the majority of these lay across the rich seams of the central coalfield.[30] However, the extent to which these resources were exploited by mercantile landowners themselves or were leased to persons experienced in the extraction industries —an option which would cut the risks inherent in any eighteenth century mining activity[31]—is very much an open question. Certainly some preferred to opt for safety. Alexander Speirs's son, Archibald, having had 'information' that 'it was supposed a considerable bed of workable coal might exist' in the estate of Elderslie granted a coal-tack to the Knightswood Coal Co. by which it was agreed that a rental of £115 per annum would be paid Speirs.[32] Others, however, did engage directly in the process and shouldered all the burdens of risk and capital expenditure. Thomas Hopkirk personally financed the working of coal on his lands of Dalbeth.[33] Archibald Smellie 'wrought extensively the coal' on his estate of Easterhill.[34] As the majority shareholder

TABLE IX
Scottish Pig Iron Firms, 1779–1810

Firm	Year of Foundation	Sources of Capital	Colonial Merchant Share	Source
Wilsontown	1779	Robert, John and William Wilson, London iron merchants		J. Butt and I. L. Donnachie, 'The Wilsons of Wilsontown', *Expl. in Entrepreneurial Hist.* 2nd ser., iv (1967), 150–168
*Clyde	1784	Thomas Edington; John Mackenzie (Rosshire landowner); The Dunlop Family (from 1810).		SRO, Register of Deeds, 260/358 DUR; 1 Currie Dal, C/11/9, Clyde Ironworks versus Colin Dunlop
*Murkirk	1787	Cramond, Dalnottar and Smithfield Iron Co (several partners were colonial merchants)	75%	SRO, GD 237/151/3, Contract of Copartnery of Muirkirk Iron Co.
Omoa	1787	1787–96: ? 1796–?: Col. W. Dalrymple (Local landowner) Messrs Francis and John Anderson, iron merchants		Sir J. Sinclair (ed) *Statistical Account of Scotland* (Edinburgh 1791–8), XV, 60; SRO, RH15/1925, Ledger of Omoa Ironworks.
Devon	1792	No information		—
Glenbuck	1795	1795–1805: John Rumney and Co, Workington		SRO, Extracted Process, Decree exonerating John Sloan, 7 July, 1821; J. Butt, 'Glenbuck Ironworks', *Ayrshire Colls*, VIII (1967–9), 68–75.
Calder	1800	Alexander and David Allan, Glasgow merchants; James Burns, David Mushet (until 1804)		H. Hamilton, *The Industrial Revolution in Scotland* (Oxford, 1932), 173.
*Shotts	1801	Walter Logan, John Baird, George Munro, Hugh Baird, Robert Baird. From 1804 Walter Logan, John Baird, George Munro, Robert Bogle, John Blackburn		SRO, Bill Chamber Process, II, 39, 288 (1816).
Balgonie	1801	Partners of Team Ironworks, Newcastle; Leith Walk Iron Foundry		SRO, Leven and Melville Muniments, GD 26/810.

*Firm with some degree of colonial merchant investment at some stage in its existence.

in the Monkland Canal, completed in 1793, and as the owner of property which bestrode the extraordinary rich Monklands coalfield, Andrew Stirling had the motivation to exploit his mineral resources on a considerable scale. He formed 'the Monkland Coal Co.' in 1798 with an initial capital of £3500. He himself had previously been sole proprietor of the two collieries which formed the basis of the company's operations and had 'expended considerable sums' in developing them. However, since 'he could not give his full time to them' he had decided to establish a partnership in which he held four-sevenths of the initial capital stock.[35]

In the later eighteenth century there was a proliferation of coal companies such as these[36] and tobacco merchants were involved in several of them. William French held half the capital in the Easter Barrachney 'coal-work' which operated mines about three miles from Glasgow.[37] From 1793 the Sandyhills and Camlachie Coal Works, formerly owned by the bankrupt tobacco lord, James Dunlop, were carried on by a syndicate which included the Dennistoun family.[38] They were also interested in the Dunmore Coal Co. in Fife.[39] Almost certainly, however, the most important example of mercantile endeavour in mining was the Dunlop-Houston stake in the Glasgow and Lanarkshire industries.

The Gorbals-Govan area on the outskirts of the town of Glasgow was said to 'abound in coal' in the later eighteenth century.[40] Mining had been carried on there since the Reformation and in the early eighteenth century 20,000 'loads' of coal were being extracted annually.[41] The parish minister reported in some wonder, in 1793, that, 'It is thought that there is such a quantity of coals in the colliery as would of itself serve the city of Glasgow for 100 years to come'.[42] Yet, despite the extensive coal measures in the area, mining had not kept pace with rising demand from manufactories and from the domestic consumer for fuel. The coalfield belonged to the Town, the Trades House and Hutcheson's Hospital, public institutions which possessed neither the initiative nor the capital to respond satisfactorily to these stimuli.[43] Development only began on a grand scale when the collieries were leased to a partnership which included the Dunlops and the Houstons, two of the most opulent merchant dynasties in Glasgow.

In June 1768 a coal tack was granted by the three institutions concerned to Colin Dunlop, Alexander Houston, Gabriel Gray and James McNair.[44] The latter two were 'experts' in mining; McNair, for instance, was 'perfectly well acquainted with the business of coal-working . . . which he had been accustomed from his earliest years'.[45] This venture was only the initial phase in a project which was eventually to include mines in three counties and which was to end in the partners being accused of trying to organise a monopoly of the West of Scotland coal trade.[46] Between 1768 and 1773, coal-tacks were awarded the company in Dumbartonshire, in Knightswood and in Jordanhill.[47] In the latter year Colin Dunlop's son, James, joined the firm and by that time the two Dunlops held half the capital while Alexander Houston contributed the remainder. Both McNair and Gray had dropped out.[48] The Little Govan Coalworks and the Knightswood Coal Co. were their 'principal objects' at this time and in them the partners had sunk much capital in the construction of waggonways to carry their coal to port for transport to Ireland.[49] In 1800 the Govan Colliery alone was valued at £20,000.[50]

The deaths of the two original partners did not interrupt the momentum of expansion. James Dunlop and Andrew Houston carried on the policies of their fathers in buying up mineral right in the barony of Glasgow and Lanarkshire.[51] It is very probable, indeed, that Dunlop himself became the most powerful coalmaster in the west of Scotland at this time. At his bankruptcy in 1793 it was reckoned the value of 'utensils', machinery and waggonways at his various collieries, exclusive of the land was in the region of £30,000.[52] He 'engaged . . . in merchandise, in shipping, in the coal trade to a great extent and embarked in almost every mercantile undertaking'.[53] His largest coal mine within his own lands was that of Fullarton in Lanarkshire. Within a sixteen year period from 1777 to 1793, Dunlop expended £10,000 in trying to improve the productivity of this single asset.[54] He also had a three-eighths share in the Elderslie Coal Co. which worked a mine in Renfrewshire, a fifty per cent interest in Rutherglen Muir Coal Co. and owned a quarter of the capital in the Sandyhill Coal Work. In addition, he was involved in the Banknock, Camlachie and Hamilton Farm coal companies and had a majority share in the New Smithills Coalwork, near Paisley.[55]

III

The relationship between colonial merchant capital and the new cotton industry is particularly worthy of examination. In the period selected for special study this sector alone experienced the rapid expansion, massive productivity gains and novel technological innovation characteristic of an 'Industrial Revolution'. Moreover, until fairly recently, it was unquestioned academic orthodoxy that the rise of this new industry from the 1780s was associated with a transfer of capital from overseas trade to domestic manufacturing as a result of the collapse of tobacco commerce during the American War of Independence. The coincidence in time between the interruption of the American trade and the foundation of the first cotton mills seemed to lend some credence to this view. According to Professor Hamilton in his classic, *The Industrial Revolution in Scotland* (1932), the explanation of the evolution of cotton manufacturing was fairly straightforward, 'Many of them (i.e. Glasgow tobacco merchants) realising the profitable nature of manufacturing industry, turned their attention and capital to the new cotton industry'.[56] Over the last two decades several writers have attacked this thesis although it is still found acceptable in some quarters.[57]

This important issue cannot be satisfactorily resolved until information on merchant investment is compared with data on the number of cotton firms which were functioning in the final two decades of the eighteenth century. Recently Dr. S. D. Chapman has compiled a list of Scottish cotton-spinning companies operating in the year 1795 and it seems feasible to use his findings as the basis of an approximate measurement of the significance of mercantile capital.[58] It is true that criticism can be levelled both at the choice of year and at the source material employed by Chapman. His list includes only those firms which held insurance policies with the Sun Fire Office in London and inevitably therefore is incomplete.[59] Clearly too there are dangers in using insurance valuations as criteria for measuring patterns in fixed capital formation.[60] Again, consideration of 1795 might underestimate the role of the colonial merchants because it antedated their investment in such major ventures as the New Lanark Co. and James Finlay and Co. which were the most important units in the Scottish industry at the time.[61]

Yet despite these objections serious discrepancies are unlikely to arise because the intention here is merely to discern in approximate terms the *proportionate* role of colonial traders in cotton-spinning. Examination of a later period might, if anything, have diminished the significance of this group. Formation of new cotton companies was rapid in the later 1790s and early 1800s and yet there was little evidence in the sources consulted of similar increases in colonial merchant investment. Moreover, as far as this analysis is concerned, where only crude figures of *the relationship between* the capital sizes of various units is relevant, Chapman's material is likely to be of some value since his list does contain most firms in which these merchants were known to have interests in the year 1795. He suggested that the policy valuations of Scottish cotton mills approached £292,180 in 1795. The valuation of companies financed at least partly by colonial traders totalled £50,100 or about seventeen per cent of the total.

It cannot therefore be said that their financial contribution was of major importance to the expansion of the industry. In addition, such investments as did occur were clearly not conditioned by a desire to transfer assets from the tobacco trade. Rather they were related to a continuing process, which had long antedated the American War, of diversification coupled with retention of major interests in overseas commerce. As Chapter 12 will show, the Glasgow tobacco firms managed to renew their links with the independent United States after 1783 and their capitalisation of industrial ventures continued to remain subordinate to their role in the Atlantic trades.[62] Indeed, of the twenty-five colonial merchants who did join cotton partnerships, seventeen were primarily involved in Caribbean rather than in North American commerce. It was these men who were importing the 'sea-island' cotton on which, until the last few years of the century, the new industry flourished. There were obvious possibilities for integration between the two sectors. The fact, however, that only a minority of overseas merchants

TABLE X

Scottish Cotton Firms and Colonial Merchant Investment, c.1795

Firm	Location of Mill	Policy Valuation (£)	Colonial Merchant Partners	Merchant Share of Capital	Source
Ballindalloch Mill Co	Balfron, Stirling	10,300	Robert Dunmore	⅓	SL, Court of Session Process 368/21
George Houston and Co	Johnstone, Renfrew	7,800	William McDowall	⅓	SRO, GD237/134
Linwood Mill Co	Paisley	7,000	James and Alex Oswald	⅓	SRO, Particular Register of Sasines (Renfrew) 48/229
Deanston Cotton Mill Co	Deanston	7,700	Messrs Leitch and Smith; Somervell, Gordon and Co	50%	Finlay Mss, Balance Book, 1789–1800
Houston, Burns and Co	Lochwinnoch, Renfrew	6,900	William McDowall		SRO, GD237/134
Reynolds, Monteath and Co	Glasgow	2,800	James Dennistoun jun. James Dennistoun sen.	⅓	SRO, Particular Register of Sasines (Renfrew) 42/217
James Monteath and Co	Anderston	8,300	James Dennistoun jun. James Dennistoun sen.	⅓	SRO, Particular Register of Sasines 42/217

Notes

1. Firms and policy valuations are extracted from Chapman, *loc. cit.*, 262–3.

2. One other firm operating at this time but for which no policy is listed was the Culcreuch Cotton Spinning Co. established 1792. The Speirs and Murdoch families, colonial merchants, held fifty per cent of the £6,000 share capital of this company. See SRO, Cunninghame Graham Muniments, GD22/1/219. Contract of Co-partnery of Culcreuch Cotton Spinning Co. 26 July, 1792.

3. Six colonial merchants (Andrew, James and William Robertson, Robert Dunmore, Robert Bogle and Robert Mackay) had earlier helped to finance an unsuccessful jenny factory on George Dempster's estate of Skibo on the Dornoch Firth. They held £500 of the £2,300 capital. See Stewart, *op. cit.*, 80; Sinclair Calder, *The Industrial Archaeology of Sutherland* (M.Litt. Thesis, Strathclyde, 1974), p. 118.

invested in cotton would tend to suggest that trade still remained more profitable or less risky than this industry.

IV

There is no single explanation which will satisfactorily account for all the instances of industrial investment which have been described in this chapter. In some cases funds flowed from commerce to industry through a straightforward process of vertical integration. The Clyde tobacco trade required access to a variety of industrial producers because, put simply, the system operated by the Scots merchants involved the exchange of European consumer goods for the primary produce of Virginia and Maryland.[63] Once financial resources allowed there was a clear advantage in having some at least of these sources of supply under mercantile control. In the West of Scotland, however, there were few manufactories in the early eighteenth century of the scale needed to cater for the bulk and quality requirements of those engaged in the Atlantic trades. Alexander Carlyle, a student at Glasgow University in the 1740s thought that:

> There were not manufacturers sufficient either there or at Paisley to supply an outward bound cargo for Virginia. For this purpose they were obliged to have recourse to Manchester. Manufactures were in their infancy.[64]

As a result several tobacco lords founded their own ventures. Their establishment of tanneries, printworks, malleable iron works and bottleworks, in particular, was designed to cater for the supply needs of their stores in the colonies. The Glasgow Tanwork Co., founded in 1738 by eight tobacco merchants and re-established twenty years later with a capital of £12,000, was set up 'for Manufacturing, Tanning, Dressing and Curing Leather of all sorts and for making of shoes, Boots, saddles and Horse furniture'. Its surviving records indicate this concern was almost wholly dependent on the American market. In 1778, for example, the firm 'had on hand goods, manufactured and unmanufactured, to a great value which they had no immediate prospect of selling . . . by reason of the present unhappy contest with America'.[65] Other organisations, such as the Pollockshaws Printfield Co., created in the 1740s, the Dumbarton Glasswork Co. and the Dalnottar and Smithfield Iron Companies had a similar bias.[66]

The search for alternative returns was likely also as merchants sought to employ spare funds, spread risk and divert at least some of their capital away from the Atlantic trades. Profits were used to extend the scale of operations in the tobacco trade but since there was a limit to the benefits of size and fixed capital requirements were few, there was an incentive also to diversify operations. Because dividends from shares in tobacco firms were rigorously controlled, persons who wished to maximise income sought to invest in other assets.[67] Thus industrial concerns with good prospects became desirable investments in the second half of the eighteenth century. For example, Neil

Jamieson, a leading partner in John Glassford and Co., looking in the 1780s for 'a good, safe business' promising 'one hundred per cent for the money' put £2000 into the Muirkirk Iron Co.[68] This process of integration was facilitated because the wealth of the tobacco lords was attractive to managers and entrepreneurs who possessed skill and trade contacts but yet lacked capital. The typical pattern was for merchants to act as sleeping partners in an industrial firm, in many cases contributing the bulk of the stock but yet relying on skilled personnel to superintend the daily routine of production and management. It was thus possible to venture capital in a whole series of manufactories in each of which the merchant held individually small shares.

TABLE XI
Gross Total of Industrial Units with some Element of Colonial Merchant Capital in Stock, c.1700–1815

Manufacture	Total No. Units	No. Outside Glasgow	No. outside W. Central Scotland
Textiles (silk, linen, wool)	23	2	—
Textiles (cotton-spinning)	12	10	1
Textiles (finishing processes)	9	4	1
Iron (malleable)	4	—	—
Iron (pig)	3	3	—
Mining (coal)	14	8	1
Mining (other minerals)	2	—	2
Sugarhouses	7	2	—
Rope and sailcloth Manufactories	3	2	—
Leather Manufactories	4	—	—
Glassworks	3	2	—
Breweries	2	2	—
Soapworks	2	—	—
Tobacco—spinners	1	—	—
Potteries and delftworks	1	—	—

Between c.1770 and 1815, twenty-one merchants held capital in one industrial firm, nineteen in two, eleven in three and nine in four. Of the remainder three traders had money in six units, one in seven, three in eight, one in nine and two in ten. The peerless James Dunlop, mainly because of his extensive coal-mining interest, held sums of varying amount in no less than seventeen different partnerships! This structure was possible because in Scots law, as a result of its Roman law antecedents, the partnership was a separate legal entity within which the rights of members, who did not actively participate in the business, could be safeguarded in a precise fashion.[69]

Undoubtedly too the role of the merchant in industry was partly connected with ownership of land. The desire to exploit all the economic possibilities of an estate could imply not simply fashionable agricultural 'improvement' but also industrial investment. After all, the 'Industrial Revolution', at least in its early stages, was very much a rural based phenomenon and for the merchant-landowner policy was partly dictated by the attraction of rising mineral rentals and mill-site values.

The relative importance of profits from the tobacco trade in the process of Scottish economic change is less easy to judge. It would be dangerous to assume, for instance, that shares held in manufactories by tobacco lords always represented a movement of profits from colonial trade into Scottish industry. As we have seen in Chapter 1, the wealth of these traders was not exclusively based on the importation of tobacco. By and large too (as Table XI shows) most of their industrial interests were concentrated in the west-central region of Scotland.

Moreover, it is plain that their role, at least in cotton production and iron manufacture, was not central to the process of development. There seems to be no evidence of a prolonged acceleration in the flow of funds from trade to industry in the critical final decades of the century and thereafter. Indeed, since tobacco firms themselves borrowed extensively from groups within Scotland to facilitate expansion of their businesses it is a matter of debate whether the domestic economy gained or lost by the consequent complicated series of credit transactions.[70]

On the other hand, the significance of merchant investment in industry must not be deflated unduly. It is possible that it was of more consequence in the first half of the eighteenth century when the nation's financial resources were limited than in the period after 1750 when they were apparently more plentiful in relation to the demands made upon them. Furthermore, the role of the tobacco merchants was important in the creation of a variety of manufactories in Glasgow and its environs which might not have evolved if they had not answered specific needs in colonial markets or within the régime of individual traders. In that sense, the later industrial pre-eminence of the region within the Scottish economy was at least in part due to their initiatives. The major material benefits which accrued to the whole of the west central region through the rapid expansion of eighteenth century Glasgow was a consequence of the rise of industries focused on the colonial trades. Paradoxically the merchant aristocracy was basically responsible for the city's slow metamorphosis from a trading into an industrial centre.

REFERENCES

1. Until the 1950s, most writers agreed that the capital of the tobacco lords was of major importance to Scottish industrial change (see H. Hamilton, *The Industrial Revolution in Scotland* (Oxford, 1932), 121; Saunders, *op. cit.*, 98; J. Cunnison and J. B. S. Gilfillan (eds.), *The Third Statistical Account of Scotland: Glasgow Region* (Glasgow, 1958), 103; Eric Williams, *Capitalism and Slavery* (London, 1944)). In the last two decades, however, opinion has shifted markedly towards a more sceptical point of view (see M. L. Robertson, 'Scottish Commerce and the American War of Independence', *Econ. Hist. Rev.*, 2nd Ser., IX (1950), 130; K. Berrill, 'International Trade and the Rate of Economic Growth', *Econ. Hist. Rev.*, 2nd ser., XII (1960), 351-9; H. Hamilton, *An Economic History of Scotland in the Eighteenth Century* (Oxford, 1963), 142, 168; R. H. Campbell, 'An Economic History of Scotland in the Eighteenth Century', *S.J.P.E.* XI (1964), 19; 'The Anglo-Scottish Union of 1707: II the Economic Consequences', *Econ. Hist. Rev.*, 2nd. ser., XVI (1964), 472; *Scotland since 1707* (Oxford, 1965), 40; 'The Industrial Revolution in Scotland: a Revision Article', *SHR*, 46 (1967), 47; 'The Union and Economic Growth' in T.I. Rae (ed.), *The Union of 1707: its Impact on Scotland* (Glasgow, 1974), 63–64).
2. GCA, Minute Book of the Merchants House of Glasgow, IV (1790–1826), 245. For similar contemporary conclusions see William Fullarton, *General View of the Agriculture of the County of Ayr* (1793), 130; James Denholm, *History of Glasgow* (Glasgow, 1804), 408; David Macpherson, *Annals of Commerce, Fisheries and Navigation* (London, 1805), III, 593.
3. See below, 177–84.
4. Calculation based on local registers of deeds and sasines and on local newspapers.
5. *Ibid.*
6. GCA, Reg. of Sasines, 23 October, 1789, F.41-3; SRO, GD1/532/1, Disposition and Assignation, the partners of the Glasgow Ropeworks to John Hay and others (1786).
7. *Glasgow Mercury*, 8 December, 1785.
8. SRO, Reg. of Deeds, 246/1/580 DAL; SRO, CC9/7/80/514, Testament of Thomas Hopkirk; GCA, Speirs Papers, TD 1/131/5, Ledger C.
9. Brown, *op. cit.*, III, 286; *Glasgow Mercury*, 8 June, 1786; 1 July, 1784; 1 December, 1785; SRO, GD 237/151/3.
10. GCA, Reg. of Deeds, B.10/15/7460, Contract of Copartnery betwixt the Glasgow Iron and Steel Manufactory.
11. *Ibid.*, SRO, Reg. of Deeds, 249/829 DUR, Contract of Copartnery of Messrs. Gordon Gillies and Co.
12. SL, CSP 180/8; 409/22; GCA, B.10/15/9342. See also G. Thompson, 'The Dalnottar Iron Co.', *SHR* XXXV (1956).
13. SRO, GD 237/151/3, Contract of Copartnery of Muirkirk Iron Co. See J. R. Hume and J. Butt, 'Muirkirk 1786–1802, the Creation of a Scottish Industrial Community', *SHR*, XLV (1966).
14. GCA, Reg. of Sasines FF 171-3 registered 11 November, 1793.
15. SRO, Reg. of Deeds, 216/802 DAL.
16. SRO, Unextracted Process Currie Mack D/5/14, Memorial for the partners of the Dumbarton Glasswork Co.
17. SL, CSP, 422/53, Answers for John Geddes; SRO, Reg. of Deeds, 246/1/570 DAL.
18. SRO, Unextracted Process Currie Mack D/5/14, Memorial for the partners of the Dumbarton Glasswork Co. . . . 2. See J. C. Logan, 'The Dumbarton Glasswork Company: a Study in Entrepreneurship', *Business History*, XIV (1972), 61–81.
19. H. Hamilton, 'Combination in the West of Scotland Coal Trade, 1790–1817', *Economic History*, II (1930).
20. Campbell, *loc. cit.* (1974), 64.
21. McCure, *op. cit.*, 229; David Loch, *Essays on the Trade, Manufactures and Fisheries of Scotland* (Edinburgh, 1778–9), I, 26.
22. SRO, Reg. of Deeds, 246/1/580 Dal; SRO, Adams Mack Misc., 22, Day Book of Dumbarton Glasswork Co. Balance Book of Dumbarton Glasswork Co.
23. GCA, Reg. of Deeds, B.10/15/5664, 6849; Speirs Papers, TD 131/4.

24. John Butt, *The Industrial Archaeology of Scotland* (Newton Abbot, 1967), 139; McCure, *op. cit.*, 170; Anon., *The Old Country Houses of the Old Glasgow Gentry* (Glasgow, 1870), XXXVI.
25. *Glasgow Mercury*, 19 January, 1790.
26. Hamilton, *op. cit.*, 140.
27. SRO, Reg. of Deeds, 295/143 DAL; GCA, Reg. of Deeds, B.10/15/8132, 9009; SRO, PRS (Glasgow), 26/97.
28. SRO, Bill Chamber Process, II, 38, 634. Bill of Suspension and Interdiction, Basil Blackburn against Glassford and Co. (1786); Reg. of Deeds, 243/458 MACK.
29. SRO, Reg. of Deeds, 279/387 DUR; 275/286 MACK; SL, CSP, 438/18, Minutes in Process, Henry Riddell and others against John Riddell, 26 February, 1802, Appendix 13–14.
30. Several estates owned by merchants were famed for their extensive coal measures. Alexander Houston's lands at Jordanhill were 'full of coal' [GCA, Smith of Jordanhill Papers, TD 1/38/27, George Oswald to Arch. Smith, 23 December, 1800]; two of Robert Dunmore's estates in Stirlingshire 'afforded plenty of coal and lime, and are most advantageously placed for an extensive sale of these commodities' [*Glasgow Mercury*, 19 January, 1796]; the lands of Dalbeth and Easterhill in the barony of Glasgow, held by Thomas Hopkirk and Archibald Smellie respectively, were fruitful mining areas throughout the eighteenth century [*Old Country Houses*, XXXII, XXXVII; GCA, Mitchell Johnston Collection, 91, Disposition by John Dunlop in favour of Thos. Edington (1795)]. On Richard Allan's lands of Barnelland and Langlee, lying about six miles from Glasgow, there was 'plenty of coal and lime'. [*Glasgow Mercury*, 30 October, 1782; 1 August, 1796].
31. B. F. Duckham, *History of the Scottish Coal Industry* (Newton Abbot, 1970), Vol. I, CH. VI.
32. SL, CSP 374/5, Petition of Andrew Houston esq. of Jordanhill and others. . . . 2.
33. GCA, Dunlop Papers, Disposition by John Dunlop in favour of Thos. Edington (1795).
34. *Old Country Houses*, XXXVII.
35. GCA, Reg. of Deeds, B.10/15/9695, Contract of Copartnership among Andrew Stirling and others.
36. Duckham, *op. cit.*, 170–199.
37. *Glasgow Mercury*, 10 October, 1787.
38. *Ibid.*, 15 October, 1793.
39. *Glasgow Herald*, 25 July, 1808.
40. *OSA*, V, 540.
41. James Cleland, *Statistical and Population Tables relating to the City of Glasgow* (Glasgow, 1828), 186, 189; J. U. Nef, *The Rise of the British Coal Industry* (London, 1932), II, 50.
42. *OSA*, V, 540.
43. Hamilton, *op. cit.*, 186. For the conservatism of these institutions see J. R. Kellett, 'Property Speculators and the Building of Glasgow, 1783–1830', *S.J.P.E.*, VIII (1961).
44. SRO, Reg. of Deeds, 259/809 DUR, Bond of co-partnery betwixt Dunlop, Houston (registered, 1793).
45. SRO, Bill Chamber Process, I, 29, 063, Answers for James McNair to the Bill of Advocation presented for Colin Dunlop and Son.
46. *Ibid.*
47. SRO, Reg. of Deeds, 259/869 DUR; 292/758 DUR.
48. *Ibid.*
49. *Ibid.*; SRO, Board of Customs and Excise, C.E.60/1/8, Account of the admeasuring of waggons and other carriages used in the shipping of coals for exportation or coastwise within the port of Port Glasgow, June, 1776.
50. SRO, GD 237/139. For the subsequent history of these works see P. L. Payne, 'The Govan Collieries 1804–5', *Business History*, III (1961).
51. *Glasgow Courier*, 13 May, 1794; SRO, Reg. of Deeds, 292/758 DUR; SRO, Unextracted Process, 1 Adams Mack, S/15/106, Information for James McNair, 3; Anon., *Abstracts of the Rules and Regulations by which Hutcheson's Hospital is governed* (Glasgow, 1800), 57.

52. SL, CSP 406/21, Petition of James Dunlop, late of Garnkirk ... 14; GCA, Dunlop Papers, State of the Funds of James Dunlop, 23 March, 1793.
53. SRO, Unextracted Process, 1 Currie Mack, D/5/14, Petition of Gilbert Hamilton. ... 61.
54. SL, CSP 406/21, Appendix, 4.
55. GCA, Dunlop Papers, State of the Funds of James Dunlop, 23 March, 1793; SRO, PRS (Glasgow), 26/215; *Glasgow Journal*, 7 January, 1794; *Glasgow Courier*, 17 December, 1791; SRO, Reg. of Deeds, 292/158 DUR.
56. Hamilton, *op. cit.*, 121
57. For critical comments on it see the works cited in ftn. 1, p. 49. For a recent example of the acceptance of this thesis see Seymour Shapiro, *Capital and the Cotton Industry in the Industrial Revolution* (New York, 1967).
58. S. D. Chapman, 'Fixed Capital Formation in the British Cotton Manufacturing Industry 1770–1815', *Econ. Hist. Rev.*, 2nd ser., XXIII (1970).
59. The Sun Fire Office's coverage of Scottish cotton enterprises seems to have been limited to the merchant manufacturers and no series of policies has been discovered for the smaller jenny-spinners.
60. See S. Pollard and J. P. P. Higgins (ed.), *Aspects of Capital Investment in Great Britain 1750–1850* (London, 1971), 108–13.
61. From 1810 three colonial traders, Robert Dennistoun, Alexander Campbell and Colin Campbell, contributed £80,000 to the capital stock of the New Lanark Co., or just slightly less than half the total [SRO, GD 64/1/247, Contract of Copartnery of New Lanark Co., 5 October, 1810]. From the mid 1790s, Leitch, Smith and Co. and Somervell, Gordon and Co., traders to America and the West Indies, held one third of the stock of £75,000 in James Finlay and Co. [James Finlay and Co., Glasgow, Finlay MSS, Balance Book, 1789–1800. I am grateful to the directors of the firm for permission to use these important records.].
62. See below, pp. 161–6.
63. See below, pp. 61–4.
64. J. H. Burton (ed.), *Autobiography of the Rev. Dr. Alexander Carlyle containing Memorials of the Men and Events of his Time* (Edinburgh, 1860), 73.
65. SRO, Reg. of Deeds, 232/817 MACK, Agreement between the partners of the Glasgow Tanwork Co., 3 September, 1778.
66. *Glasgow Mercury*, 1 January, 30 December, 1784; 8 June, 1786.
67. See below.
68. SRO, GD 237/151/3, Neil Jamieson to Archibald Tod, 21 October, 1793.
69. R. H. Campbell, 'The Law and the Joint-Stock Company in Scotland' in P. L. Payne (ed.), *Studies in Scottish Business History* (London, 1967), 139–49.
70. See below, pp. 93–8; for a discussion of some of the problems raised by an analysis of this kind see M. W. Flinn, *The Origins of the Industrial Revolution* (London, 1966), 45 and S. L. Engerman, 'The Slave Trade and British Capital Formation in the Eighteenth Century', *Business History Review*, XLVI (1972), 430–43.

Part II

TRADING METHODS AND ORGANISATION IN THE GLASGOW TOBACCO TRADE

4

The Organisation of the Glasgow Tobacco Trade, c.1740-90

IN the eighteenth century the British tobacco trade was conducted in a variety of ways. For our purposes however the two most important were the 'consignment system' and the 'store system'. The first of these flourished in the seventeenth century and in the first three decades of the eighteenth and was the typical method used by the London tobacco merchants. There were generally three parties in the arrangement—the London merchant house, its factor in North America and the planter-customer. The latter consigned his tobacco to the factor whose parent company disposed of it in British and continental markets. The important element in this transaction, however, was that the planter retained title of ownership until his tobacco was sold by the merchant and so he, rather than the London house, shouldered all the burdens of risk, insurance, freight charges and port dues. In other words, in this system the merchant was merely an agent acting on behalf of his American client. Yet the relationship between the two necessarily became more complicated than this. When the tobacco was sold, the merchant deducted his commission and handling charges plus the cost of the goods he had been requested to deliver to the planter in the colonies. If there was anything left the profits would go to the planter but more often than not there would be a balance owing the London house. This would then be incorporated in an account which the merchant carried over from year to year. The system operated in mutually beneficial fashion to both parties. The trader obtained his commission payment and cut his risks; the planter, in return for consigning his tobacco to a particular agent, was entitled to expect the credit which was the basis of his rising material standards and expanding tobacco production.[1]

The trading method which concerns us more directly in this chapter is, however, the second of the important variants, the store system, practised by traders in certain of the English outports and most successfully of all by the tobacco merchants of Glasgow. By the beginning of our period, c.1740, this was easily the most popular system there and a knowledge of the nature of its operation is vital to an understanding of the success of the Glasgow firms in American commerce at this time.[2] The major difference between the consignment and store systems was that in the latter agents of the parent company purchased the tobacco outright from planters before shipping it to Britain. Firms established stores all over the tobacco colonies, not simply in order to collect the annual crop but also to service the consumer needs of their customers. Planters were allowed to acquire store goods on credit on condition that they sold their tobacco to the factor. As in the consignment system these grants of credit were rarely self-liquidating at the end of a crop year; more commonly running accounts developed since the planter's tobacco and the price offered for it were normally insufficient to repay advances. The store system also therefore became a medium for the extension of long-term credit to the American tobacco colonies.

As a preliminary to examining in detail the ramifications of this direct-purchase system its origins in the Scottish tobacco trade will be discussed. Precious little, unfortunately, is known about its organisation before the 1730s. To historians of Glasgow it was a simple, uncomplicated arrangement by which merchandise was exchanged for tobacco, with no credit and accounts closed after a single voyage. According to this interpretation, merchants chartered a vessel, a supercargo was appointed and the ship dispatched to the colonies to return as soon as possible with tobacco acquired in exchange for goods.[3] Yet even before the end of the seventeenth century this rather primitive type of commercial organisation was being superseded by one based on a series of stores under the control of resident factors. Much of the valley of the Potomac had been settled in this way by the 1680s and gradually the word 'supercargo' lost its original meaning and was used instead to describe a permanent storekeeper.[4] This is scarcely surprising. The few Glasgow men who ventured to the colonies had never had the reputation to attract consignments from the wealthier planting families of tidewater Virginia; rather than acting as commission agents they had always bought and sold, peddling their wares in the traditional fashion of the Scots merchant in Europe. Their concentration on the direct purchase of tobacco and the supply of goods would inevitably encourage them, once sufficient capital was available, to establish more permanent contacts than the old supercargo system allowed. It was in their interest, much more so than that of the London consignment houses, to ensure that vessels when they arrived in the colonies would have a freight more or less guaranteed and that customers could be expected for their merchandise. Only through resident factors buying up tobacco in advance and establishing a permanent clientele could the Scots merchants turn over their capital quickly and cut their risks.

As population expanded westwards in the tobacco colonies merchants planted many temporary stores near the falls of the rivers flowing into Chesapeake Bay. These could satisfactorily play the role of marketing centres among a dispersed and less wealthy planter class whose petty wants and small crops hardly justified the time and trouble of the greater London commission houses.[5] However, emphasis in catering for the needs of this group was subsequently a major factor in the success of the Glasgow merchant houses. After c.1720 tobacco cultivation expanded most rapidly in the inland areas of Virginia and Maryland which were dominated by the smaller planters. In the commission system the risks and expenses were mainly retained by the planters; the smaller men however did not have the financial reserves to enable them to deal directly with European markets. A recent calculation suggests that their disposable income in the 1760s was between £6 and £15 per annum.[6] They therefore much preferred transacting business through the storekeepers who, as intermediaries, could offer credit, goods and uncomplicated disposal of crops.

Thus, at the beginning of the period chosen for detailed study, the Glasgow store system was already firmly established. One typical concern at the time, that headed by John Murdoch and Archibald Buchanan, had been operating for many years in Hanover County, Virginia. There they owned two stores under the direction of a superintending factor, William Millar. Their turnover was nearly £3000 per annum, debts owed them by planters amounted to £200 and goods held in the stores were valued at over £1200.[7] The Bogles, one of the first families to make their fortune in the American trade, were operating the store system at least from the 1720s yet still describing their resident factors as 'supercargoes'.[8] Even temporary ventures, common at the time, by which a few traders came together for a single voyage, normally required the setting up of a store outlet for a time under the charge of a representative of the group. Thus in 1741 John Gartshore, Robert Boyd, Matthew Bogle, Allan and Robert Dreghorn intended to freight the ship *Boyd* for a single voyage to Virginia after which it was intended to dispose of the vessel. Yet previous to this arrangement they had settled a factor in the colonies to purchase tobacco in advance by importing goods from London and drawing bills on the partners in Glasgow.[9]

What seems then at first glance to be a fairly simple type of commercial organisation had, in reality, become a sophisticated one. This is not to say that most merchants had necessarily developed a long-term commitment to the tobacco trade by c.1730. The Bogle papers indicate that often these stores were temporary affairs and much smaller than the types which were to characterise the trade in subsequent decades.[10] They sprang up near the fall line tobacco warehouses during the inspection season, were essentially peripatetic and only some became permanent retail outlets.[11]

The marketing season in the tobacco trade extended from 10 November when inspection of the crop began to the end of the following August, leaving September and October as a slack period in which merchants took inventory of their stocks and made out accounts. Theoretically ordinary trading in the store system was based on barter. Planters exchanged their staple commodity for merchandise or for a combination of goods and money. However, cash purchases were usually essential to attract new customers and common also when tobacco supplies were scarce. Yet, storekeepers were always directed to keep their bill-drawings to a minimum and instructed to offer better terms to those customers who would accept store commodities in exchange for their tobacco rather than cash.[12] This was because some merchants estimated their profit from the sale of goods as important as income from tobacco sales in Europe; and, in addition, once cash was given the risks went up for it meant an outlay of capital long before there could be any commensurate return.[13]

Within this commercial structure, the Scots' crucial advantage seems to have been their ability to offer higher prices for tobacco produced by the smaller planters. This apparently partly accounted for their early successes in the trade in the last few decades of the seventeenth century.[14] Again, as late as 1769, a leading American merchant in Yorktown, Virginia, confided to a London trader concerning his fears that the Glasgow houses would monopolise the commerce: 'certain it is they give more real money for Tob(acc)o here than can be had at your Market except for a few particular Crops'.[15] The reason for the better prices offered by the Glasgow merchants probably lay within the logic of the store system itself. The aim was to acquire as much tobacco in advance as was necessary to cut down the turnaround time of incoming vessels in order to save on freight costs, the biggest single expense in the trade after the prime cost of tobacco. By cutting an important element in capital costs and (as we shall see below) turning over capital quickly by selling tobacco rapidly in bulk to European customers, the Glasgow men were able to achieve the necessary low operating expenses which allowed them to quote attractive prices to clients in the colonies.[16] The planters realised how the storekeepers regulated prices in accordance with expected ship arrivals. In 1772, for instance:

> So great is the demand for tobacco all over the Colony arising from the number of ships employed on the trade that the planter has been able to establish his own terms and to procure what part money he chuses.[17]

It was little wonder then that the estimated time of arrival of vessels was one of the most closely guarded secrets of company representatives in the colonies ... 'as when the Planters find a merchant pressing for tobacco and know he has a ship in the country it is generally difficult to procure their tobacco as they endeavour to enhance the value'.[18] But this drawback was not an insurmountable obstacle. The normal policy by the 1760s seems to have been to increase the circle of customers at all costs even if this meant inflating prices because the return to the merchant accrued not simply through the sale of tobacco in Europe but also through the retail of goods to planters in the colonies.[19]

In practice the two elements in a transaction between storekeeper and planter did not occur at the same time. The tobacco part of the exchange took place most frequently at the meetings of the county courts in the plantation colonies and many Scottish stores were thus sited adjacent to these administrative centres.[20] The selling of merchandise was, however, an all the year round activity carried on at the store. While some articles were sold across the counter for tobacco, the total amount was small. Commerce was based on credit. The regular tobacco unit of exchange—a hogshead—had so large a money value that it was hardly ever practicable for a planter to buy enough store goods at any one time to equal the value of one of these. Hence business was carried on most suitably through running charge accounts. The 'storekeepers generally sell their goods on trust, or time and receive payment in tobacco as the planters get it ready'.[21]

New firms or established companies setting up additional stores found that to gain custom it was imperative to extend credit over a considerable period before a profit was made. Glassfords founded a new outlet at Occoquam, Virginia, in 1759. From that date, an annual consignment of goods valued at £1250 was delivered to it but as their storekeeper, Alexander Henderson, informed them, 'remittances from this store will be small for some time but in the end it may turn out a very good place'.[22] Another contemporary considered that for every hogshead imported a sum of £25–30 had to be invested in America exclusive of shipping charges and other expenses.[23] Indebtedness of planters to Glasgow stores thus increased as tobacco imports rose. One estimate in the early 1760s, by John Glassford himself, suggested that he and his fellow merchants were owed a total of £500,000 by American planters.[24] In 1778 the estimate of debt had nearly tripled to £1,306,000.[25]

The origins of this vast sum are varied. Some observers at the time regarded it as the fruit of planter prodigality or middleman exploitation. The truth is more complex. The tobacco colonies were in a unique position as debtor areas in British North America. In 1776, Virginia, with about 21% of the population of the thirteen colonies, yet accounted for 46% of the amount owed Britain when the Revolution took place. Virginia and Maryland combined, with 30% of the population owed 57.4% of the debt.[26] These figures give us a clue to the origins of credit. The tobacco colonies were geared to satisfying international needs for an important commodity. Yet production was primarily controlled by a planter class with little capital in an area which also lacked an indigenous merchant group of any size. It followed that the investment needed to increase cultivation had to come from outside. Planters responded to a growing market not by improving their modes of production but by purchasing more (slave) labour. Even a single extra field hand could double and perhaps more than double the output of a household hitherto dependent on the labour of the planter alone.[27] So marginal was the small planter's financial position that he could only acquire slave assistance by borrowing.

The credit advanced meant too that the colonists could work through the months between harvests without having to deny themselves clothing, food and other items. It made it possible for them to cope with the differences in timing inherent in agricultural marketing—the fact that before the proceeds of one year's crop were in, the planter had to live and to plant the next crop.[28] In turn, storekeepers were instructed by their principals in Glasgow to be fairly liberal with credit when financial circumstances at home allowed in order to attract custom.[29] Again, one must take into account competition between firms as a factor encouraging extension of credit. To the radical colonial politician the Glasgow companies may have resembled the agents of a Scottish conspiracy intent on the co-operative exploitation of rural Americans. As William Lee had it:

A North Briton is something like the stinking and troublesome weed we call in Virginia wild onion. Whenever one is permitted to fix the number soon increases so fast, that it is extremely difficult to eradicate them, and they can poison the ground so, that no wholesome plant can thrive.[30]

In reality, however, competition between the Glasgow merchants was often savage and one of the most effective weapons in the struggle to gain an extended clientele was competitive offer of credit. So William Cunninghame and Co. directed one of their factors in 1768 to mount a campaign against rival firms by granting generous sums, 'such advances will assist towards enabling you not only to retain the former customers but also to engross the whole business'.[31] Similarly, Glassfords regulated their credit policies in accordance with the strategies of rival Glasgow companies.[32] There is some evidence too that over-zealous debt collection was considered inadvisable except in a most serious crisis. Storekeepers had to be careful lest they encourage planters to move their business elsewhere.[33] A more common response was therefore to obtain security on the property of those planters too deeply in debt to make speedy repayment. This bond obliged the debtor to pay interest on the sum owed, was negotiable and could be discounted for cash.[30]

The running charge accounts which formed the mechanism of the credit system could only work on the basis of rough standards of prices for the annual tobacco crop. Various factors governed these: the weather, condition of growing crops, intelligence from company headquarters as to potential demand in Europe for each of the different varieties of tobacco, and the number of purchasers in the trade. Since commerce in Virginia was decentralised and ultimate markets far away, the colony's business community evaluated all the information bearing on these influences at four annual meetings at a central point, in Williamsburg, the administrative and legal focus of the Chesapeake region. Since people from all over Virginia met in the capital at the sessions of the General Court in April and October and the Oyer and Terminer Court in June and December, it was convenient to use these times to produce a market price for the colony's most important commodity. After merchants and planters at the meetings balanced the probable size of the crop against the latest information from Britain concerning demand, a few would begin to buy and sell a little tobacco. When these opening prices were accepted by any considerable number of buyers and sellers, the price was said to have 'broke' or to have become the prevailing market price.[35] Thereafter the 'Court price' became the standard for dealings between planters and storekeepers.[36] As one Glasgow house pointed out in the early 1770s:

> The general practice there (i.e. in Virginia) is for the factors to receive tobacco in exchange of debts due to the stores and to allow the current prices for the same, which shall be fixed thereafter. This is called the market price, the same as the fiars in Scotland.[37]

Not all customers, however, were given the same price. Higher offers were always made to those who were prepared to supply tobacco in discharge of debts rather than for cash. To take one example, William Cunninghame and Co. gave twenty per cent more on the former transaction than on the latter.[38]

On occasion, too, some attempt were made to fix prices by presenting a united mercantile front against planters. In 1767 it was agreed to offer 22/6 per 100 lbs until 10th June and then lower it 'after having held a consultation on the subject with the Merchants of Fredericksburg'. Again, in December, 1772 a meeting of 'the most considerable of the merchants' in and around Falmouth in Virginia unanimously decided not to exceed 16/8 until May, 1773 'much to the dissatisfaction of the planters'.[39] Despite the propaganda which pro-planter politicians could make out of such efforts, one must remain dubious about their effectiveness. Individually the different Glasgow firms sought their own salvation and normally (except in a crisis) maintained highly competitive policies towards one another. Co-operation was based on expediency and was short-lived because the economic situation which encouraged merchants to look to their mutual interest was usually itself ephemeral. It only required one factor to agree to a higher price for price-fixing endeavours to collapse. Thus the attempt of December, 1772, already referred to, came to an end a month later when T. and A. Donald and Co. offered a substantially higher price; 'such', wrote the factor of another firm bitterly, 'is an instance of the pernicious consequences of misunderstandings or jealousy amongst purchasers'.[40] Moreover, the operation of the store system itself normally provided adequate protection for the planter. The need to freight ships in the shortest possible time and to buy up tobacco in advance of the arrival of others virtually guaranteed that planters' reluctance to sell at what they considered a low price would effectively destroy mercantile price-fixing. To reduce prices to an unrealistic level was self-defeating anyway since it could only result in inflation of book debts and antagonise the clientele.

Glasgow firms regarded the variety and quality of goods in their stores to be as important in the attraction of customers as offers of credit. To service their needs for supplies of provisions, ironmongery, textiles and luxuries merchants had to develop trade contacts throughout the Western World, from South America to Canada in the north and to the flax-growing areas and textile centres of Russia and the German states in the east. Undoubtedly, however, the two main sources of supply were the islands of the British Caribbean and the manufacturing areas of the United Kingdom itself.

The West Indies trade was a necessary corollary to the tobacco trade. Most Glasgow houses had correspondents there who supplied sugar, rum and molasses for their North American outlets.[41] Sometimes vessels outward bound from the Clyde were directed firstly to the Caribbean before proceeding to the tobacco colonies; alternatively merchantmen awaiting a cargo of tobacco were occasionally dispatched to the West Indies to load store provisions.[42] Some factors, either separately or in combination with their British employers, engaged also in Caribbean commerce. As planters often paid for their imported articles in wheat and corn, the storekeepers found the West Indies market a profitable outlet for grain.[43] For instance, Neil Jamieson, the chief colonial representative of John Glassford and Co., carried on an extensive trade with the Caribbean, particularly Antigua, and with the Azores and the Mediterranean, dealing in provisions, lumber and wine. He also financed shipbuilding and owned coastal shipping and was involved in the salt trade from Bordeaux to Lewiston and in the slave trade to the Carolinas.[44]

The West Indies, however, although important, was but a specialist provision centre for the Glasgow stores. Manufactured articles had to come from Europe and, in particular, from Britain. The extent to which manufacturers in Scotland supplied the colonial markets has in recent years attracted the attention of a number of historians since it raises the interesting issue of the impact of the Union of 1707 and of the colonial trade as a factor in the growth of Scottish industry.[45] The problem at the moment is still unresolved although the orthodox view would suggest a 'duality' in the Scottish experience with domestic manufacturing developing broadly independently of market stimulus from North America. As Professor R. H. Campbell has remarked:

> ... the growth of the entrepôt trade [in tobacco] may be attributed to the Union, though only with some qualifications, but any consequential stimulus to economic growth in other sectors of the economy is less certain. The Glasgow merchants who traded with the colonies could not always find the goods they wanted to export in Scotland and had to call on supplies from London.[46]

Thus far, however, discussion of this question has been based on an examination of eighteenth century trade figures which do not always accurately reflect the source of the commodities sent out to the colonies. Here material taken from merchant letterbooks and accounts will be utilised.[47]

Several conclusions can be drawn from these data. Firstly, there is little evidence that Glasgow houses, after c.1750, acquired much in the way of manufactured articles outside Britain. Only salt and wine from France and Spain and linen from Germany appear with any regularity in their accounts and order-books. Not surprisingly, after 1783 an independent United States still preferred to acquire the bulk of its clothing, plantation equipment and luxuries from the U.K., which was the source of goods to which Americans had become accustomed.[48] This view would correlate with recent research on the Scottish linen trade which shows that between 1747 and 1749, only 13.4% of linen exported from Scotland (with the colonies as a major market) was made in Europe, from 1757–59, 17% and between 1766–8, 8%.[49] A second point, based on a previous chapter of this book, is that many of the industrial units developed throughout the eighteenth century in the Glasgow area were capitalised by tobacco merchants and were geared to satisfying

TABLE XII

Scheme of Goods Ordered from London, 27 May, 1760 by Lawson, Semple & Co.

---

1 Pair of midling hand Cologne Milstones
½ doz. of old fashioned leather chairs with leather backs and double nails.
1 doz. leather bottomed chairs the seats the natural colour of the leather
1 Silver Tea Pot
1 doz. pint cans of the newest fashion
2 doz. salt cellars with shovels and glasses
1 Silver Cream Pot and let the Somervells crest be engaged on each of them
1 doz. mahogany chairs with leather bottoms fitt for a hall and two smoking chairs
1 doz. silver handed knives
4 doz. leather bottomed chairs such as we had March, 1759 from Samuel Seabroch

---

Source—SRO, RH 15/1179, James Lawson Letterbook, 1758–62, Lawson to James Russell, 27 May, 1760.

colonial demands for soap, beer, nails, shoes, saddles and a host of other articles. At the same time it is clear that these same merchants ordered goods from all over Britain, from Liverpool, Manchester, Newcastle and especially from London. Indeed, outward bound cargoes from the Clyde formed only a proportion of goods sent to the colonies on Glasgow's account. Many firms retained agents in southern ports who freighted vessels returning from Europe in ballast after delivering tobacco. One however ought not to exaggerate the role of English producers in meeting their needs. In the second half of the eighteenth century, for instance, they appear to have used London mainly as a source of luxury goods. One such order from the capital is illustrated in Table XII.

Furthermore, the evidence from a series of companies at different times and of varying size indicates that the *bulk* of the articles they sent out to the colonies was indeed purchased north of the Border. George Oswald and Co.

in the 1760s had accounts with a variety of Scottish manufactories, including W. and J. Fleming, coppersmiths, Neil Bannatyne's stocking works, Young and Trotter, calico printers, the Glasgow Ironworks and the Pollockshaws Printfield Co.[50] In 1731 the Bogles spent a total of £1300 on goods for the Virginia market yet only £300 of this amount went to buy articles produced in England.[51] Similarly, in the late 1750s, Lawson, Semple and Co. ordered £3000 worth of commodities for their stores in the colonies and about £7–800 of this stock originated south of the Border.[52]

While some Glasgow tobacco firms in the second half of the eighteenth century seem therefore to have primarily bought from Scottish manufacturers it is less easy to gauge the overall effect of their demand on the development of domestic industry. The only systematic study which has so far been carried out on the markets of a major Scottish industry suggests that between two periods 1758–62 and 1768–72 19.7 per cent and 18.3 per cent respectively of Scottish linen was exported from Scottish ports. About ninety per cent of this was sold in the North American and West Indian colonies.[53] It can hardly be said therefore that the tobacco colonies formed the *major* outlet for Scottish linens—domestic consumption and English demand were clearly much more important. At the same time they did apparently represent the industry's biggest single overseas market. One suspects indeed that the dynamic of colonial demand for Scottish manufactures operated much more strongly at the regional rather than the national level and affected the composition of output more than the volume of production.

The supply of British commodities to the planters of North America was one method by which the merchants attracted custom to their stores. Their main function, however, was to sell tobacco in European markets, thus transforming the planter's product into cash and facilitating exchange of goods. Tobacco was not homogeneous. The two basic varieties, oronoco (strong in flavour) and sweet-scented (mild) were themselves differentiated by the influences of climate, soil and the level of planter skills. In turn, the distinctive flavours of each type meant that some were more acceptable in certain markets than others. Maryland increasingly specialised in strong, bright-leaf tobaccos which were preferred in Holland and Northern Europe; from the upper valley of the James River in Virginia came the leaf most desired in France.

The relative importance of the different markets was reflected in the location of the stores of the Glasgow firms. Because French demand was most significant in the second half of the century it followed that Glasgow's trade became predominantly a Virginian affair. When a meeting of the city's merchants estimated the extent of debt due them from North America in 1778 they concluded that Maryland owed £155,810, North Carolina, £29,924 and Virginia no less than £719,038.[54] Professor Price has indeed suggested that 'the golden age of the Scottish tobacco trade, 1740–75, is the age of the French market'.[55] In this period the French began to buy most of their tobacco from Glasgow suppliers. Scottish export to France as a proportion of total British exports rose from 52% between 1757–62 to 72% between 1766–75.[56]

It would be unwise, however, to see Glasgow's triumph in the tobacco trade as an achievement *only* based on the rich prize of the French order. In *most* years during the 'golden age' the French market took little more than one third of total re-exports from the Clyde. For example, between 1757–62, Scottish exports to France as a proportion of total Scottish exports was 35%; between 1766–75, the corresponding figure was 34%.[57] Just as significant therefore during this period was an increase in supply to other markets, notably to Holland and Ireland. Again, although Glasgow traders specialised in the re-export trade—over 98% of all imports to the Clyde were later shipped out again—several firms also sent cargoes direct to Liverpool, Bristol and, most importantly, to London for sale in the south.[58] Their success then was built on their ability to cater effectively for a series of different markets. Although it is clear from merchant correspondence that 'the French price' was the single most influential element in their reckonings, few companies were entirely dependent on the French market. Table XIII

TABLE XIII
Tobacco Exports from Greenock and Port Glasgow, April–July, 1775

Firm	France	Holland	Ireland	Norway	German Ports
'Glassford Group' (3 companies)	703	1359	163	—	989
'Speirs Group' (2 companies)	576	363	498	137	—
'Cunninghame Group' (2 companies)	543	391	94	18	—
Colin Dunlop	206	89	—	—	—
McCall, Elliot	193	—	29	—	30
Hamiltons	237	—	—	—	—
George Oswald	158	—	—	—	—
Bogle, Jamieson	189	—	—	—	—
J. and H. Ritchie	121	—	—	—	—
J. McDowall	—	55	49	—	—
Snodgrass, Thomson	—	—	127	—	—
Dinwiddie, Crawford	97	—	45	—	—
Ramsay, Monteath	87	—	—	—	—
Donalds	114	—	229	—	—
Grays	—	140	—	—	—
McCalls	45	—	—	—	—
W. and J. Ballantine	18	—	—	—	—
Murdoch, Dreghorn	—	1	—	—	—
TOTALS (Hogsheads)	3287	2398	1234	155	1019

Source—SRO, E.504/28/24; E.504/15/25.

shows that only seven of the twenty-two firms freighting outwards from the Clyde in the second quarter of 1775 were sending tobacco only to French ports. French purchasing was subject to some fluctuation because buyers in that market frequently seem to have stockpiled in one year and only purchased spasmodically the next. Between 1774 and 1775, Scottish tobacco exports to France were less than half those of the preceding two years. To have depended entirely on such a market would have been to invite financial suicide. The greater firms therefore tended to have interests in a variety of tobacco-growing regions in the colonies the produce of which was geared to the differing tastes of European customers. McCall, Elliot and Co. were in business in both Virginia and North Carolina with two stores in each. One of John Glassford's group of companies had nine stores in Maryland while his other interests were in Virginia. Similarly Cunninghame, Findlay and Co. traded with Maryland while William Cunninghame and Co. were entirely concerned with Virginia commerce.[59] What therefore has to be explained in the final section of this chapter is not simply why the Glasgow houses were able to dominate the French market but also why they were successful elsewhere.

It is no coincidence that the dramatic rise of the Clyde ports to a position of importance in the tobacco trade after c.1730 was parallelled by the triumph of the direct purchase method of trade over the consignment or commission system. Not only did Glasgow merchants gain in these years but so also did traders in the English outports (most notably, albeit temporarily, those of Whitehaven) who bought tobacco from planters rather than acted as commission agents for its sale.[60] It follows therefore that part of the reason for Glasgow's rise is to be sought in the special advantages of the direct purchase method over the commission system. There were two main ones. Firstly, after the first quarter of the eighteenth century the frontier of tobacco cultivation began to move westward across the fall lines of the various rivers flowing to Chesapeake Bay into the piedmont country beyond. Here production was broadly concentrated in the hands of a less wealthy planter class, who, unlike their more powerful fellows of the established tide-water regions, did not have individual crops of sufficient size to attract the interest of the London commission houses. The store or direct purchase system was however ideally suited to solving the marketing problems of these groups. The merchant rather than the planter incurred the risks and the expenses of transporting the tobacco across the Atlantic and credit and goods were freely available from the stores. The planter necessarily became indebted but his compensation was a rising standard of living and assured demand for his crop.

The second major benefit of the direct purchase system was that it was geared to the needs of the French purchasers who, as we have seen, formed the single biggest market for tobacco in eighteenth century Europe.[61] From 1674 to 1791 the buying of tobacco from foreign sources for the French customer was not in the hands of independent merchants. Purchasing was controlled by a state monopoly farmed out to private interests. It followed that the 'Farmers General of the French Customs', as they were described in our period, bought mainly in bulk to satisfy national requirements. They do not appear to have purchased much in Britain before the early eighteenth century but subsequently seem to have become very interested in that market because of the cheapness and versatility of British colonial leaf and as a result of Walpole's decision in the 1720s to eliminate most of the fiscal burden on re-exports through U.K. entrepôts. Consumption within the monopoly area increased seven fold from 1715 to 1775 and between 1730 and 1744 France surpassed Holland to become the first market for British tobacco.

It is significant that during these years the buying agents of the French began to place more orders among those outport merchants who were now big enough to deliver the bulk cargoes which they required. In 1730 they were buying approximately less than ten per cent of their needs in Glasgow;[62] by 1757-62, however, this had risen to fifty-two per cent of an increased purchase.[63] There were short-term considerations involved in this process. For instance, insurance premiums were lower in the northern sea lanes during the war of 1744-8. But a more decisive and ultimately more important influence was the nature of the tobacco trade of Glasgow (and of Whitehaven) compared to that of London. Because the Glasgow firms actually owned the cargoes they imported they could dispose of it in huge sales to the French buyers in Scotland, who, in the 1750s and 1760s, were William Alexander and Sons, an Edinburgh firm with close personal and matrimonial ties with some leading Glasgow merchant families.[64] The consignment system was much less suited to French needs because the commission agent's obligation to the planter was to achieve the highest possible price for his hogsheads when sold on an individual basis. Such methods were far too expensive and time-consuming for the agents of the French monopoly.[65]

Underpinning this advantage not only in the French but also in other markets was the cost at which the Glasgow firms were able to sell. It was recognised in the trade that they could bring home their tobacco more cheaply than their competitors. A correspondent of the London consignment house of John Norton and Sons wrote in 1768:

> ... they [the Scots] sail their ships so much cheaper than you can from London and they have some other advantages in the Trade, to which you and I are strangers, that it is my opinion, that in a few years that London Market will be chiefly supplied thro' that Channell.[66]

Data on prices paid by the French agents in various British centres confirms that tobacco sold in Glasgow and Whitehaven was often cheaper than that bought in London, Liverpool and Bristol. For example, in 1760 they offered $3\frac{3}{4}$d per lb. in London and $3\frac{1}{4}$d in Glasgow. In 1763, the prices were 2d in the former market and $1\frac{3}{4}$d in Scotland.[67]

One reason for these price differentials, which helped them in other markets apart from the French, was that Glasgow firms seem to have been keener to achieve rapid turnover of capital than to extract the last farthing of profit from their tobacco sales. Partly this may have been because of their shortage of liquid funds, but probably it was more basically a result of their commercial methods. As owners of the tobacco they were supplying they could not afford the risk and time of the lengthy bargaining procedures conducted by the consignment houses who were merely selling agents. Since the primary income of the latter came from commission on tobacco sales, they *did* want to hold out for the highest possible price. Time and again the London men scathingly criticised their fellow merchants in Scotland for accepting lower offers from buyers than the market, in their view, merited.[68] The Glasgow companies on the other hand were able to compensate for their lower returns from selling tobacco by practising economies of scale, by their income from retail of goods to planters and by cheaper operating costs.

The 'store system' facilitated advance purchase of tobacco thus cutting turnaround times in the colonies to a minimum, in the process shortening the length of voyages and adding to Glasgow's advantage of having the shortest sea-route to the colonies around Ireland. Speedy sales to customers in Europe meant that capital costs were also cut at the other end of the voyage. This resulted in a substantial gain in the productivity of merchant vessels. In Atlantic commerce generally it was rare for ships to make a double voyage in one year. Not so apparently in the Glasgow tobacco trade. The *Blandford*, owned by Dinwiddie, Crawford and Co. made five voyages to Virginia and one to Rotterdam between 1768 and 1771.[69] The *Cochrane*, a vessel belonging to William Cunninghame and Co. delivered tobacco at Havre de Grace in France in the late summer of 1772, sailing thereafter directly for the James River in Virginia where she loaded 460 hogsheads of tobacco. After delivering these in the Clyde, she was due to return to the Rappahanock valley in June of 1773, with a cargo of store goods and there load a further 460 hogsheads.[70] Costs were also cut by firms establishing their own industrial units to supply articles in demand in the colonies or by exploiting their oligopolistic position in relation to independent manufacturers. Thus in the linen trade in the 1760s competition among Scots, Irish and German producers enabled the exporter to force profit margins down, a common practice being for the latter to demand a five per cent discount for cash payment or long credit of twelve months.[71]

REFERENCES

1. For the consignment system see Samuel Rosenblatt, 'The Significance of Credit in the Tobacco Consignment Trade: a Study of John Norton and Sons, 1768–1775', *William and Mary Quarterly*, 3rd. ser., (1962), 383–99; F. U. Mason (ed.), *John Norton and Sons: Merchants of London and Virginia* (Richmond, 1937).
2. In my research I have come across only one Glasgow house practising the consignment method after c.1740.
3. Gibson, *op. cit.*, 206; Stewart, *op. cit.*, 5.
4. C. B. Coulter, 'The Virginia Merchant' (Unpublished Ph.D. thesis, University of Princeton, 1944), 9.
5. *Ibid.*; A. C. Land, 'Economic Base and Social Structure: The Northern Chesapeake in the Eighteenth Century', *Journ. of Econ. Hist.*, XXII (1965), 649.
6. *Ibid.*, 643.
7. GCA, Reg. of Deeds, B.10/15/5943, Statement from William Millar, 27 July, 1744.
8. ML, Bogle MSS, George Bogle of Daldowie's Letterbook, Bogle to Captain William Dunlop, 29 January, 1730.
9. GCA, Reg. of Deeds, B.10/15/5523 (1741).
10. ML, Bogle MSS, George Bogle's Letterbook, Bogle to Matthew Bogle, 20 October, 1731.
11. Coulter, *op. cit.*, 18.
12. GCA, Alexander Henderson's Letterbook, 1758–64; SRO, GD 247/158/0, William Cunninghame and Co. Letterbooks, 1769–1774.
13. LC, Glassford Papers, John Glassford to Neil Jamieson, 4 June, 1761. Merchandise exchange was safer. Goods purchased in Britain at 12 months credit and sent to Virginia during the summer should have been sold for tobacco that would be remitted the following summer.
14. Coulter, *op. cit.*, 16.
15. Quoted in Price, *loc. cit.*, 306.
16. See below, pp. 84–5.
17. SRO, GD 247/158/0, James Robinson to William Cunninghame and Co., 18 October, 1772.
18. *Ibid.*, James Robinson to John Turner, 25 October, 1768.
19. See, for example, various letters in GCA, Alexander Henderson's Letterbook, 1758–64. One practice consisted of rating store goods in sterling and allowing accounts to be paid in Virginia currency at an increase of 50% or 100%, and in paper money at an increase of 200% or 300%, thereby beguiling unwary planters into buying more high-priced goods than if they had been rated in currency. See A. P. Middleton, *Tobacco Coast: a Maritime History of Chesapeake Bay in the Colonial Era* (Newport, Va., 1953), 107.
20. See the situations of some of William Cunninghame and Co.'s stores in PRO, AO 12/56/307–8 at Mecklenburg Court House, Brunswick Court House, Fauquier Court House.
21. Quoted in Coulter, *op. cit.*, 106.
22. GCA, Alexander Henderson's Letterbook, Henderson to John Glassford and Co., 5 June, 1759.
23. SL, CSP 162/3, Information for James Dougal...44. This statement was made in a court action concerning Alexander Cunninghame and Co.
24. BM, Add. MS. 33030/31.
25. GCA, Speirs Papers, TD 131/10–12, Diary of Alexander Speirs, 2 March, 1778. For the debts of individual companies see below.
26. Jacob M. Price, 'Capital and Credit in the Chesapeake Tobacco Trade, 1750–1775', read to the 27th Conference in Early American History, Ohio Academy of History, October, 1970.
27. A. C. Land, 'The Tobacco Staple and the Planter's Problems: Technology, Labour and Crops', *Agricultural History*, XLIII (1969), 79–81.
28. Emory G. Evans, 'Planter Indebtedness and the Coming of the Revolution in Virginia', *William and Mary Quarterly*, 3rd. ser., (1962), 511–33.

29. SRO, GD 247/58/0, James Robinson Letterbooks, *passim*.
30. W. C. Ford (ed.), *Letters of William Lee* (Brooklyn, 1891), 2 vols., II, 424, n.
31. SRO, GD 247/58/0, James Robinson tp John Turner, 25 October, 1768.
32. GCA, Alexander Henderson's Letterbook, Henderson to John Glassford and Co., 28 February, 1759.
33. The extent of competition can be seen clearly in a letter from the chief factor of William Cunninghame and Co. to his parent house in 1774. According to this the firm's Richmond store was not doing well; it had attracted some of the former customers of Messrs. Donalds but they were now being wooed by 'Mr. Buchanan who has again opened a store in company with Alexander Donald James McDowall and Co.'. The other competitors were A. Speirs and Co. and Henderson, McCall and Co. Even large advances of credit had not produced the expected results, 'I understand some of the Customers at this store and those too for whom large sums of money have been advanced, have disposed of their Crops to other merchants—partly because Mr. Gordon had declined paying any money for them; and partly I suppose from an inclination to shift. This shows the absurdity of advancing large sums of money for any men, as they will only deal with you while it is so conducive to their interest'. (SRO, GD 247/158/0, J. Robinson to W. Cunninghame and Co., 16 April, 1774).
34. J. H. Soltow, 'Scottish Traders in Virginia, 1750–1775', *Econ. Hist. Rev.*, 2nd. ser. XII (1959), 96.
35. J. H. Soltow, 'The Role of Williamsburg in the Virginia Economy, 1750–1775', *William and Mary Quarterly*, 3rd. ser., XV (1958), 467–482.
36. SRO, GD 247/158/0, James Robinson to John Turner, 22 April, 1769.
37. SL, CSP 162/23, Information for Elizabeth and Barbara Cunninghame, ..7.
38. SRO, GD 247/59/S, W. Cunninghame and Co. to John Turner, 18 July, 1774.
39. SRO, GD 247/158/0, James Robinson to John Neilson, 25 May, 1767; to W. Cunninghame and Co., 19 December, 1772.
40. *Ibid.*, Robinson to W. Cunninghame and Co., 8 January, 1773.
41. SRO, RH 15/1179, James Lawson's Letterbook, 1758–62, Lawson to John Semple, 25 August, 1761.
42. GCA, Reg. of Deeds, B.10/15/6183, 6123.
43. Middleton, *op. cit.*, 107.
44. Neil Jamieson Papers, 1757–89, typescript in Glasgow City Archives.
45. Hamilton, *op. cit.*, 142–5; Campbell *op. cit.*, 46–7; A. J. Durie, 'The Markets for Scottish Linen, 1730–1775', *SHR*, LII (1973), 30–49.
46. 'The Union and Economic Growth' in T. I. Rae (ed.), *The Union of 1707: Its Impact on Scotland* (Glasgow, 1974), 63.
47. The following sources were examined in the course of this analysis: ML, Bogle MSS, George Bogle of Daldowie's Letterbook, 1729–42; SRO, RH 15/1179, James Lawson Letterbook, 1758–62; SRO, Letter Books, Accounts and other Papers of William Cunninghame and Co., 1768–1801, GD 247/39; 58–9; 141; GCA, Speirs Papers; GCA, Journal of Baird, Hay and Co., 1772–1816; GCA, TD 188, Oswald Account Book.
48. See below.
49. Durie, *loc. cit.*, 39.
50. GCA, TD 188, Oswald Account Book.
51. ML, Bogle MSS, George Bogle's Letterbook, Bogle to Matthew Bogle, 11 September, 20 October, 1731.
52. SRO, RH 15/1179, James Lawson Letterbook, Lawson to John Semple, 16 February, 1759.
53. Durie, *loc. cit.*, 38
54. GCA, Speirs Papers, TD 131/10–12/1, Diary of Alexander Speirs, entries for April, 1781.
55. Price, *op. cit.*, 610.
56. *Ibid.*, 611.
57. *Ibid.*
58. ML, Bogle MSS, George Bogle's Letterbook, Bogle to Captain William Dunlop, 29 January, 1730; SRO, RH 15/1179, James Lawson Letterbook, Lawson to John Semple, 13 October, 1760.

59. GCA, Reg. of Deeds, B.10/15/8123, Bond of Copartnership betwixt Messrs. John McCall etc.; PRO, AO 12/9/35; PRO, 12/56/292-301. The secondary interest of Alexander Speirs, William French and John Bowman, Speirs, French and Co., traded exclusively with Maryland. Speirs, Bowman and Co., the other member of the organisation, was solely concerned with the importation of tobacco from Virginia. See GCA, Speirs Papers, TD 131/4, Ledger B, 1773-80; SL, CSP 190/13, Petition of Messrs. Speirs, French and Co.
60. Price, *op. cit.*, 594-604.
61. The following two paragraphs are based on Price, *op. cit.*, *passim* and on his article 'The Economic Growth of the Chesapeake and the European Market, 1697-1775', *Journ. of Econ. Hist.*, XXIV (1964), 497-510.
62. ML, Bogle MSS, George Bogle's Letterbook, Bogle to John Carstares, 27 November, 1730.
63. Price, *op. cit.*, 611.
64. For the Alexanders see Charles Rogers, *Memories of the Earl of Stirling and the House of Alexander* (Edinburgh, 1877), 2 Vols. The Alexanders were related through marriage to the Murdochs and the Cochranes.
65. Price, *op. cit.*, 658-9.
66. Mason, *op. cit.*, 66.
67. Price, *op. cit.*, 671-76.
68. *Ibid.*,
69. GCA, Lockhart Papers (on microfilm), Master's running accounts of the ship *Blandford*, August, 1768-July, 1771.
70. SRO, GD 247/158/0, James Robinson to William Cunninghame and Co., 18 October, 1772.
71. Durie, *loc. cit.*, 45.

5(a)

The Emergence of the Glasgow Tobacco Companies

IT first becomes possible to analyse the structure of Glasgow tobacco importation from 1742 when the Customs Accounts for the Clyde ports are extant.[1] These data confirm evidence from other sources that the trade was undergoing a process of transition at that time. Already several features which were to characterise the large companies of the 1760s and 1770s were apparent; yet in addition, the nature and type of unit in operation suggests also the survival of the characteristics of a less sophisticated era. It is clear, for instance, that the trade was already controlled by a small group of wealthy merchants who were often the descendants of famous Glasgow trading families. Between October and December, 1742 over two-thirds of the 3783 hogsheads imported were shipped by four groups, the Dunlops, the Bogles, the Oswalds and the McCalls. Most of the remaining cargoes were landed by a further six associations of merchants.[2] This oligopolistic pattern was to continue and be consolidated during the following two decades of expansion. The 'top' groups changed in personnel and size but the unchallenged predominance of a handful of major firms remained.[3]

However, organisation was almost certainly much less formal in the 1740s than it was to become later. Only a minority of the groups importing at this period were established companies operating under deeds of partnership. Indeed for the 1740s only one contract of copartnery has been discovered—that which governed the business of Archibald Buchanan, John Bowman, Thomas Hopkirk and three others in Virginia from 1744.[4] The more common organisation was for a group of merchants, most often related by blood or marriage, or known to one another through long acquaintance, to share importation of a given cargo of tobacco. These associations were linked to the merchant's single biggest capital cost, the purchase of a ship. Given the risks of eighteenth century commerce, combined with the effects of war, marine insurance bankruptcies and weather it was only prudent to pool resources and to ensure that one's capital was spread over a few such associations rather than concentrated in one. Thus when the Bogles were building a new vessel for the Jamaica and Virginia trade in 1736, four 'interests' were involved in the project, George Bogle ($\frac{3}{8}$), Messrs. Robertsons ($\frac{2}{8}$), John Jamieson ($\frac{2}{8}$) and Captain William Dunlop ($\frac{1}{8}$).[5] Such ventures were designated by the name of the vessel concerned and could be wound up on completion of a single voyage and the ship sold.[6]

Their flexibility probably explains the popularity of these associations at this time. Most merchants perhaps did not envisage long-term commitment to any one sector of commerce and therefore had less need of the formal partnership deed to lend a framework of stability to their operations. Such devices, which normally endured for at least four-five years, would have circumscribed their activities to too great an extent.

Nevertheless it is possible to detect, behind the apparent informality of business organisation, the emergence of several merchant groupings whose association persisted over long periods of time and whose links were cemented not by legal regulation but by family loyalty and trust. Provost Andrew Cochrane from the 1720s participated with the Buchanans in the tobacco trade. This connection was to persist, with various changes of personnel up to the 1780s. All the original principals were dead but their relatives and protégés were still firmly in control.[7] The rapid settlement of stores in North America by Glasgow merchants which characterised the period after c.1730 accelerated this process towards stable associations of merchants. This more full-blooded commitment to the tobacco trade increasingly resulted in the formation of formal partnerships based on earlier looser associations. The steadily rising level of importation and the increase in the size of individual groupings meant that the informal and personal basis of mercantile relationships might no longer suffice. It is also probable that the evolution of partnerships was an attempt to extend the capital base of individual units as commerce developed. To do so would mean the recruitment of sleeping partners whose rights would have to be safeguarded in law.

From the middle of the eighteenth century, then, the company form of organisation began to spread in the Glasgow tobacco trade. At what date it became typical it is not possible to say with any claim to certainty. However, by the end of the 1750s, some of the principle associations—Kippen, Glassford and Co., Archibald Buchanan and Co. (later to emerge as Speirs, Bowman and Co.) and the Berries and Grays conformed to this type.[8] By the end of the next decade the vast bulk of the Clyde's imports were shipped by merchant groups incorporated in formal partnerships.[9]

This new sophistication, however, did not alter the concentration of control of imports in the hands of a few rich merchants, despite the fact that by the early 1770s the Clyde trade was about ten times what it had been in the 1730s. In 1774, 31,090 hogsheads of tobacco were landed at Greenock and Port Glasgow by a total of 36 firms.[10] Yet 21 of these units only shipped together 4200 hogsheads. Not one of these imported individually more than 500 hogsheads and ten landed less than 200. It ought to be borne in mind, on the other hand, that even these smaller ventures often imported more than the largest groupings of an earlier generation. They were dwarfed, however, by the massive syndicates which dominated the trade by the 1770s.

Three groups of interlocking partnerships, the Cunninghame, Speirs and Glassford groups, handled over fifty per cent of the tobacco in that decade. The major interest of the first of these, William Cunninghame and Co., had nine partners in 1776. Three of these held eighty per cent of the shares in a second firm, Cunninghame, Findlay and Co. William Cunninghame and his nephew, Robert Findlay owned ninety per cent of the stock in a third and much smaller venture, Cunninghame, Brown and Co.[11] The two Speirs companies conformed to a similar pattern. Speirs, Bowman and Co. and Speirs, French and Co. each shared three partners, Alexander Speirs, John Bowman and William French, who had a controlling interest in the capital stock of each.[12] Both these groupings represented the climax of several decades of growth. Speirs and Bowman had first signed a formal partnership deed with the Buchanans in 1744 but before that date had been 'concerned together in the Virginia trade and in several ships and cargoes'.[13] The Cunninghame companies were of even older vintage. Their antecedents can be traced back to the business activities of the Cochranes, the Buchanans and the Lukes in the 1720s.[14] The size of these organisations by the 1770s was thus a consequence of the steady reploughing of profit by several generations of merchants.

The third group of the trio which controlled the Clyde tobacco trade at this time was headed by John Glassford. Arguably this syndicate was the most complex and highly integrated of all. On superficial examination it would seem that Glassford's interests were represented by two firms, John Glassford and Co. and Glassford, Gordon and Co.[15] Yet closer analysis reveals that he and some of his fellow partners had important shares in no less than four other companies in the 1770s, all of them extensive importers of tobacco. In two of these, Archibald Henderson and Co. and James Gordon and Co., the three names of Henry Riddell, James Gordon and Glassford himself recur. In addition, the two latter, together with Archibald Henderson, held shares in Henderson, McCall and Co. Finally, five of the merchants in this venture formed the partnership of George Kippen and Co.[16] In the three years before the outbreak of the American War in 1775 these Glassford firms on average imported about one-fifth of all Glasgow-owned tobacco.[17]

The web of integration and concentration also included companies operating in a slightly smaller scale. The Buchanan-Jamieson group comprised four firms, the Snodgrass-McCall syndicate also four and the Donald group, two.[18] The structure of the trade was completed by a handful of important family businesses[19] and some smaller ventures which were only infrequently listed in the customs accounts and probably only indicate a limited and ephemeral commitment to the tobacco trade. By contemporary standards the average Glasgow tobacco company was a very large-scale enterprise. Initial stocks of capital ranged between £5000 and £20,000 divided into a number of individual shares.

However, because of partnership regulations which controlled dividends and the difficulty of extracting book profits in the short term these initial capital sums could rise very sharply over time. So it was reckoned that by 1779 the total capital of the Cunninghame group hovered on the £100,000 mark while that of James and Robert Donald was estimated at £65,000.[20] Most contemporary industrial units were small fry compared to these giants; linen firms normally had capital stocks of under £2000 and only sugarhouses, glassworks and the few ironworks of the day demanded more than £4000.[21] The costs of the tobacco trade were a prime factor in accelerating the trend

TABLE XIV
Capital Stock of Sample Glasgow Tobacco Partnerships, c. 1740–83

Firm	Capital Stock	Date
George McCall and Co.	£5000	Uncertain
Findlay, Hopkirks and Co.	£8000	1783
Buchanan, Bowman, Speirs	£16,400	1744
Buchanan, Hastie and Co.	£10,500	1772
William Cunninghame and Co.	£20,000	1770
Cunninghame, Findlay and Co.	£15,000	1770
G. and A. Buchanan and Co.	£8000	1768

Sources—GCA, Probative Writs, B.10/12/4, 9; Reg. of Deeds, B.10/15/8123; SRO, RH 15/2232; SRO, Reg. of Deeds, 309/2/58 DUR; SL, CSP 162/3.

towards oligopoly. In the colonies the large syndicates were fearsome competitors, able because of their standing to attract loans in Britain and organise efficient extension of credit across the Atlantic to planters. Such firms adopted a self-consciously imperialist policy towards their smaller competitors. So in 1767, a Cunninghame storekeeper was advised to strike hard at the operations of another Glasgow firm consisting of Robert Lawson and William Bogle. As Cunninghame's superintending factor observed:

> I believe there is no other concerned [i.e. in Lawson and Bogle] if so ... as their capital will not afford it, consequently his customers who want large sums of money advanced to them at times for to purchase negroes etc. will be obliged to leave him and this concern [i.e. Cunninghame and Co.] is as able to answer their purpose in that respect.[22]

The size of companies was reflected in the number of their partners. Tobacco houses at Whitehaven, Liverpool, Bristol and London consisted of merchants acting alone or in partnerships of two or at the most three.[23] In Glasgow, however, such organisations were the exception rather than the rule. Twenty-four Clyde firms were examined spanning the period c. 1764 to 1783. (See Table XV). Fifteen had more than four partners. Of this number, two companies consisted of nine individuals. A further three had eight partners and two had seven. The minimum number of merchants in any one group was three.

In addition, as has already been noted, merchants tended to distribute their funds among several companies, in some of which at least they were

TABLE XV

Number of Partners in Glasgow Tobacco Firms, c. 1764–83

Firm	No. of Partners	Source
Henderson McCall	9	SRO, CE 60/1/10
W. Cunninghame	9	PRO, AO 12/56/292–305
Glassford, Gordon	8	*Glasgow Mercury*, 19 Jan., 1790
Speirs, French	8	PRO, AO 12/9/53
James Jamieson	8	GCA, Reg. of Deeds, B.10/5/9593
John Glassford and Co.	7	PRO, AO 12/9/37
Thomson, Snodgrass	7	GCA, Probative Writs, B.10/12/4
Speirs, Bowman	6	GCA, Speirs Papers, TD 131/7, Ledger, 1785–88, 45
Cunninghame, Findlay	6	PRO, AO 12/56/292–305
Buchanan, Hastie	6	GCA, Probative Writs, B.10/12/4
George Kippen	5	*Glasgow Advertiser*, 22 Jan., 1790
P. Colquohuon	5	GCA, Speirs Papers, TD 131/09, Sederunt 54 of P. Colquohoun and Co.
James Brown		PRO, AO 12/9/59–61
Baird, Hay	5	GCA, Journal of Baird, Hay and Co.
McCall, Elliot	4	GCA, Reg. of Deeds, B.10/5/8123
Arch. Henderson	4	*Glasgow Mercury*, 19 Jan., 1790
Bogle, Jamieson	4	GCA, Reg. of Deeds, B.10/5/8045
George McCall	4	GCA, Probative Writs, B.10/12/9
McCall, Smellie	4	*Glasgow Courier*, 19 April, 1794
T. and A. Donald	4	*Glasgow Herald*, 14 June, 1811
Thomas Donald	4	*Glasgow Herald*, 7 Feb., 1812
Cunninghame, Brown	3	PRO, AO 12/56/292–305
Colin Dunlop	3	GCA, Probative Writs, B.10/12/7/349
George Oswald	3	SRO, CE 60/1/8

sleeping partners. The spreading of assets in this way among a limited number of ventures was bound to result in multiple partnerships. How is this structure to be explained?

At its base was the Scottish law of partnership and the specific regulations adopted in contracts of copartnery. In Scotland, unlike in England, the partnership was a separate legal entity able to sue, be sued and draw up regulations governing the conduct of members which found acceptance at law.[24] It was thus possible to safeguard the rights of partners who contributed their capital but could not supervise all their financial commitments on a day-to-day basis. The amount which might be borrowed by managing partners was rigorously controlled, limitations on risk incorporated in contracts and individual obligations defined.[25] Again, members were only allowed an annual return of five per cent interest on their shares until the company was dissolved. Given this limitation, it served both to maximise profit and minimise risk to disperse one's assets.

Another factor responsible for the Glasgow pattern was the operation of the store system itself. So much responsibility was placed on a firm's chief storekeepers in America that it was only prudent to encourage their initiative, stimulate diligence and promote loyalty by allocating to them shares in the partnership. Thus nine of the forty-two shares in Findlay, Hopkirks and Co. were set aside for the concern's colonial representatives. Matthew Blair, 'merchant in Potomack' and John Campbell, 'merchant in Blandensburg', received 5/42 and 4/42 shares respectively.[26] Similarly John Craig and David Walker were full partners in Alexander Cunninghame and Co. who 'resided in America, where they had the most considerable stores under their management and likewise the superintending of the other factors'. Three of the eight partners in Speirs, French and Co. were resident storekeepers in Maryland.[28]

Finally, there was a financial attraction in extended partnerships. Throughout history, Scottish merchants had tried to alleviate problems of national capital scarcity by pooling scarce funds.[29] It was perhaps inevitable that this system would be carried over into the tobacco trade with its distinctive financial burdens. It is possible, indeed, to plot a rough correlation between numbers of partners and the importance of a company as measured by its annual importation of tobacco. Four of the five firms with most members (8-9) belonged to either the Speirs, Cunninghame or Glassford groups. Such a system allowed merchants to mobilise the capital of moneyed elements in the West of Scotland, who wished to seek a rentier income.[30] There was no gulf between the mercantile, landed and professional classes of the region and close social relationships helped to promote a vigorous market in partnership shares.

It followed, because of the nature of the investing group, that only a minority of partners were actively involved in the day-to-day running of the firm. One member of the concern acted as managing partner, resided in Glasgow and was assisted by clerks who would not normally be shareholders. For this he was paid an annual salary which in the contracts examined was normally between £60 and £100, and in addition, allocated allowances for his counting-house, coal and candles. His major financial reward, however, came from his personal shares in the firm. In the bigger ventures, for example, the managing partner normally held the single largest share. Where he did not, partnership articles tried to ensure that he discharged his onerous responsibilities to his fellow members. Thus William Buchanan, managing partner in Buchanan, Hastie and Co. had only a minority interest in the firm. As a result his associates introduced sanctions to encourage him. He was directed to carry out the tasks of manager and book-keeper 'and obey the orders of his fellow partners under the penalty of £1000 sterling in case of transgressions or disobedience'.[31]

The managing partner was thus the central figure in the organisation of Glasgow tobacco companies. He—

> ... was trusted implicitly by the other partners. By him the agents and factors abroad were chosen; by his advice factors were assumed as partners, by him the ships were purchased and freighted; goods sent out to a great amount, tobaccos ordered to fill those ships; stores established in different places; and every transaction of the Company directed; the factors abroad acting under him, taking their general orders from him and doing of themselves only those things which fall within the ordinary province of a factor.[32]

It followed, therefore, that the success or failure of a firm depended to a considerable extent on the personal qualities of the chief partner and his ability to control the company's employees in America. The great problem in this respect was the distance between store outlets in America and company headquarters in Glasgow. The condition of the tobacco crop in the colonies and market and credit conditions in the colonies could change so swiftly that general strategy formulated at one period could have little relevance a few weeks later. Such hazards were exacerbated in the years before 1775 as the volatile fuel of political controversy was added to existing problems intrinsic to the trade. In the sixties and seventies, too, the expansion of extended series of stores throughout Virginia and Maryland belonging to Glasgow firms meant that the managing partner in Britain was often only capable of exercising an essentially supervisory function. Especially in the larger companies a highly complex form of business organisation had developed, the ramifications of which stretched from the colonies to London, Glasgow and the European continent.[33] The chief partner was still responsible for the overall purchasing and credit strategy of the company but delegation of power to men on the spot in Virginia and Maryland had become inevitable.

This fact was increasingly recognised. Occasionally the function of managing partner was divided between two men, the one responsible for operations in North America and the other controlling company interests in the United Kingdom. In this way, Robert Findlay and William Cunninghame were appointed 'joint-managers' of Cunninghame, Findlay and Co.[34] In addition, the position of 'superintending factor' was created in the bigger organisations. Among the smaller firms the importance of the American representative in the partnership was illustrated by new salary levels which approximated to those of the chief partner in Britain.[35] In addition such responsibility was placed on the leading factors in the colonies that very often only kinsmen of the managing partner were recruited to that position.[36]

The main function of most of the remaining partners in a tobacco firm was simply to supply funds to the capital stock. Yet they also met and conferred when an important decision on general company policy was to be taken.[37] No alteration in shares could be made without their consent and in the event of disagreement among the partners each share counted as one vote and the majority decision was final. Although partnership deeds were signed for fixed limits of time—usually varying between four and seven years—a majority of votes could dissolve the firm at any point during this period. Finally some contracts contained a clause encouraging participants in a copartnery, other than the managing partner, to take a bigger share in the company's affairs. Thus Article I of the contract of George Bogle and Co. enjoined the other partners 'to give their help and assistance always when needful'.[38]

As Professor Price has observed, the larger Glasgow firms were miniature prototypes of later private joint-stock organisations.[39] Through elaboration of specific articles of copartnery and exploitation of the Scottish law of partnership, merchants were able to alleviate many of the problems implicit in eighteenth century commercial relationships. When individuals subscribed to a partnership deed their shares became part of the common stock and these could not be withdrawn until the company's debts were paid.[40] On the death or bankruptcy of a partner there was strict control over the re-allocation of his shares. Precautions were normally taken against the entry of an unwelcome member into the firm. If an original partner wished to withdraw his share, he was usually required to make first offer of it to his fellow members. In the contract of Findlay, Hopkirks and Co., for example, the remaining partners if they agreed to accept the share, were permitted to purchase it over a three year period in annual instalments.[41] If no existing partner wished to acquire it, the share could be offered to an outsider but only with the consent of the majority.[42]

Companies also sought to protect themselves against the possible insolvency of their members. Extraction of a bankrupt's share by creditors might invite disaster for his associates particularly since it was likely to occur at a time of general credit crisis. Firms could not refuse to pay the trustees of a sequestrated estate but they could at least prolong the process over a long period. For instance, in several contracts, solvent partners were designated preferred creditors on the stock of a bankrupt colleague. The latter's share could not be withdrawn until his debts to the company and *all* its debts were paid.[43] In the real world this could mean that the process of retrieving a bankrupt's stock by less fortunate creditors could go on indefinitely. Other contracts set a time limit of between eighteen months and two years on payment of the share of the insolvent partner.[44] Creditors were perhaps less likely to sue for a writ of sequestration with the foreknowledge that a merchant's assets were tied up for long periods in a series of different companies. This partnership regulation may help to explain why Scottish tobacco merchants were relatively *less* vulnerable to bankruptcy than their colleagues elsewhere. Another advantage might have been the controls which existed in partnership deeds to ensure liquidity. Factors in the colonies were always advised to make a distinction between good debts and bad or dubious ones and precautions taken lest liquid assets be over-estimated.[45] So, McCall, Elliot and Co. annually made a deduction of $12\frac{1}{2}$ per cent from 'good' debts, 50 per cent from 'dubious' debts and the summary of bad debts was not included in the annual valuation at all.[46]

REFERENCES

1. SRO, E.504/28, Customs Accounts, Port Glasgow; E.504/23, Customs Accounts, Greenock.
2. *Ibid.* John and James Ritchie; James and Robert Berrie; John Robertson and Co.; John Baird and Co.; Thomas and William Wallace; Ramsay, Baird; Allan and Robert Dreghorn.
3. See below.
4. GCA, B.10/15/6653, Copartnery, Arch. Buchanan, Speirs etc.
5. ML, Bogle MSS, George Bogle of Daldowie's Letterbook, 1729–42, George Bogle to William Bogle, 29 March, 1736.
6. See, for instance, GCA, B.10/15/5357, Disposition, James Robertson to Robert Robertson, 1740; B.10/15/5528, Contract and Assignment among Andrew Aiton etc.
7. GCA, B.10/15/4747; SRO, RH 15/2232, Contract of Findlay, Hopkirks and Co. See also, below, pp. 109–10.
8. GCA, B.10/15/6653, 6188; Probative Writs, B.10/12/2, folio 54.
9. Generalisation based on GCA, Register of Deeds, and SRO, Port Glasgow and Greenock Customs Accounts.
10. SRO, E.504/28/23–4; E.504/15/23–5.
11. PRO, AO 12/56/292–305. For partners see Appendix II.
12. *Ibid.*, AO 12/9/53; GCA, Speirs Papers, TD 131/7, Ledger, 1785–88, 45.
13. GCA, B.10/15/6653, Copartnery, Arch. Buchanan, Speirs etc.
14. *Ibid.*, B.10/15/4538.
15. PRO, AO 12/9/37; *Glasgow Mercury*, 19 January, 1790.
16. *Ibid.*; SRO, CE 60/1/10, Petition of Henderson, McCall and Co. to H.M. Board of Customs; *Glasgow Advertiser*, 22 January, 1790.
17. SRO, E.504/28; E.504/15. However they were still behind the Speirs firms.
18. GCA, Probative Writs, B.10/12/4; *Glasgow Courier*, 19 April, 1794; *Glasgow Herald and Advertiser*, 14 June, 1811. For members of these partnerships see Appendix II.
19. For example, Colin Dunlop and Sons, George Oswald and Co., James Ritchie and Co. and Peter Murdoch and Sons.
20. GCA, B.10/15/7606; PRO, T 79/15, 18.
21. GCA, Register of Deeds, *passim*.
22. SRO, GD 247/58/O, James Robinson to Bennet Price, 7 October, 1767.
23. Price, *loc. cit.*, (1967), 309.
24. Campbell, *loc. cit.* (1967).
25. Generalisation based on examination of a series of contracts preserved in local and national registers of deeds.
26. SRO, RH 15/2232, Contract of Copartnery of Messrs. Findlay, Hopkirks and Co.
27. SL, CSP 162/23, Information for Elizabeth and Barbara Cunninghame . . . 36.
28. RPO, AO 12/9/53; SL, CSP 190/13, Petition of Messrs. Speirs, French and Co. . . . 2.

29. S. G. E. Lythe, *The Economy of Scotland in its European Setting, 1550–1625* (Edinburgh, 1960), 116–141.
30. GCA, B.10/15/6195; Probative Writs, B.10/12/9; *Glasgow Mercury*, 1 January, 1784. Thomas McFie, a wealthy Glasgow lawyer was in company with the Berries in the 1740s. Local lairds had shares in George McCall and Co. and Buchanan, Hastie and Co.
31. GCA, Probative Writs, B.10/12/4, Contract of Buchanan, Hastie and Co.
32. GCA, Dunlop Papers, Additional Observations for James Dougal . . . 6.
33. SRO, GD 247/59/5, Cunninghame-Robinson Correspondence.
34. SRO, GD 247/58/P/1, Minute of Meeting of the partners of Cunninghame, Findlay and Co., 29 January, 1773.
35. GCA, Reg. of Deeds, B.10/15/8123, Contract of McCall, Elliot and Co.
36. NLS, Charles Steuart Letterbooks, MS 5026, James Ingram to Charles Steuart, 25 April, 1771. See Henry Riddell's position in John Glassford and Co. and William Cunninghame's in Cochrane, Murdoch and Co.
37. SL, CSP 162/23/4–5.
38. GCA Probative Writs, B.10/12/9, Contract of George McCall and Co.
39. J. M. Price, 'Capital and Credit in the Chesapeake Tobacco Trade, 1750–1775'.
40. GCA, B.10/15/8123, Bond of Copartnership betwixt Messrs. John McCall etc. Similar regulations were made in the case of Buchanan, Hastie and Co. (GCA, Probative Writs, B.10/12/4), Alexander Cunninghame and Co. (SL, CSP 162/23), William Cunninghame and Co. (SRO, Reg. of Deeds, 309/2/58 DUR).
41. SRO, RH 15/2232, Contract of Findlay, Hopkirks and Co.
42. GCA, B.10/15/8123, Contract of McCall, Elliot and Co.
43. GCA, B.10/15/6653, Copartnery, Arch. Buchanan, Speirs etc.
44. SRO, RH 15/2232; SL, CSP 162/23/2; GCA, Probative Writs, B.10/12/9; GCA, B.10/15/8123.
45. GCA, Probative Writs, B.10/12/9, Contract of George McCall and Co.
46. GCA, B.10/15/8123, Bond of Copartnership betwixt Messrs. John McCall etc.

5(b)

The Tobacco Firm in Virginia: William Cunninghame and Co., 1768-1775

WILLIAM CUNNINGHAME and Co. were among the giants of the tobacco trade. Regularly in the 1770s they were among the five largest Glasgow importers. The firm was composed of nine partners each holding shares of the total capital of £20,000 which was divided into 458 parts.[1] At least three of these individuals, however, were company factors and storekeepers in America who were allocated a total of thirteen shares as an incentive to diligence. One of these was James Robinson, 'General Superintendent of the Company', who was responsible for organising and supervising business in Virginia and controlling the activities of the concern's various store outlets. The real financial power, however, lay with the representatives of three merchant dynasties, the Cochranes, the Murdochs and the Bogles. William Cunninghame, managing partner and kinsman and protégé of Provost Andrew Cochrane, owned 229 shares or exactly fifty per cent of the stock. Cochrane, founder of the firm and by this time an old man, held 48 shares, Robert Bogle of Shettleston, 64 and the two Murdochs, Peter and John, a total of 104.

Here was an organisation of great stability and commercial influence. Three of the partners had direct access to the Glasgow banking world. Andrew Cochrane and John Murdoch were two of the founders of the Glasgow Arms Bank (Cochrane, Murdoch and Co.); Peter Murdoch was later a prominent shareholder in the same institution.[2] The Bogles and the Murdochs were trading families of ancient lineage, already well-established by the later seventeenth century.[3] All four leading partners in the firm had extensive investments elsewhere in trade and industry. In addition to his Virginia interests, Cunninghame was the major shareholder in two Maryland houses, Cunninghame, Findlay and Co. and Cunninghame, Brown and Co.[4] Robert Bogle also owned capital in the first of these. Peter Murdoch, in addition, was involved in Murdoch, Dreghorn and Co. and Speirs, Bowman and Co., the latter a major rival of the Cunninghame firm in the Virginia trade.[5] The partners also had interests in a variety of industrial enterprises which included the Port Glasgow Sugar House, the Pollockshaws Printfield Co., the Dalnottar Iron Co., the Glasgow Tanwork Co., the Glasgow Bottleworks and the Anderston Brewery.[6]

This important firm controlled fourteen stores in Virginia.[7] Most of these were centred on the piedmont area of the state in new tobacco land which gave leaf of superior quality and better crops. This region lay above the navigable limits of the James, Rappahannock and Potomack rivers. The firm thus established headquarters stores near the heads of navigation at Petersburg and Richmond and at Fredericksburg and Falmouth on the Potomack. James Robinson, the company's superintendent, resided in this latter town. These major centres were then linked to dependent stores in the interior.[8] In these areas there lived and worked the smaller planters to whose needs the Glasgow houses geared their sale and credit policies. The siting of the company's stores was also influenced by the requirements of the French market. For instance, in 1775 about two-thirds of their imports originated from the Upper James river valley and eight of their stores were also located in that region which specialised in production for the French.[9] Moreover, company correspondence continually refers to the significant role played by the French agents in tobacco sales. The firm was in some unease in November, 1772 when 'the French by Messrs. Herries and Co. came to Markett . . . very unexpectedly'. Again, in 1769, concern was expressed over whether the French had started to buy before the account of a storm in Virginia in that year reached the United Kingdom. In Robinson's correspondence with company headquarters in Glasgow primary attention was always concentrated on the behaviour of French prices and new storekeepers were specifically advised to purchase tobacco 'fit for the French manufactory'.[10]

The store outlets themselves probably varied in size according to function. Some of the headquarters units were probably quite large affairs. The one at Fredericksburg was valued at £1700 and that situated in Richmond was apparently commodious enough to be used after the Revolution by the Virginia Assembly until the state building was completed in 1789.[11] Of eleven stores valued, the smallest was worth £200 and together the eleven were assessed at £11,450 exclusive of stock on hand, store furnishings or slaves. Most of the bigger units had negro labour—Falmouth store had seven slaves—to work in the adjacent company farms which provided food for the storekeeper and his assistants and also to carry out general labouring tasks.[12]

All the Cunninghame storekeepers were young Scots recruited from families known to the company principals. The first stage in their career was often service on an indentured basis as assistant to an established storekeeper. So by an agreement of 1769, John Craig, son of James Craig, laird of Braidland, in the parish of Dalry, Ayrshire, 'bound and obliged himself, honestly, diligently and faithfully, to serve William Cunninghame and Co.

in Virginia'. Craig was to be indentured for a period of five years from the date of his arrival in the colonies and to be employed as an assistant storekeeper. During this time, 'he was not to absent himself from the company's service and was to obey at all times the orders of the Company'. He, in turn, was provided with bed, board and washing and a salary which rose on a scale from £5 to £25 over five years.[13] There apparently was no shortage of sons of the gentry, or of the mercantile and professional classes in Scotland able and willing to take up such positions.

The five year training period given to assistants was vital to company success. Despite James Robinson's formal control over the chain of stores most outlets were separated from one another by hundreds of miles over difficult country. Necessarily, therefore, the storekeeper had to be given some independence and allowed some initiative and consequently the company in its turn was dependent on the loyalty and character of its servants. This partly explains the preference for their fellow countrymen and for young men whose families were known, or even better, related to the partners. Nepotism had its uses. Thus, although storekeepers and assistants were advised to mix in local planter society in order to gain custom, they remained in the main a separate group, essential to the functioning of local business but often a target for radical abuse against the middleman. The social position in the community was demonstrated vividly in the Revolutionary crisis. All remained loyalist, despite much physical persuasion, and continued to respond conscientiously to company orders.[14]

Because of the size of the Cunninghame enterprise, an elementary career structure evolved to reward those who had demonstrated ability. Whenever a vacancy arose among the stores or when a new unit was established, the chief factor chose the most promising of the new assistants to fill the post. Thus, Mr. Dobbie, assistant to Thomas Gordon, in a store in Halifax County, was appointed to a second establishment there because 'of his own knowledge of the business, care and assiduity' together with the good reports Gordon had given of his loyalty to the company.[15] Similarly John Turner, 'bred to business' at the Rockeyridge store replaced Bennet Price at Farquar Court House.[16] A further possibility was the offer of a minor share in the partnership or the signing of a salary contract with the company by which pay rose from £40 to £100 per annum in accordance with ability.[17] These were very substantial wages by eighteenth century standards[18] and provide further evidence of the financial standing of these large enterprises and the premium put on good service from storekeepers. It meant that their salaries alone (exclusive of payments to assistants) cost Cunninghame and Co. annually a maximum of £1400 and a minimum of £560 in the 1770s.

In return for such financial rewards, total commitment to the company's business was expected and employees, unlike those of other firms, were forbidden to trade on their own account.[19] Sometimes company demands could reach bizarre extremes. One Bennet Price was dismissed the firm's service in 1768. Unfortunately Price had taken a wife, and, 'They cannot agree to be served by a married man, if a single one can be got, thinking the former must often be necessarily call'd from their business by his family affairs'.[20] Even the company's patient training of potential storekeepers occasionally proved inadequate amid the temptations and stresses of frontier life. High salaries unfortunately were sometimes as much an encouragement to corruption as an incentive to industry! Francis Hay, 'gave loose to dissipation. A purchase was made of a servant girl which he kept for sometime; and gaming to excess soon became common—so much addicted was he to this Vice that he has lost as I have been informed £60 at a sitting . . .'.[21] William Johnstone's sins were regarded as unmentionable but his 'behaviour was such that we look on him as totally unworthy of continuing in our service'.[22]

Perhaps there were bound to be failures. Success in the management of a store depended on a rare blend of qualities. Shrewd business sense, charm in order to ingratiate oneself into the confidence of customers, a deep concern for the company's interest and dutiful application to the labour of compiling accounts were all important. The cultivation of good relationships with planters was deemed particularly desirable by James Robinson. His storekeepers had to develop a 'knowledge of People's disposition' in order to extend the circle of his customers and ascertain their credit-worthiness.[23] The supreme combination in attracting a fresh clientele was what he called 'good usage' and 'plenty of money'. The latter as a purchasing medium for tobacco was always limited by the company but was considered a sure means of drawing new customers to the store. 'Good usage' consisted of more subtle but none the less apparently effective techniques to encourage planters to offer their crop to the firm. In this respect, the twentieth century salesman or marketing expert would have little to teach these merchants. Robinson counselled one of his storekeepers to use 'drink in abundance' when soliciting custom and in addition, every effort was to be made to 'conciliate the affection and esteem of the people and to gain their confidence' by showing honesty in every transaction.[24] At the same time, however, there was danger in too much intimacy: 'Secrecy in all your Transactions of Business even to the most simple is what I would strongly recommend'.[25]

All this advice was designed to ensure that there would be a satisfactory annual equilibrium between the company's shipping capacity and the tobacco crop which could be expected from planter-customers. Each year in October James Robinson drew up a grand plan of crop estimates and shipping schedules for the following season. The smooth functioning of this mechanism depended on storekeepers achieving their estimated levels of purchase before the company's vessels arrived. Only thus would loading time be cut to a minimum, and full utilisation of a ship's carrying capacity be achieved. So in 1772 Robinson calculated that a gross total of 5250 hogsheads could be exported from the firm's fourteen Virginian stores in six vessels (Table XVI).

This system was clearly intended to be highly efficient. In the eighteenth century, most shipowners involved in the Atlantic trades accepted that one annual crossing was all that could be expected from most vessels.[26] Yet half of Cunninghames' fleet (and doubtless also the ships of other Glasgow houses) achieved two voyages per annum.

The effectiveness of the operation, however, was dependent on two variables which could only be partially estimated—the weather and European market prices. The need to offer a full freight to vessels on arrival meant that storekeepers had to bid up the prices of scarce tobacco, offer cash or delay ship departures until prices levelled out. Doubtless, these disadvantages were sometimes cancelled out by higher prices in Europe. These, however, did

TABLE XVI
W. Cunninghame and Co.'s Shipping Estimates for 1772–3

Ships	Rivers		
	Rappahanock	Potomack	James
Cochrane via Havre de Grace arrive December	—	—	460
Janett via France arrive December	—	390	—
Cunninghame straight out arrive December	500	—	—
Neptune with goods arrive April	—	—	460
Venus arrive April	—	450	—
Ocean from London arrive April	560	—	—
Cochrane with goods arrive June	460	—	—
Cunninghame with goods arrive June	—	—	500
Neptune with goods arrive September	—	400	—
Venus arrive September	450	—	—
Ocean arrive September	—	—	560

Source—SRO, GD247/158/0, J. Robinson to William Cunninghame and Co., 18 October, 1772.

not always offer satisfactory compensation. In 1772, U.K. prices were in the doldrums because of the depression of that year. Yet,

> ... such is the overdone situation of the trade on every river in this colony that little tobacco can be bought without paying a great part money to the Planter ... So great is the demand for tobacco all over the Colony arising from the number of ships employed on the trade that the planter has been able to establish his own terms and to procure what part money he chuses.[27]

The risks inherent in the system could be avoided to some extent by altering erroneous estimates in the light of crop and market developments in time for the arrival of vessels in the late summer and early autumn. So Robinson in April, 1773 concluded that 'the second ships' for each river could not expect an immediate cargo and 'must lie a considerable time for the collections'. He therefore suggested that they should be put to alternative uses, indicating that one might call at Liverpool for salt before crossing the Atlantic.[28]

Cunninghame storekeepers obtained their annual tobacco shipments in three ways; for cash, for bills of exchange or in payment of goods earlier supplied to planters. The latter method was the most popular since money was scarce and profit was made on goods sold. Mark-ups of 65–75 per cent were most common on articles sold in the Cunninghame stores, a figure which was made up of freight and handling costs plus profit to the firm.[29] Because of the returns from sales of store goods and their function in attracting fresh tobacco supplies to the firm, great care was always taken in ensuring that storekeepers procured articles to suit planter preferences. Managers who sent vague orders for goods to company headquarters in Glasgow were severely reprimanded.[30] At the same time the firm was quick to take advantage of any scarcity in the supply of goods to raise the level of its advances. Immediately before the implementation of the colonists' non-importation agreements in 1774–5, Robinson was urging his storekeepers to increase prices 'as they will soon be scarce' and William Cunninghame himself counselled his employees to 'most secretly adhere' to the non-importation policy for the company's benefit.[31] Evidence like this does perhaps lend some substance to the accusation that the Scots merchants were grasping middlemen charging exorbitant profits. Yet J. H. Soltow's verdict is more sensible:

High advances on goods did not end with the expulsion of the Scottish merchants during the American Revolution. In the early nineteenth century wholesalers generally charged a mark-up of 100–150 per cent of the original cost of merchandise, to which southern retailers added a similar advance. Thus, the high prices of imported goods resulted not so much from deceit and collusion among sellers as from the high costs of marketing in a rural economy.[32]

REFERENCES

1. SRO, Reg. of Deeds, 309/2/58 DUR, Contract of Copartnership among the partners of William Cunninghame and Co., Glasgow.
2. Buchanan, *loc. cit.*
3. McCure, *op. cit., passim.*
4. PRO, AO 12/56/300, 305.
5. GCA, Speirs Papers, TD 131/7, Ledger; 1785–88, 45; PRO, AO 12/56/292.
6. SRO, Reg. of Deeds, 216/802 DAL; Andrew Scott, 'The History and Progress of the Four Leading Articles of Foreign Origin', *Trans. Glasgow Arch. Soc.*, I (1859), 366; SRO, Reg. of Deeds, 232/817 MACK; GCA, Probative Writs, B.10/12/5; GCA, Reg. of Deeds, B.10/15/7460.
7. PRO, AO 12/56/288; SRO, GD 247/59/S, General Inventory of Slaves and other personal estates belonging to William Cunninghame and Co.
8. *Ibid.*; Price, *op. cit.*, 666–7.

9. R. P. Thomson, 'The Tobacco Export of the Upper James Naval District, 1773-5', *William and Mary Quarterly*, XVIII (1961); Price, *op. cit.*, 667.
10. SRO, GD 247/58/0, James Robinson to William Henderson, 11 March, 1772, 14 November, 1769.
11. PRO, AO 12/56/293; I. S. Harrell, *Loyalism in Virginia* (Durham, North Carolina, 1926), 95.
12. SRO, GD 247/59/S, General Inventory of Slaves and other Personal Estates belonging to William Cunninghame and Co. . . . 1777.
13. SRO, Unextracted Process, I Currie Mack, C/4/13, W. Cunninghame and Co. versus Craig (1777).
14. See below.
15. SRO, GD 247/58/0, James Robinson to Thomas Gordon, 23 August, 1770.
16. *Ibid.*, to Bennet Price, 11 September, 1768; to John Turner, 6 October, 1771.
17. PRO, AO 12/56/292; SRO, GD 247/158/0, James Robinson to Andrew Chalmer, 31 May, 1771.
18. H. G. Graham, *Social Life of Scotland in the Eighteenth Century* (Fifth ed., London, 1969), 4.
19. SRO, GD 247/158/0, James Robinson to John Turner, 6 October, 1771.
20. *Ibid.*, to Bennet Price, 11 September, 1768.
21. *Ibid.*, to John Turner, 18 March, 1773.
22. SRO, GD 247/141, William Cunninghame to William Henderson, 18 July, 1774.
23. SRO, GD 247/158/0, James Robinson to John Turner, 25 October, 1768.
24. *Ibid.*
25. *Ibid.*, 4 October, 1768; 6 October, 1771.
26. Ralph Davis, *The Rise of the English Shipping Industry in the Seventeenth and Eighteenth Centuries* (London, 1962).
27. SRO, GD 247/158/0, James Robinson to William Cunninghame and Co., 18 October, 1772.
28. *Ibid.*, to William Cunninghame and Co., 27 April, 1773.
29. *Ibid.*, 6 October, 1771.
30. *Ibid.*, 22 April, 1769.
31. *Ibid.*, Robinson to William Cunninghame and Co., 26 February, 1773; SRO, GD 247/59/S, William Cunninghame to John Turner, 18 July, 1774.
32. Soltow, *loc. cit.*, 94.

6

Sources of Capital for the Glasgow Tobacco Trade, 1740-80

THE successful financing of the Glasgow tobacco trade is one of the paradoxes of eighteenth century Scottish history. American commerce was dependent on much capital but Scotland, according to several scholars, was in the first half of the century an impoverished country, apparently incapable of sustaining an enterprise of such dimensions.[1] In this chapter an attempt will be made to resolve this apparent contradiction. It will be argued that even an apparently deprived economic region, by gaining access to finance elsewhere and by exploiting its own resources, could accumulate the necessary capital to dominate an important branch of international trade.

In order to carry out this analysis satisfactorily a distinction must be drawn between 'working' capital, designed to cover specific transactions in day-to-day business activity, and 'long-term' finance representing the investment in goods and credit to planters so vital to growth in the tobacco trade but not producing returns for several years. In practice such a division is to some extent an artificial one but it does allow the discussion to be conducted in a clearer fashion. In the first category one of the problems was the need to cover the time between purchase of marketable commodities in Europe, acquisition of tobacco in North America and its sale in British and Continental markets. For the Glasgow men, as we have observed,[2] the issue was somewhat more complicated because, unlike most of their competitors in London and the other outports, they tended increasingly to purchase tobacco outright in the colonies rather than act as commission agents for its sale for planters who retained title of ownership. The Glasgow merchants thus tied up more of their capital by shouldering all the financial burdens of insurance, freight, customs duties and other port charges.

By the later seventeenth century the use of bills of exchange for settling accounts without transmission of coin or bullion was already familiar to Scots merchants. It was the most efficient method of covering the time between sale to customer and payment to supplier.[3] The letterbook of Adam

Montgomery, a late seventeenth century Glasgow merchant, trading to Stockholm in tobacco and other commodities, indicates that overseas commerce of the time was conducted almost entirely by bill operations.[4] By the second half of the following century this system had become particularly well-developed in the Glasgow tobacco trade. For the mechanism between drawer, bill-broker and banker to operate effectively two things were necessary. The first of these was security of payment when the bill had matured. Undoubtedly a major element in providing this was the bulk sales to the French Farmers General, the most important single purchasers in the trade. The French buyers also paid in cash or in immediately discountable bills of exchange and the consequent dependence of the Glasgow men on the French order was shown vividly in anxious mercantile correspondence concerning it and in the regularity with which the French agents were able to force down prices and break even the most determined mercantile front.[5] Significantly in the credit crisis of 1772, Sir Robert Herries, the French buyer 'was received with open arms' by the great Clyde traders.[6] Again, the French agents were often willing to make advances to hard-pressed firms to pay port charges if the anticipated cargo was first promised to them. Probably the greater houses had no need of such a facility but it was taken advantage of by merchants operating closer to the financial margin. Thus in 1762, when it was difficult to procure credit and sales were sluggish, William Alexander and Sons, acting for the French, advanced cash for customs duties to Lawson, Semple and Co.[7]

A second prerequisite for the healthy functioning of the bill mechanism was personal knowledge and trust within the international commercial community. Perhaps the most valuable assets possessed by the eighteenth century businessman was not his capital but rather his reputation and his connexions. The prestige and influence of the well-known families in the Glasgow tobacco trade meant that they seem to have had little difficulty in securing credit from contacts in other parts of the United Kingdom or Europe. One of the Bogles borrowed freely in London in the 1720s because his father's credit 'was as good as ever' and consequently his son 'can never want money when you think to borrow it and that without paying Interest on it'.[8] James Lawson secured sums of varying amounts from fellow merchants in Bristol, Liverpool and London by drawing bills for between six and twelve months.[9] The system of credit was particularly well developed with London, the financial capital of Western Europe at this time. The repeated references to 'London bills' in merchant letters and the effect of the withdrawal of London loans in 1761-2 and 1772 provide eloquent testimony to their importance in the Glasgow financial structure. Firms drew bills on their agents in the capital, payable in twenty to sixty days, before which time the latter would draw on their principals for the same sum plus interest and commission. This device could be repeated several times and costs included an annual interest rate of five per cent plus a commission of one-half of one per cent for each bill drawn.[10] George Bogle's financial dealings illustrate the mechanism in operation:

> I have yours this day with Inclos'd 2nd Bill of Exchange on Messrs. Alexander and James Coutts merchants in London for Sixty pounds sterling payable 20 days after date you may send me the first bill by next post Inclos'd to Ralph Fairley the Sugar House Manager, who was accepted of your offer, and who will take three hundred pounds payable at London in thirty days after Date you indorsing them to them or his Order and Sending two bills to him by next post of the Same tenor and Date by which Bills you may have your money payable here on Demand, or if you chuse to have your money at Edinburgh payable in fourteen or twenty days at furthest Including your ¼ per cent.[11]

Moreover, it was commonplace to borrow against the security of tobacco shipments before sale. The Dutch tobacco market, for instance, was notoriously sluggish. Consignments were auctioned in small lots over a period of weeks or even months and capital was tied up in stocks accumulating in Dutch warehouses.[12] To preserve liquidity bills were drawn on correspondents in Holland in anticipation of sales.[13]

It was not possible, however, to depend on the bill mechanism for all capital needs. Companies which traded to North America 'in the store way' were committed to long-term investments and the bill system, with repayments dependent on short time schedules, and quick return on capital, could only partially satisfy their requirements. The structure of the Glasgow trading community was partly responsible for the accumulation of longer-term investment funds. Although a proportion of income was always shed in estate purchase, conspicuous consumption and in the provision of dowries and annuities, merchant families normally also set aside cash resources for the continuation of trading connections. Sons, grandsons and great-grandsons succeeded one another. It was rare for the second or third generations to dispose of their interests in commerce. As we have seen ownership of land need not conflict with business activities.[14] Through inheritance therefore the accumulated profits of earlier generations could be incorporated within the capital structure of the new. Only bankruptcy, financial recklessness or a childless marriage might interrupt the momentum of development. Commonly merchant fathers directed that money left to their descendants was to be used in trade. Colin Dunlop granted his son, John, £3000 as 'stock in trade'; John McCall advanced his two eldest sons 'a considerable sum' specifically for the purpose of 'setting them up in business'. Thomas Hopkirk allowed his son James £4000 on the condition that he invested it in commerce.[15] The evidence suggests that the generation of the 1720s, 30s and 40s already consisted of men of wealth whose sons were likely to inherit substantial sums. Robert Bogle, for instance, in the 1720s, had accumulated a considerable surplus and utilised it in lending to a series of landowners on heritable bond.[16]

Endogamy within the merchant group, a natural result of the limited supply of socially acceptable partners in a small community, also helped to consolidate cash resources and limit the risk of haemorrhage of capital. Commonly junior partners in tobacco firms married the daughters of their senior colleagues[17] and such romantic attachments were yet another of the methods by which the new generation gained access to the resources of the old. The provision of a substantial dowry (in Scotland 'tocher') could be the key to later financial success for an ambitious young merchant and his descendants. Space allows only one illustration of this. When Alexander Speirs married into the wealthy Buchanan clan he was 'possessed of but a modest fortune'. His ability, drive and financial connections with the Buchanans made him 'the mercantile god of Glasgow' by the 1770s. When his own daughter, Martha, wed one of Speirs's associates, George Crawford, a dowry of £5000 was promised.[18]

Yet, as earlier discussion has shown, in spite of the dominance of the great families, the openings in trade were sufficiently wide to permit the emergence of new figures who had saved enough to rise to full partnership level.[19] This mobility within the community was indicative of the trade's capacity for generating its own investment capital.

Just as crucial, however, was the retention of profits within the capital structure of individual firms. Since partners were only allowed five per cent interest on the value of their shares, it followed that the vast proportion of company earnings were ploughed back. To some extent, of course, this was inevitable since most accruals took the form of book profits which were difficult to realise in the short term.[20] Nevertheless, strict control over dividends helped to preserve liquidity and to diminish the need for external borrowing. This was necessary anyway because many firms prohibited loans above a certain figure. Thus in the case of Speirs, Bowman and Co., the managing partner was only authorised to borrow sums to a maximum of twenty-five per cent of the paid up capital. Capital growth occurred by retention of profit. In 1744, total capital was £16,200. Three decades later the managing partner, shares alone were valued at £57,000.[21]

It would be wrong, on the other hand, to give the impression that all firms were able to survive and extend their activities from their own resources. At any one time, there would be a significant group which had to seek long-term credit from elsewhere because they were in the early stages of expansion, because of under-capitalisation or because of pressure on existing resources as a result of market problems. These difficulties were perhaps most likely to prevail in the period of rapid growth in tobacco importation after c.1750. Perhaps for this reason, some historians have suggested a close relationship between the formation of the Glasgow banks in the 1750s and 1760s and the successful financing of the tobacco trade. To Soltow, the capital supplied by the Glasgow banks 'which specialised in mobilising credit for the tobacco trade' was one of the prime reasons for Scottish dominance in Virginia commerce and Price was almost equally emphatic in his praise of them.[22] Here it will be argued that these institutions were *one* of the channels through which capital flowed to the trade but that they were by no means the most important.

The ventures concerned were the Ship Bank (founded in 1752), the Glasgow Arms Bank (founded in the same year) and the Thistle Bank (established 1761). All three partnerships were dominated by tobacco lords. The Cochranes and the Murdochs were leading members of the Arms Bank (and later the chief partner was Alexander Speirs) while the founders of the Ship Bank were Colin Dunlop, Allan Dreghorn, Andrew Buchanan, Robert Dunlop and two wealthy West India merchants, Alexander Houston and William McDowall.[23] The first partners of the Thistle Banking Co., apart from a local laird, Sir John Maxwell, were all tobacco traders viz. John Glassford, James Ritchie, John Coats Campbell and John McCall.[24] To some extent at least these enterprises were simply larger and more formal

TABLE XVII
Sums Borrowed on Bond by Bogle, Somervell and Co. at 5 July, 1768

Bonded Creditor	Loan (£)
Robert Lawson, late of Virginia	1,200
John Anderson, portioner of little Govan	1,000
James Graham, surgeon of Paisley	1,000
John Bell of Autermoney	1,000
James Russell, commissary clerk of Dunblain	600
Cochrane, Murdoch and Co. (Arms Bank)	500
Christina McGilchrist, relict of Robert Cross, merchant in Glasgow	500
Mary Maxwell, daughter of deceased James Maxwell of Bogtown	433
Margaret Buchanan, daughter of deceased William Buchanan of Carbeth	300
Henry Wardrop, portioner of Dalmarnock	330
John Sym, writer in Glasgow	150
Martha Bogle, relict of Andrew Leitch, merchant	100
	£7,113

Source—GCA, Register of Deeds, B.10/15/8045.

versions of established banking activities. In the first half of the eighteenth century, successful merchants with surplus funds had received deposits, handled exchange business and provided credit facilities. The father, grandfather and uncle of Peter Murdoch, a founding member of the Arms Bank, had been engaged together long before the 1730s in a 'banking business'. For the time the venture seems to have carried on on a considerable scale since Murdoch père's own share in the undertaking was £2000 sterling.[25]

Too much ought not to be read into the coincidence between the formation of the three banks and rapid expansion in the tobacco trade. The extant records of the Ship and Thistle do not indicate that their services were geared specifically to the needs of tobacco companies. The largest groups among their customers seem to have been West of Scotland landowners and merchants or industrial firms with no direct connection with American trade.[26] Evidence of the sources of credit for two tobacco companies trading in the 1760s and 1770s presented in Tables XVII–XIX confirms this impression. The question 'how typical' these credit structures were of other firms cannot be answered

TABLE XVIII

Abstract of Sums owed by Buchanan, Hastie and Co. to 1777 with interest calculated to 1783

Creditors	Loan (to nearest £)
Merchants, industrial firms, craftsmen	18,201
Banks in Glasgow	9,201
Landowners in Scotland	7,780
Trust funds of widows, orphans, spinsters, institutions	7,492
Professional groups (lawyers, clergymen, military officers, etc.)	5,388
Creditors with English addresses	2,015
Unclassified	12,165
	£62,242

Source—SRO, Currie Dal Sequestration, B1/1 (1777).

TABLE XIX

Sample of Sums Borrowed on Bond by Buchanan, Hastie and Co., 1768–1772

Creditor	Amount (£)	Date
William Clavil, landowner	2,000	1768
John Alexander, purser H.M.S. *Panther*	500	1769
James Smollett of Bonhill	100	1771
John Murray of Blackbarony	300	1771
Daniel Baxter, bookseller in Glasgow	400	1773
Factor for children of James Glen, Goldsmith in Glasgow	400	1773
Dr. William Macfarlane, physician in Edinburgh	250	—
Sir Kenneth Pringle of Stithill, Bart	500	—
John Yuill, Shoemaker in Glasgow	600	1772
John Wilson, Town Clerk of Glasgow	600	1772
Marquis of Annandale	1,500	—

Source—GCA, Register of Deeds; SRO, Register of Deeds.

with complete certainty but examination of several hundred bonds in local and national registers of deeds does at least *suggest* similar patterns elsewhere. Furthermore, the sources for funds borrowed by these two companies are remarkably similar to those of the loans of Robert Robertson, a merchant trading to Virginia before the 1750s (see Table XIX).

SOURCES OF CAPITAL FOR THE GLASGOW TOBACCO TRADE

Bank finance was clearly not of central importance to either of the two firms or to Robertson. Seven per cent of Bogle, Somervell and Co.'s loans were provided by the Arms Bank and Buchanan, Hastie and Co. owed fifteen

TABLE XX

Bonded Debts of Robert Robertson and his Nephew James Robertson, 29 September, 1740

Creditor	Amount (£)
Robert Robertson, preacher of the Gospel in Glasgow	250
Margaret Thompson, daughter of deceased Thomas Thompson, merchant in Glasgow	166
John Montgomery, minister of Gospel at Stewarton	100
Hugh Smith of Thorntown and the rest of the Curators of Matthew, Helen and Elizabeth Strang in East Kilbride parish	277
Alexander Dunlop, Professor of Greek, Univ. of Glasgow	100
John Robertson, bookbinder in Glasgow	100
Robert Rae, portioner of Little Govan	500
Joseph Baxter, Cork-Cutter in Glasgow	74
William Stirling, surgeon in Glasgow	55
Arch. Govan, merchant in Glasgow	200
Lieut. John Rawson, of the Hon. Col. Guises Regiment of Foot in Glasgow	100
Richard Hill, son of John Hill in Greenock and his curators	287
John Hunter, merchant in Glasgow	93
Benjamin Thompson	90
Helen Wells, relict of George Thompson, merchant in Glasgow	50
William and Andrew Gray, merchants in Glasgow	200
Jean Mair, relict of Andrew Lang, in Greenock	120
Capt. William Dunlop, merchant in Glasgow	100
Deacon Convener of Trades House	80
Alexander Andrews, merchant in Rotterdam	94
Bank of Scotland	500
Claud Johnstone	1,000
TOTAL	£4,536

Abstract	Amount (£)
Professional groups (ministers, surgeons, lawyers, teachers, army officers, etc.)	605
Trustees, widows, minors, spinsters	900
Landowners	500
Banks	500
Craftsmen	254
Merchants	1,777
TOTAL	£4,536

Source—GCA, B.10/15/5402, Disposition and Assignation, Robert Robertson to his Creditors, 1740.

per cent of their total debt to the Ship, Arms and Thistle Banks. Robertson obtained about eleven per cent of his credit from the Bank of Scotland.

It would seem therefore that the role of bank finance in the tobacco trade was not to provide the bulk of the capital but rather to cater for some of the more specific needs of merchant firms. In their willingness to act as bill discounters these institutions plainly provided an important service. The value of bills accepted in the Ship Bank rose from £8,854 in 1752 to £54,135 ten years later.[27] Probably another valuable function was to meet short-term cash requirements for customs, port and freight charges. Thus most firms held 'cash accompts' with either the Glasgow or Edinburgh banks on which they could draw overdrafts to a specified amount. For instance, the Berries had credit from the Arms Bank for £800 in the 1750s.[28] By 1751, the Royal Bank of Scotland had sanctioned 'cash accompts' to the value of £15,000 for 24 Glasgow firms. Three were for £1000, one for £1500 and one for £2000; the remaining nineteen were for £200–£600.[29] The 'cash accompt' system was perhaps particularly useful to the smaller company which was more likely to be under-capitalised and perhaps more dependent on external sources of credit at critical periods. Certainly in 1761–2, James Lawson of Lawson, Semple and Co. complained bitterly when the banks called in their overdrafts: 'this breeds great Confusion and Distress amongst us'. He argued three years later that:

> Our Banks are at war with one another which by ruining upon one another they are obliged to call in People's cash accounts in a most rigorous manner which adds greatly to the present distresses of this place.[30]

Apart, however, from these overdraft services, banks also helped merchants with urgent customs and freight charges to meet through their own note issues so by the end of the 1750s, the Ship had notes to the value of around £100,000 in circulation and twenty years later its smaller rival, the Thistle, had an issue of £30,000.[31]

Despite this impressive catalogue of benefits accruing from the expansion of Glasgow banking, Tables XVII–XX have indicated that merchants obtained the bulk of their credit by borrowing not from institutions but from other individuals with capital to spare. As Andrew Brown, one of the first historians of Glasgow and himself a tobacco merchant, observed, 'the strength of the monied interest of the West of Scotland was embarked in it' (i.e. the tobacco trade).[32] Landowners, professional people, trustees, widows and spinsters—groups traditionally associated with the funding of government stock, land and mortgages—were apparently prepared to channel at least some of their savings into more speculative fields. Buchanan, Hastie and Co. obtained loans from sources as diverse as the Marquis of Annandale, the Faculty of Advocates, medical practitioners, a naval purser and the trust funds of widows and orphans.[33] Registered bonds among Glasgow deeds show that in the eighteenth century a vigorous capital market functioned in the city drawing together the funds of a surprisingly diverse series of social groups. How is this pattern to be explained?

It must be stressed firstly that Scottish Lowland society, especially at élite level, was very closely-knit and integrated by a series of kinship, friendship and marriage ties. Wealthy traders, as important and well-known members of this regional community and, often scions of established landed and professional families within it, exploited their contacts for business purposes. The movement of merchants into land and their political and administrative influence in the counties around Glasgow lent them that essential 'respectability' without which borrowing on a grand scale could not take place. While social relationships were more fluid, society in the Scottish Lowlands was also less rigidly demarcated along religious lines (unlike some regional centres in England). Dissent was never as great an obstacle to social intercourse as it was south of the Border. The age of 'Moderatism' had cooled the tempers of all but the most dedicated of zealots. Certainly some of the tobacco lords were Episcopalians but this surely made them more intimate with some of the fashionable leading families in the West who were of a similar persuasion.

The merchant thus first sought credit from his kin and associates. James Lawson was assisted by James Dunlop in procuring a loan from William and James Manson of Rotterdam:

> Our mutual friend Mr. Jas. Dunlop of this place tells us that if we are in want of money (which is the case with us at present, having a deal of Tobacco Laying here for want of ships to carry it to your Market) that we may draw upon you for 6000 or 7000 guilders.[34]

He then contacted his brother at Mauchline, his other acquaintances and 'several of our Richest and knowingest merchants'.[35] Table XVII (p. 93) which lists the bonded debts of Bogle, Somervell and Co., provides further evidence of this pattern. Robert Lawson, who lent the firm £1200 was a member of a family of tobacco importers which had previous business connections with the Jamiesons, one of whom was a shareholder in Bogle, Somervell and Co. A total of £900 was subscribed by the widows of three traders who had prospered in American commerce, Robert Cross, William Buchanan and Andrew Leitch. James Russell, 'commissary clerk of Dunblain' who lent £600 was the father of David Russell who acquired his burgess ticket in 1779 through marriage to Susanna Bogle. William Bogle, managing partner in Bogle, Somervell and Co., was her uncle.

Nevertheless, personal relationships alone might not guarantee loans if interest rates were not competitive or security unsatisfactory. Here the great magnet was probably the more favourable rate of financial return offered on bonded loans which meant in most years higher earnings than were possible by investment in government securities. Five per cent was the normal interest on personal bonds and only rarely during wartime did Consols reach this level.[36] Significantly when they did, as for instance in the American War of Independence, merchants complained of the scarcity of credit and the difficulty of obtaining bonds.[37] Yet one suspects that five per cent on these loans was simply a base rate employed to conform with the usury laws. An actual transaction could result in a much higher return. Thus 'liquidate penalties' were always included by which the debtor promised to pay the creditor a specified annual amount (usually twenty per cent of the principal sum) for each year that the loan remained outstanding. Since most bonds endured for several years,[38] one wonders whether these penalty clauses were collusive negotiations, the agreement being drawn up on the assumption that the additional sum would in fact be levied.

Finally, efforts were made to render lending on bond a secure investment. That merchants succeeded in doing so is effectively demonstrated by the evidence of the large numbers of trustees, widows and well-to-do spinster ladies who entrusted a portion of their life savings to tobacco firms. Partnership law permitted loans to be raised both on the company's joint stock and on the person of the individual partners. The 'heritable bond' gave additional security by linking the loan to a specific part of the creditor's heritable property. In the event of insolvency the holder of such a bond would be a preferential creditor on the bankrupt's assets. This was an important consideration before the Scots Bankruptcy Law of 1772 (12 Geo. III, c.72) because up till then a few creditors could receive satisfaction without the claims of others being consulted.

The broad impression gained therefore from the evidence examined during this analysis is that at least after c.1750 there was no shortage of investment funds in Scotland among the higher and middling social classes. Long-term loans in the tobacco trade were apparently negotiated against a background of abundant supplies of savings in relation to investment opportunities and some firms were quite capable of solving their own problems of undercapitalisation by borrowing extensively in the market. These companies gained because there were few major competing areas for commercial investment in the West of Scotland apart from American and Caribbean trade. Even the industrial ventures of the period were often ancillary to this commerce or financed by merchants who controlled it. Only in the last two decades of the century did this monopoly situation change.

REFERENCES

1. Smout, *op. cit.*, 239–53; Hamilton, *op. cit.*, 291–313.
2. See above, Chapter 4.
3. Smout, *op. cit.*, 117.
4. ML, Adam Montgomery's Letterbook, *passim*.
5. Price, *op. cit.*,
6. *Ibid.*,
7. SRO, RH 15/1179, James Lawson's Letterbook, W. Alexander and Sons to Lawson, 5 January, 1762.
8. ML, Bogle MSS, George Bogle's Letterbook, Bogle to Robert Bogle, 18 July, 1727.
9. SRO, RH 15/1179, James Lawson's Letterbook, *passim*.
10. Soltow, *loc. cit.*, 95.
11. ML, Bogle MSS, George Bogle's Letterbook, Bogle to William Alexander, 29 September, 1729.

12. GCA, TD 132, Letters of Kippen, Glassford and Co., William Davidson to George Kippen, 20 February, 1759.
13. ML, Bogle MSS, George Bogle's Letterbook, Bogle to John Cartairs, 23 September, 1729, 14 May, 1733; SRO, RH 15/1179, James Lawson's Letterbook, Lawson to James Russell, 26 December, 1759, to William Davidson, 16 December, 1760.
14. See above, pp. 26–7.
15. ML, MS Notes on the Family of Dunlop of Garnkirk, 59; SRO, Reg. of Deeds, 231/1/937 MACK, Discharge of John Dunlop to Colin and James Dunlop; GCA, Reg. of Deeds, B.10/15/9961; SRO, Reg. of Deeds, 231/135 MACK, Disposition by Thomas Hopkirk in favour of James Hopkirk.
16. ML, Bogle MSS, George Bogle's Letterbook, Bogle to the Hon. My Lady Shaw, 30 December, 1734; to Earl of Dundonald, 25 August, 1735; Registered Heritable Bond and Disposition, the Earl of Dundonald to Robert Bogle, 1729.
17. See above, Figure I, p. 12.
18. SL, CSP 180/7, Answers for Archibald Speirs . . . 1; GCA, Register of Deeds, B.10/15/8435, Settlement, Alexander Speirs, 16 December, 1782.
19. See above, pp. 4–7.
20. Price, 'Capital and Credit'.
21. GCA, B.10/15/6653, Copartnery, Arch. Buchanan, Speirs etc., 8 December, 1759; Speirs Papers, TD 131/6/1A, States of private affairs, Alexander Speirs esq.
22. Soltow, *loc. cit.*, 85; Price, *loc. cit.*, 305.
23. John Buchanan, 'Banking in Glasgow during the Olden Time', *Glasgow Past and Present* (Glasgow, 1884); GCA, Speirs Papers, TD 131/4 Ledger B; GCA, TD 161/1, Ship Bank Balance Book (Xerox copy, original in Bank of Scotland, Glasgow).
24. GCA, Reg. of Deeds, B.10/15/8314, Bond by Sir James Maxwell, James Ritchie and Co.
25. *Ibid.*, 7145, Discharge of £2000 bond by Peter Murdoch, jun.
26. GCA, Ship Bank Balance Book, 1751–1761; Ship Bank Ledger TD 161/3, Part I, 1769–1772; TD 161/2, Thistle Bank Journal, 1778–9.
27. GCA, Ship Bank Balance Book, 1751–61.
28. GCA, Reg. of Deeds, B.10/15/6188.
29. Price, 'Capital and Credit'.
30. SRO, RH 15/1179, James Lawson's Letterbook, 1762–66, Lawson to John Semple, 24 February, 1762; 21 January, 1764.
31. GCA, Ship Bank Balance Book; Reg. of Deeds, B.10/15/7432.
32. Andrew Brown, *History of Glasgow* (Glasgow, 1795), II, 143.
33. SRO, Currie Dal Sequestrations, B1/1, Buchanan, Hastie and Co., 1777.
34. SRO, RH 15/1179, James Lawson's Letterbook, Lawson to Messrs. William and James Manson, 22 February, 1761.
35. *Ibid.*, Lawson to John Semple, 14 January, 1763; 21 January, 1764.
36. T. S. Ashton, *Economic Fluctuations in England, 1700–1815* (Oxford, 1959). *passim.*
37. NLS, MS 8794, Foreign Letterbook of Alexander Houston and Co., Houstons to Messrs. Turner and Paul, 1 December, 1778; SRO, GD 247/59/Q/2, William Cunninghame to Robert Dunmore, 27 July, 1778.
38. In 1720 Arthur Tran received 1000 merks from James Hamilton of Aikenhead. This was still unpaid in 1737 [GCA, B.10/15/5185]. Thomas Orr, borrowed from Andrew Tait, minister of the Church, 1000 merks in 1730; the sum was unpaid in 1737 [GCA, B.10/15/5195].

Part III

GLASGOW MERCHANTS AND THE AMERICAN WAR OF INDEPENDENCE

7

Merchant Reaction to the American War of Independence 1775-83

I

FOR over a decade before 1775 the political and commercial relationships of the United Kingdom and her American colonies were punctuated by a series of crises as tension built up in the years before the Revolution. These events were matters of major significance to the Glasgow trading community. Between 1755 and 1775 the estimated values of imports from America ranged each year from one-third to one-half of total Scottish imports. The vast proportion of this consisted of tobacco shipped by Glasgow merchant firms. The influence of political action, especially by non-exportation agreements, could disrupt this lucrative commerce. Thus, until the War of Independence had begun in earnest, the Glasgow traders tried to protect their interests by officially favouring colonial aims and condemning any coercive or punitive policies adopted by the British Government which were likely to cause hostility and reaction in America. In 1765–6 they opposed the Stamp Act which obliged the colonies to pay a duty on a wide range of legal documents and publications and was widely unaccepted as an intolerable tax. When it was repealed, 'all concerned in the trade and manufactures of this place (i.e. Glasgow) who are so deeply interested in the prosperity of the colonies expressed a more than common joy and satisfaction'.[1]

Company representatives in America had to tread carefully because often their desire to expand trade conflicted with radical intentions to influence the British government by prohibiting imports and exports. In addition, Scots storekeepers were vulnerable to political diatribe as a class to whom all planters were indebted and who were universally suspected of being of 'Tory' sympathies. In 1774, it could be said that a Scotsman in Virginia was 'in danger of his life (at least of being tarred and feathered) if he says a word that does not please them'.[2] The most virulent attacks were reserved for the Glasgow men:

The Glasgow factors seem to be great objects of their resentment, the case is plain; to them they owe the money, some of them have been roughly handled ... James Dunlop, son of Mr. William of Glasgow ... who resides at Port Royal refused to sign the association, a mob gathered soon and put it in his option to be hanged, have his storehouse burnt or sign.[3]

In such a situation it was only politic to pay at least lip service to the wishes of the radicals. Factors of William Cunninghame and Co. were instructed to 'most secretly adhere' to any non-importation agreement. Indeed the firm recognised that there was commercial advantage in doing so: 'We hope they will thereby be enabled to pay off part of their debt to Britain during such an agreement subsisting'.[4]

The long series of difficulties in colonial relations meant that the Glasgow houses were always kept well informed by their agents about political conditions in Virginia and Maryland. Moreover, such journals as the *Caledonian Mercury*, the *Glasgow Journal* and the *Scots Magazine* faithfully reported successive crises, incorporating transcriptions of news and comment originally published in London newspapers and including items of specific Glasgow interest concerning the colonies, the sources of which were often private letters received from Scots resident in America. The fact that merchants were fully aware of the problems developing across the Atlantic is certain; what is perhaps more debatable is how they interpreted the information received and, more important how their analysis of the situation affected their business decisions in the years and months before the outbreak of armed rebellion in 1775. A review of the correspondence of important firms in this period appears to indicate that although a further deterioration in colonial relations was expected, no outright rebellion was anticipated and radical attempts at economic blackmail by prohibiting exports of tobacco would probably prove ephemeral. The political climate in 1774–5 was such that the most optimistic appraisals of the situation were given. The resident factor in Virginia of James Brown and Co. reported to his parent house in April, 1775 (a mere five months before the ports were due to close in implementation of a non-exportation agreement) a rumour in the state that the United Kingdom Parliament had 'put a stop to any proceedings against the Americans for a certain number of years'. This he added had cooled many colonial tempers.[5] The instructions of Messrs. Speirs, French and Co., one of the largest firms trading to Maryland, demonstrate that they expected a non-exportation agreement to be put into effect but that this would only be a temporary disruption. If the export of the year's crop should be halted, their factor was advised in June, 1775 to keep his stores open and to dispose of goods to those planters whose payment could be depended upon. Bonds were to be taken for existing debts, although no special effort was to be made to liquidate outstanding advances. Such a course of action, it was pointed out, 'will procure you the good will of your customers which may be of use when trade is open'. In other words, the firm saw the emerging confrontation as yet another in a series which had plagued their activities since the early 1760s and not as a water-shed which would end in permanent adjustment of the political structure on which the Clyde tobacco trade was based. Their final directive illustrates their optimism over future commercial links with Maryland:

> We desire you may contribute all in your power to dispose of the goods you have . . . as we would wish to have all our old goods disposed of before a new importation is allowed.[6]

Evidence from the Cunninghame records is of special interest in the discussion of this issue because William Cunninghame has long played the role in Glasgow hagiography of the shrewd man of business, skilfully extricating himself from an impossible situation as commercial collapse loomed and, in the process, making vast windfall gains on imported tobacco as wartime prices spiralled.[7] The firm's correspondence shows, however, that his firm was very much in a dilemma in 1774 and the first few months of 1775. In the autumn of 1774 William Cunninghame himself was fairly confident that both non-importation and non-exportation agreements would be unsuccessful. 'I imagine', he noted in September of that year:

> all your associations will come to nothing, the prudent Pennsylvanians will no be pushed into such violent plans . . . what madmen the Virginians are. How can they live or keep their negroes alive without coarse linens and cloths?[8]

The previous July he had equally firmly rejected the possibility of the radicals interrupting the export of tobacco:

> . . . they will never think seriously of stopping the exportation of tobacco . . . everything would soon be destroyed by the Fly and Worm.[9]

Then his aim had been the extension rather than the contraction of his company's interests in North America. He planned to set up 'a lasting establishment' on the upper Potomac in Virginia to counter the competition from the stores of Messrs. Buchanans.[10] As late as March, 1775 he was still unwilling to accept the possibility of a wholesale disruption of trade, maintaining that any attempt by the colonials to stop exportation must come to naught in the same way as their previous efforts had collapsed ignominiously in the past.[11]

Because of these assumptions, Cunninghame gradually found himself in a position of indecision as evidence began to accumulate in the early months of 1775 that the radicals were determined to implement their threats. There is little indication, for instance, in the correspondence between his chief factor, James Robinson and his storekeepers in that year that a grand strategy was being marked out to extract maximum commercial advantage from the developing political situation. In April, 1775, a few months before the ports were closed, the manager of the Cunninghame store in Dumfries wrote anxiously to Robinson:

I really am at a loss how to act with regard to the purchase of cargoes and postpone doing anything until I heard from you, but from Findlay's letter now before me, informing me with certainty that all our ports are to be shut instantly I wish I had attempted purchasing. *The merchants here at present are undetermined what to do.*[12]

Robinson himself in May agreed that 'purchasing tobacco in these times would be imprudent' and that the wisest course would be to await political and market developments.[13]

With hindsight it is possible to criticise the Scottish firms for short-sightedness and failure to appreciate the seriousness of the situation. Yet several points help to explain their attitude and allow us to understand the real problem which confronted them. In the first instance Glasgow traders had been accustomed since the early 1760s to political instability in the colonies and to the sanctions on trade which accompanied it. Such agreements had been adopted in 1765, 1768–9 and 1770 and had collapsed soon afterwards. Familiarity with such failures and with the traditional lack of solidarity shown by the colonists made merchants sceptical of the effectiveness of the more vigorous tactics of 1774–5. In this they were supported by letters such as the following which appeared frequently in the Scottish press:

> Some of the merchants on your side of the water will doubtless take the alarm; but they must be very green indeed, who can suppose that we shall execute our threats; we have no more thought of dropping trade in earnest than you have of becoming a Mussulman. We shall rather submit to being taxed a few shillings by the parliament, than to tax ourselves with the ruin of our whole estates, by breaking off trade.[14]

Indeed, some firms were sending out large cargoes of goods to the colonies at the time in anticipation of the speedy re-opening of ports. Andrew Sproule had 'no fear in bringing in a vessel with osnabrughs, Irish linens and other portable goods' which would later be retailed at scarcity prices. Robert Shedden, an independent merchant, asked for a £10,000 shipment of goods if his credit would stretch to that amount, urging his correspondents that it was 'a favourable time to strike a bold stroke'.[15] Undoubtedly speculative purchases such as these were important elements in the Scottish domestic production boom of 1775–6.[16]

In the second place, even when armed conflict began, it was accepted that the colonists could not resist the counter-measures of British regular troops for any extended period. The military power of the rebels was regarded with contempt. As one Scots factor observed,

> ...it was the general opinion both among civil and military men that our provincials would not fire a single gun in the contest and that all their preparations were meant only to intimidate and to exhort terms.[17]

To contemporaries the colonials were 'puny Americans' and their land 'a petty little province, the creature of our own hands, the bubble of our breath'.[18] Readers of the Scottish press were gaily informed that the colonials had only forty pieces of cannon of which not more than twenty-five were fit for service. A few weeks after hostilities began,

... the rebel army are in great distress for want of clothing so that it is certain one half of them will desert, or be obliged to be disbanded when the cold weather sets in ... the opinion of the people in America who have not lost their reason by enthusiasm is, that if a proper force is sent out in the spring, one of their principal towns destroyed by way of an example, and a few regiments sent to the southern provinces, that there is not the smallest doubt but that the rebellion will be crushed in one campaign and the rebels brought to a proper sense of their duty.[19]

Only a few voices questioned the general optimism. Richard Oswald's nephew noted how most had a 'mean opinion' of the Americans but he himself thought they were 'far from being despicable, they are unanimous, regularly trained and proper subordination gaining ground every day among them'. To him Washington was a 'man whose prudence was to be feared more than his courage'.[20] This, however, was written in August, 1776 and was still apparently a minority view at that date. It took the British defeat at Saratoga in late 1777 and the French entry into the war in the following year to produce a more realistic appraisal of the situation.

Because of the consensus in early 1775, Glasgow firms were unwilling to purchase tobacco in quantity for the first few months of that year. Previous crops from 1773 had glutted the market and forced prices downwards.[21] One suspects also that many companies still held unsold stocks from 1774 and wisely were unwilling to begin buying on any scale until the situation had clarified. William Cunninghame, whose three firms imported more than one-fifth of the total shipments to the Clyde in 1775 concluded as late as March that 'Purchasing tobacco in the present term is in my opinion a greater risk than ever as the intended crop this year will by all accounts be as large as ever'.[22] Merchants were supported in these views by the persistent difficulties they had encountered in negotiations with the French buyers since early 1774 in their efforts to achieve a higher price. As late as spring 1775 these attempts had proven unsuccessful because of the French agent's belief that 'the dispute between mother country and the colonies would be amicably adjusted' and as a result prices would fall.[23]

Yet in the atmosphere of that final year of peace political and commercial conditions could change very rapidly. It would appear that from April–May, several Glasgow firms began to accept that the non-exportation agreement, scheduled to come into force in September, would in fact be implemented. From the early summer one can indeed speak of a concerted and feverish[3] attempt to buy up tobacco and load ships for home as the reality of incipient rebellion crystallised before company representatives in the colonies. By June, for instance, a virtual seller's market had been established in Virginia; factors eschewed the normal method of acquiring tobacco as payment for debts incurred at their stores and instead cash purchases were increasingly employed.[24] Transport costs rose as extra vessels were hired to ship the annual crop before ports closed. At Alexandria in Virginia, for example, 'there was no such thing as craft to be got' in August, 1775 and one observer noted how the decks of Glasgow vessels, traditionally used to store staves and barrel hoops, were, in this particular summer, loaded with tobacco.[25]

The Scots were very successful in buying up the valuable crop of that year. Imports were about four million lbs more than in 1774 although vessels had had to be freighted within a shorter time.

Undoubtedly the Glasgow firms gained because they practised the direct purchase method of acquiring tobacco. This, rather than the commission system, was most suited to obtaining bulk supplies in short periods of time. Since credit conditions in 1775–6 were good, companies were able to draw extensively on their London correspondents to cover cash purchases in the colonies. In early 1776, for instance, Glassford, Gordon and Co. obtained credit of £30,000 from the London house of Edward and Rene Payne.[26] Evidence from one of the most important tobacco-exporting districts in Virginia, the Upper James River valley, shows that English merchants and

TABLE XXI
Scottish Imports of Tobacco, 1771–5

Year	Total (lb)
1771	47,268,873
1772	45,259,675
1773	44,543,050
1774	41,348,295
1775	45,863,154

Source—P.R.O, Customs 14/2.

factors shipped approximately the same amount of tobacco as in 1774. Yet the larger Scottish firms managed to substantially increase their exports. Cunninghame shipments rose from 1,654 hogsheads in 1774 to 1,771 in 1775; Speirs, Bowman and Co. cornered the lion's share, their exports increasing from 4,853 hogsheads in 1774, to 5,451 the following year. Significantly, however, the shipments of several of the smaller companies fell sharply in relation to 1773 and 1774 levels.[27] Apparently they were vulnerable to the competition of their more powerful countrymen when tobacco prices were high and purchasing was mainly done in cash.

Almost certainly, however, Glasgow managed to acquire more of the vital 1775 crop than any other port in the United Kingdom. Warehouses at Port Glasgow and Greenock were so overstretched that 'temporary sheds' and private stores had to be filled but in early 1776 there was 'still a good deal of tobacco which cannot be landed for want of the places to put it in'. Messrs. Dinwiddie, Crawford and Co. complained to the Board of Customs that they were unable to discharge their 322 hogsheads of tobacco from the *Blandford* in August, 1776: 'On examining the cellars and enquiring at the person who has the management of them . . . we find we cannot get room'.[29] Yet, as previous discussion has shown this good fortune was not the result of a master-plan worked out to gain maximum advantage from an anticipated political crisis; rather it was based on a tardy recognition of the reality of the situation and anxious adjustment to it. As John Glassford and Co., Colin Dunlop and Sons and Bogle, Somervell and Co. confessed in the autumn of 1775:

> . . . our factors in these parts (Virginia and Maryland) were obliged to *hurry away* our ships with tobacco and other goods, then on board, otherwise we had been precluded from bringing them to a European market.[30]

The Glasgow merchants were also fortunate because they held extensive stocks of tobacco as a result of the operation of objective market forces. Importers benefited through the uniquely large crops and relatively sluggish demand of 1773–5 and this meant that *of necessity* they had considerable unsold stocks on hand. Market reports in the summer and autumn of 1774 complained how the French Farmers General were offering only $1\frac{3}{4}$d per lb. for tobacco, that crops that season had been immense and that 'every mercatt in Europe . . . is full'.[31] Demand nearer home was no more vigorous and dullness in markets continued into the following year.[32]

Whatever the reasons for their position, several Glasgow firms were able to achieve windfall gains in the first few years of the American War. A vigorous direct trade between the rebellious colonies and Europe failed to develop and scarcity prices for tobacco ensued.[33] Between 1770 and 1775 prices had averaged below 2d per lb. From the spring of 1775, however, the rise began, only slowly at first with an average price of 3d per lb. until the ports closed in September.[34] From then on the bonanza commenced. A year later, the highest quality tobacco at Port Glasgow was selling at 1/6d per lb., the 'meanest' at 8d. A month later the merchants were demanding 10d for the latter.[35] Some qualities were selling as high as 2/- and so intoxicated was the Scottish press at the spiralling profits that it was suggested:

> . . . the West India merchants of Glasgow and Edinburgh should advise their correspondents to plant tobacco there, as it would afford a far greater profit to the planter than sugar and rum and the sale is quick and certain.[36]

A major influence on this trend was that between 1773 and 1775, the purchasing agents of the French monopoly in Scotland had cut back their orders in an effort to push prices downwards.[37] Thus, when the war broke out, they were left in an exposed position with insufficient stocks and the possibility that supplies would be interrupted for at least several months. Inevitably, therefore, they entered the market vigorously in 1775–6. By early March, 1776, Sir Robert Herries, the French buyer, was negotiating with Glasgow for 10,000 hogsheads but only offered $3\frac{1}{2}$d per lb. The Clyde merchants insisted on $3\frac{3}{4}$d and when Herries agreed they then demanded

4d.[38] The important factor here was that traders were not subjected to any pressure on credit at this time. The widespread confidence in the ability of British arms to end the war speedily, an upsurge in commerce with Holland and England and the beginning of tobacco speculation were all factors in this boom.[39] The *Scots Magazine* was only one of the contemporary journals which 'noted a great plenty of money now in circle'. Importers were not therefore compelled to release their large tobacco stocks on to the market in order to satisfy pressing creditors; rather the period of relaxation allowed them to retain supplies and await developments. Thus, although only 1,521 hogsheads were landed in the Clyde in 1776, there still remained 14,404 hogsheads, or about twenty-five per cent of the 1775 importation, in cellars there in August, 1776.[40] In early 1777, one of the Oswalds alleged that there were 7000 hogsheads at Port Glasgow and a further 8000 at ports abroad 'belonging to this place and the whole quantity at Market is reckoned to be about 30,000 hogsheads, so that half of the quantity at Market belongs to this place'.[41]

In August of that year Glasgow firms 'sold a great quantity of tobacco to the French at a very great price'. A gross figure of £150,000 was quoted in press reports as the month's return on sale.[42] There was now no restraint in selling. The total of 14,000 hogsheads on hand in August, 1776 had shrunk to 670 by February, 1778.[43] Demand proved inelastic throughout Europe because imports from North America fell to a trickle in the first years of war and consumers refused to take the cheaper Dutch, German or Ukrainian tobacco without a mixture of Virginia-Maryland leaf. The Glasgow merchants were in a semi-monopoly position in a market where prices were burgeoning. By March, 1776 London houses had sold off almost all their stocks. One London trader wrote enviously to his friend in Glasgow, 'the quantity of tobacco now in Britain is chiefly in your hands and the price rests with you'.[44] As a result even the inferior qualities of tobacco normally only acceptable in the export market were now welcome in the capital. Indeed the price rise there seems to have been even more significant than on the Continent. By the end of 1777 some Glasgow firms were taking advantage of this by shipping back to Britain cargoes previously exported to France, Holland and the German states.[45] In petitioning the Board of Customs to permit this, they stressed that tobacco had become so difficult to obtain in London that it was now fetching exorbitant prices there and even 'the meaner sort' was in much demand.[46] As one contemporary noted, by re-shipping 'they imagine they shall sell off their large stocks of an inferior sort of tobacco to London traders and that after the rate of 2/- per lb.'.[47] Such returns were clearly enough to justify the additional freight and customs expenses involved in the operation. In the spring of 1778, 325 hogsheads exported by Speirs, Bowman and Co. to Dunkirk were returned and in the period April-October 1778, the Cunninghame group of companies shipped back a total of 648 hogsheads from Rotterdam and Hamburg.[48]

Undoubtedly a number of tobacco traders in Glasgow in the years 1775–7 did achieve massive windfall gains. As the *Caledonian Mercury* pointed out 'the loss of the American trade has been of great advantage to that place (Glasgow)'.[49] Merchants made up for the leaner years of 1773–4. Then Speirs, French and Co. had made 'no profit equal to our debts on remittance'; so great were the returns in subsequent years, however, that Alexander Speirs was able to acquire a series of estates in Renfrewshire and Stirlingshire valued at £60,000 and pay in cash for almost all of them.[50] Yet, while admitting the successes of some, one must be careful not to be misled by contemporary euphoria. Press commentators witnessed the spiralling prices for tobacco but generally failed to balance these against the high cost of buying the crop of 1775 within a restricted time schedule. Reports to firms' headquarters in Glasgow indicated that planters were taking advantage of the political situation to hawk their supplies around various companies, that purchasing could only be done in cash or good bills and that some stores had run out of coin as a result.[51] Again heavy importation in such a short period could only occur in a context of rising transport costs. Because there was a seller's market in the Chesapeake in the summer of 1775 only larger firms with sufficient resources were able to acquire large tobacco stocks.[52] Probably, therefore, most of the profits were creamed off by the giant companies. Significantly over eighty per cent of the tobacco export of 1777 was handled by enterprises belonging to the Cunninghame, Speirs and Glassford syndicates.[53] They were able to retain stocks until prices rose. As late as August, 1776 Glassfords still held 1,823 hogsheads and Cunninghames almost 5,000, just 1,108 less than they had shipped from America throughout the previous year. These three groups together with Dinwiddie, Crawford and Co. owned 8,839 of the 14,404 hogsheads in storage at the Clyde at that date. Only another seven firms retained stocks of more than 100 hogsheads viz. George Oswald and Sons (546), Alexander Grindlay and Co. (343), Ramsay, Monteath (277), John and William Ballantyne (259), John and William Gray (217), Dreghorn, Murdoch and Co. (277) and Colin Dunlop and Sons (192). Thirteen companies held less than fifty hogsheads and of these, seven had less than ten.[54]

II

The nature of the Scottish tobacco trade meant that large sums had to be sunk in long credits to North American planters[55] which were not easily liquidated in the short-term. Glasgow opinion was well aware of the apparent vulnerability of the American debts. Professor Thomas Reid noted with dismay in 1765 the serious situation developing in the colonies and estimated the city's effects there 'at above £400,000'; John Brown, the Glasgow banker, put the figure closer to one million pounds sterling.[56] During the Stamp Act crisis, one of the town's leading merchants, John Glassford, when questioned on the possibility of recovering these vast debts, replied pessimistically that this was 'uncertain' and that 'if these circumstances continue we may be unpaid'.[57] Despite this warning, however, all the indications are that the indebtedness of colonial planters to the Glasgow houses continued to expand in the years before the Revolution.[58] Tobacco importation increased because merchants invested ever larger sums in credit since only through such loans could planters afford to settle new land and extend their labour forces.

Nevertheless, especially after the credit crisis of 1772 which ruined several London tobacco firms, the Glasgow companies' instructions to their agents to retrench and liquidate outstanding advances became more pressing. William Cunninghame in April, 1772 urged his chief factor in Virginia 'to force payment of many of our overgrown large debts' and two years later envisaged a grand programme of debt collection.[59] Yet he feared 'do it in what manner you will, it will cause much fear and disturbance amongst the people'. No stranger should be employed in settling debts; instead an assistant ought to be spared from each of the stores 'who is acquainted with the people ... the people would be better satisfied by assurance of time and partial payments from a person they know and have been used to deal with'. Care was to be taken also lest the planters should suspect that the company had been forced into action 'of necessity ... or the Company being in the least distress'.[60]

Yet, no matter how well-laid the plans or how diplomatically storekeepers behaved there were formidable and possibly insurmountable obstacles to debt collection in the years immediately preceding the Revolution. The logic of the 'store system' meant that reduction of debt was unlikely while the trade expanded. As a contemporary lawyer observed:

Everyone who is acquainted with the trade must know that this was unavoidable; for it is impossible at any one time to get more out of the debts due by the planters than about a fourth part. They have credit at the several stores with which they deal for four years produce, and they never can deliver more than the produce of one year.[61]

An additional difficulty was caused by the very nature of the debts. John Glassford alleged that the vast majority were for relatively small amounts, most for under £30 sterling in individual accounts.[62] Recent research has confirmed this pattern (see Table XXII).

Superficially it might seem that since most debts were for small sums recovery would be easier than if they were for large amounts. Yet this interpretation fails to take account of the fact that they were not trivial to the less wealthy planters of interior Virginia who were the Glasgow firms' best customers. The issue of their recovery was also complicated by the fact that debtors often had outstanding accounts with several different companies and the total sum owed might therefore be considerable.[63] One Scots merchant confided in his brother despairingly that 'they (the debts) commonly are endless—they are so small and numerous that it requires posterity to finish a concern'.[64] The agricultural economy of Maryland and Virginia suffered from a profound scarcity of specie in the colonial era and was not capable of repayment on the scale which would be necessary. After all it was the planter class's perennial need for working capital which encouraged indebtedness in the first instance. One storekeeper of Dunmore, Gilmour and Co. put the matter in a nutshell:

> I never knew money so hard to collect as at present, the Courts' business being stopped. Indeed, were they willing, I know not whether it would be in their power, there being so little money in circulation among us.[65]

At the very best, successful collection would imply a major administrative operation involving the power of the law on the creditor's side. Increasingly,

TABLE XXII

Frequency Distribution of Virginia Debts claimed by selected Merchants in England and Scotland in 1776 (Pounds Sterling)

Range (£)	Number of English Debts	Number of Scottish Debts
0–100	—	161
100–299	27	32
300–499	13	8
500–699	6	7
700–999	7	—
1000–1999	9	—
2000–2999	12	—
3000–4999	6	—
5000–7999	2	—
TOTAL	82	208

Source—Richard B. Sheridan, 'The British Credit Crisis of 1772 and the American Colonies', *Journ. Econ. Hist.*, XX (1960), 180.

however, before 1775, such activity took place not in an atmosphere of relative goodwill but rather in one of explicit hostility towards the Scots factors. James Lawson, of Lawson, Semple and Co., travelled to America in 1772, hoping to wind up his interests there by the autumn of that year. Two years later he was still in Maryland and writing home that there was now little possibility of collecting the company's debts because of planter antagonism and the recalcitrance of the courts.[66] Some argued that even the threat of legal action was enough to encourage a debtor to flee into the back country. Alternatively court actions tended to be protracted, according to one factor because of

> ...the tediousness of the law ... and the generally litigious disposition of the people who are well-acquainted with every chicanery that the law will admit of to keep off paying their debts.[67]

Another Glasgow man at a much later period put the colonial 'ingenuity to procrastinate a just debt' down to 'a distemper', peculiar to the climate!⁶⁸ Even if an action in court was successful, judgement in a merchant's favour could simply mean the transfer of debt from one individual to another rather than the collection in cash of the sum owed. So limited was the property of many planters and so profound the cash shortage that sequestration of debtor assets was unlikely to bring about a speedy sale and release the sum due. The threat of imprisonment was reduced by the widespread knowledge of the expense the creditor had to bear to keep the debtor in custody and the hope of a quick release if the creditor's resources and/or his determination gave out.⁶⁹

Such intrinsic problems were considerably exacerbated in the years 1774–6. Maryland and Virginia courts were shut from the summer of 1774.

TABLE XXIII
Estimates of Glasgow's Debts in North America, 1778

Area	Amount (pounds sterling)
Virginia	719,038
Maryland	155,810
North Carolina	29,924
Undistinguished	401,313
TOTAL	£1,306,085

Source—GCA, Speirs Papers, TD131/10–12, Diary of Alexander Speirs, 2 March, 1778.

One court in Berkshire County, Maryland did try to sit but a mob invaded the courtroom, seized the chief judge and kept him prisoner until he consented to adjourn the sitting *sine die*. One witness coyly observed that 'by such methods they meant to avoid the payment of their just debts'.⁷⁰ Direct intimidation might prove equally effective. It was freely admitted at the time that 'the Glasgow factors seem to be the great objects of their resentment, the case is plain to them they owe the money'.⁷¹

Because of all these obstacles the level of debt owed Glasgow merchants remained considerable when commercial intercourse with the colonies was interrupted in 1775. The trading community itself estimated unrecovered assets and debts at over £1,300,000.

Although there was doubtless some exaggeration in these figures, evidence from merchant accounts confirms that the amount of debt owed did remain considerable. As befitted its position as one of the largest organisations, the

Cunninghame group of companies had the huge sum of £111,300 outstanding to them.[73] Dinwiddie, Crawford and Co. was owed £40,000.[73] The 'subject' of Colin Dunlop and Sons in Virginia, exclusive of fixed property, calculated in October, 1776 stood at £24,041.18s.7.[74] Around £20,000 were owed John Glassford and Co., one of the four firms which made up the Glassford syndicate.[75] Logan, Gilmour and Co. and Baird, Hay and Co., much smaller ventures had debts of £20,000 and £16,000 respectively.[76] The two major companies in which Alexander Speirs was primarily concerned were owed over £46,000 and four leading Virginians were indebted to George Kippen and Co. for £10,000.[77]

III

War exacerbated the ordinary hazards of trade and at the same time produced opportunity for windfall gains. However, because the collapse of Glasgow's American commerce after 1775 seemed so complete and the sums owing the city's traders so immense, nineteenth century writers tended to stress the more negative effects of the war on the merchant community. In their view its immediate effect was to cause financial and economic chaos in Glasgow. James Denholm, writing about thirty years after the rebellion, thought that it had dealt 'a dreadful stroke to Glasgow' and that 'it proved the ruin of great numbers who before reckoned themselves possessed of independent fortunes'. In similar vein, Robert Reid argued that the dispute with the American colonies, 'nearly annihilated the foreign commerce of the city, and ruined a great proportion of her enterprising merchants'; another nineteenth century antiquarian, George Stewart, described how 'heavy failures were of daily occurrence' among the tobacco aristocracy.[78] All these writers proceeded on the assumption that because of trade disruption and unpaid debts financial disaster must have overwhelmed Glasgow. However, a careful examination of the fortunes of the tobacco firms during these years indicates that they seriously over-estimated the numbers which incurred losses and became insolvent.

It seems probable in the first instance that much of the confusion concerning the extent of bankruptcy was caused by the preconception that merchants who experienced difficulty in the 1770s and 1780s inevitably did so because of the American War. In several cases this was almost certainly not so. William French, according to one Glasgow historian 'was ruined by the American War'.[79] French's assets, on the other hand, were not sequestrated until July, 1787 and between the end of the war and his insolvency four years later he had been actively engaged in land speculation in Lanarkshire.[80] Furthermore, he was an influential member of the Speirs group of companies which, as will be noted, successfully adjusted to the exigencies of wartime commerce.[81] Another firm usually listed in the catalogue of those which went under was Wilson, Brown and Co. *Senex* thought that 'they failed for

£40,000 due to the collapse of the tobacco trade'; yet the firm was still operating in the final year of the war and rather than being 'importers of tobacco to a considerable extent' were at the time manufacturers of roll tobacco principally engaged in the Irish export trade. Again, since the company did not fall into difficulties until 1786, their problems were unlikely to be directly connected with the war itself.[82] The same point probably applies to James Brown and Co. One printed source suggests that they were 'ruined' during the period of hostilities but other data contradict this. For instance, in evidence to the Loyalists Commission in 1786, the firm described how they were in the process of re-establishing pre-war links with Maryland. There is no mention of any past or impending financial disaster which might have strengthened their case for compensation from the government.[83]

Because of this discrepancy between the printed version of events and the picture which was beginning to emerge through study of relevant manuscripts, it was decided by this author to conduct a full-scale investigation into the fortunes of the tobacco companies between 1775 and 1785. A table of those firms engaged in the trade in the early 1770s was compiled and an examination begun through a wide variety of sources to obtain proof of a company's survival into the later 1780s. If the concern was found not to have continued it was scrutinised, where source material allowed, to determine whether its demise had occurred through bankruptcy, mutual agreement among the partners or termination of a contract of copartnership. There were thirty-seven firms involved in the trade in 1774-5 and it was possible to trace thirty-three of these and reach conclusions on their experience during the American War.[84]

On the basis of the information thus assembled, it is scarcely possible to describe the effects of the war on the Glasgow merchants as catastrophic. Seven units did fail between 1775 and 1785 and their disappearance may have been associated with the hazards of wartime commerce. Yet these companies together only imported a minor proportion of the tobacco landed at Clyde ports in 1774-5. Only one bankrupt concern was numbered among the eleven firms which shipped more than 500 hogsheads each and four of the insolvencies (those of Hugh Wylie, Wylie and Mackenzie, Baird, Hay and Co. and Jamieson, Johnston and Co.) were concentrated among the ten firms which imported the least. As a speculative trade, tobacco commerce was always likely to produce bankruptcies. In this respect therefore there was nothing especially significant about the American War period.

The bankruptcy of one group of companies has however attracted the attention of posterity. In December, 1777 Buchanan, Hastie and Co. and its sister concerns Bogle, Jamieson and Co. and James Jamieson and Co. failed for over £62,000.[85] The repercussions of this disaster were felt among the moneyed classes of lowland Scotland because the Buchanan firms had been borrowing heavily on bond for several years and had had to default on many of their loans. Equally significant was the fact that this crash represented the failure of one of the most famous and influential merchant families in the city. The Buchanan dynasty had been prominent in the commercial and political life of Glasgow throughout the eighteenth century. Andrew Buchanan, senior, aged fifty-two when the bankruptcy occurred, had been Provost of the town and in the early 1770s was adding to his reputation by developing 'Buchanan Street'. His kinsman, James Buchanan, had likewise been Provost (in 1768 and 1774) and was married into the family of the Earls of Haddington.[86] Their influence in local circles was made apparent after the collapse when both were offered positions in burgh administration, James being appointed Inspector of Police and Andrew, Town Chamberlain. Unfortunately the melancholy effects of their financial problems did not end at that point. A year after taking up his post Provost Andrew was dismissed in disgrace for embezzling almost £1500 from town funds.[87]

Despite the stir which the Buchanan bankruptcies caused among contemporaries they seem to have been only partly due to the interruption of American commerce. James Gourlay, a pioneer historian of the tobacco trade observed that the Buchanan group was one of the few which actually owned plantations in the colonies and so suggested that the sequestration of these assets by the colonists in 1778 was the immediate cause of their failure.[88] The interpretation, however, conflicts with other evidence. The Glasgow banker, John Brown, whose firm was a major creditor of Buchanan, Hastie and Co., pointed out that their total 'subject' in America was £13,000.[89] This compares very unfavourably with the figure of over £60,000 owned by the Buchanans and indicates that even if their American assets had been under company control their ultimate fate would have been little affected.[90]

It would probably be fairer to argue that the firms concerned suffered defects in capital structure and possibly also from failings in business qualities among the partners. These in turn were exacerbated by the pressures on credit which began in late 1777. From the 1760s they had been accumulating a series of large loans on personal bond and several partners had mortgaged their estates to attract additional credit.[91] What is indeed most interesting in the list of debts is the very small amount owed to those who can be identified as 'trade creditors'—about £8000 out of the total of £62,000.[92] In other words, the vast proportion of creditors were persons who had deposited money with the company on loan, not other firms who were awaiting payment for goods received. Obviously such a structure would be extremely vulnerable as pressure built up on credit from the closing months of 1777.

In that period the boom conditions of the early phase of the war began to wane as wartime costs rose and relations between the United Kingdom and France deteriorated. Business confidence faltered. By December, 1777 markets were 'perfectly dull', according to one Glasgow merchant house, and firms were making special efforts to restrict credit, curtail plans and recover debts.[93] In a word, there was general movement towards liquidity.

The survival of Buchanan, Hastie and Co. and its sister concerns at such a time was unlikely. Since they were chronically short of working capital they could not continue indefinitely. Significantly they succumbed fairly early in the period of depression. Their experience with one creditor might well have been typical. Thomas Buchanan and Co. had sold a parcel of hats valued at almost £110 to Bogle, Jamieson and Co., one of the Buchanan firms. The hatmakers applied for payment in June, 1777 but were fobbed off with a bill payable six months later. The acceptance fell due in December of that year but still Buchanans failed to offer a remittance.[94] In the same month a writ of sequestration was taken out against them by their creditors.

The very fact that this syndicate had such a disastrous experience while the vast majority of merchants survived could also suggest that its members lacked qualities which others possessed. John Brown, the knowledgeable city banker, certainly thought that the Buchanans had brought trouble upon themselves:

> It seems one of the great causes of the failure was when others of the tobacco trade were getting home great quantities of tobacco which on account of the troubles were giving a very great price, the Company was delaying and arguing with their agents and factors abroad. Besides their affairs seem to have been miserably managed at home. Instead of the partners minding the business they are making pleasures and advocations at their town and country houses. From a state of their affairs laid before their creditors, they appear to be owing £50,000, mostly bonded money.[95]

Material on the other insolvencies is scarce. It seems that Hugh Wylie's property was not divided by a formal process of sequestration but when he died in 1782 it was evident his family was impoverished because of his business losses. His widow was awarded 'an interim supply of money' by the Town Council until his funds could be recovered from America.[96] Wylie's affairs had been in difficulty since the middle of 1777 when one of his business associates, John Mackenzie, had failed because 'the loss on his American property was unequal to his engagements'.[97] According to another colleague, Henry Ritchie, his misfortunes had begun even earlier:

> I cannot say I know any particulars of his circumstances, but in general they cannot be good, as the company he was connected with had a great subject in Virginia, and were unfortunate to sell the little tobacco they had in 1775 at the low price of 4d p. lb.—but it is not I alone that suspect him. He is generally suspected to be in poor circumstances and yet he has lived and does live at considerable expense.[98]

At his death in 1782 his debts amounted to £2000 net.[99] A firm experiencing similar problems, Baird, Hay and Co., appear to have ceased operations in 1777 with £16,100 outstanding to them in Virginia; three years later another tobacco concern, McCall, Smellie and Co., consisting of Archibald and Richard Smellie and George McCall, had its assets sequestrated by the Court of Session.[100]

Small units, such as those described above, would find survival very difficult in the period 1777–81. Operating on slender financial margins they probably did not have the capacity to increase their imports substantially in the last few months of peace especially since much of the purchasing at that time was done with cash. They were thus unable to make substantial gains during the period of boom prices. Again, small companies were more dependent on an annual flow of remittances from North America than their opulent rivals. Negotiating loans in local capital markets would over time become more difficult as lenders discovered the weak financial position of prospective borrowers and as rising government interest rates attracted investors to the Funds.[101] Even the greatest units experienced temporary difficulty when the steep rise in wartime operating costs was accompanied by scarcity of commercial credit.[102]

However, this section has shown that it was not the relatively few failures of the period which require emphasis but rather the remarkable ability of most firms to come through the crisis and adapt to the new pressures and opportunities of wartime trade. Undoubtedly many of the features of the Glasgow merchant community already described in this volume were of importance in this respect. By the early 1770s the city's tobacco trade had evolved to a level of organisation which was well adapted to coping with the stresses of a financial crisis. The merchant group was so small, power within it was so concentrated, and companies were so inter-linked by family and partnership bonds that firms were unlikely to indulge in a *sauve qui peut* as pressure on credit developed from the later months of 1777. Merchants were so involved in one another's affairs as insurers, as fellow partners, as creditors, as cautioners, as co-obligants and as members of the same social and political élite, that salvation lay in mutual restraint.[103] The train of financial disaster might well begin when the balance of the bill of exchange mechanism was upset. Mutuality at least helped to restrict the danger of this happening.

It is also probably true that the vast sums owed Glasgow which remained unrecovered in the colonies when commerce was interrupted were not of major significance to the liquidity of most firms. Companies which operated the 'store system' were geared to large-scale extension of credit over long periods; the huge organisations which dominated the trade did not exist on such a shoe-string basis as to require comprehensive debt recovery to escape collapse. On the contrary, since by the 'store system' merchants became owners of the tobacco, their primary concern was the price that a year's crop was likely to fetch in home and, above all, in European markets. Credit to planters was a vital cost in the mechanism of the trade which would only prove a drawback if prices over time were depressed or if loans were not carefully rationed in relation to the capacity of a particular firm. Income from tobacco sales was in effect the return for the sum invested in loans. As has been seen, the direct purchase method of the Glasgow men was very well suited to acquiring cargoes quickly in the crisis atmosphere of the summer of 1775. The resulting boom prices for tobacco probably more than compensated most merchants for their outstanding American debts. Just as importantly, the trading community seem to have been able to create a satisfactory balance between the flow of American commodities during the war and prices gained for them in Britain and Europe. If importation at anywhere near pre-war levels had been sustained the picture would have been much gloomier. Scarcity prices were necessary to compensate merchants for rising costs and these were maintained at most times between 1775 and 1781.[104] Of essential importance in this respect was the fact that neither the colonials nor European competitors were able to organise a direct transatlantic commerce in American commodities. Thus British merchants continued to control the flow of trade and directed their factors in New York and the Caribbean to purchase only the amount necessary to keep up prices.[105]

Only firms with a low liquidity preference were likely to encounter extreme difficulty during these years. Yet probably only a minority of concerns fitted into this category. Normally, annual accounting procedures ensured that assets were not over-estimated; indeed often as much as fifty per cent of the value of American debts were written off. Because fixed costs formed such a minor proportion of their commercial régime, diversification by tobacco merchants was a fairly easy matter and rapid adjustment in trade patterns very possible. As will now be seen, existing interests in landowning and in Caribbean, European and Canadian trade could be expanded. Investment in privateering and hiring of merchant vessels to government were other profitable expedients.

REFERENCES

1. *Caledonian Mercury*, 8 March, 1766.
2. *Ibid.*, 22 November, 1774.
3. NLS, MS 5028, Charles Steuart Letterbook, 1773-4, James Parker to Steuart, 29 September, 1774.
4. SRO, GD 247/59/5, William Cunninghame to John Turner, 18 July, 1774.
5. EUL, Mercantile Accounts, Virginia and Maryland, Alex. Hamilton to Messrs. John Brown and Co., 25 April, 1775.
6. SL, CSP 190/13, Extract of a letter from Messrs, Speirs, French and Co., to George Sherriff, 15 June, 1775.
7. See, for example, Stewart, *op. cit.*, 195.
8. SRO, GD 247/141, W. Cunninghame to J. Robinson, 29 September, 1774.
9. SRO, GD 247/59/S, W. Cunninghame to John Turner, 18 July, 1774.
10. *Ibid.*
11. SRO, GD 247/59/Q/1, W. Cunninghame to J. Robinson, 28 March, 1775.
12. *Ibid.*, William Cunninghame jun. to James Robinson, 25 April, 1775. My italics.
13. *Ibid.*, 4 May, 1775.
14. *Caledonian Mercury*, 27 August, 1774, 'Extract of a letter from a gentleman in New York, to a friend in Glasgow, dated July 2, 1774'.
15. Coakley, *op. cit.*, 121.

16. For this see below,
17. NLS, Charles Steuart Letterbooks, MS 5209, James Murray to Charles Steuart, 15 May, 1775.
18. *Scots Magazine*, May 1774.
19. *Caledonian Mercury*, 25 November, 1775.
20. SRO, Oswald Papers, GD 213/53, John Anderson to Richard Oswald, 26 August, 1776.
21. Price, *op. cit.*,
22. SRO, GD 247/59/Q/1, William Cunninghame to James Robinson, 28 March, 1775.
23. Sir William Forbes of Pitsligo, *Memoirs of a Banking House* (London, 1860), 45–6.
24. SRO, GD 247/59/Q/1, W. Cunninghame to James Robinson, 21 May and 4 August, 1775; SL, CSP 190/13, G. Sherriff to Speirs, French and Co., 3 June, 1775.
25. SRO, GD 247/59/Q/1, Cunninghame to Robinson, 17 and 26 August, 1775; James Crosby to Robinson, 20 July, 1775.
26. PRO, AO 12/55/47.
27. Thomson, *loc. cit.*, 405–6.
28. SRO, CE 60/1/8.
29. *Ibid.*, Dinwiddie, Crawford and Co. to H.M. Collector of Customs, 13 August, 1776.
30. SRO, CE 60/1/8, Petition of John Glassford and Co. etc. to H.M. Board of Customs, September, 1775. My italics.
31. SRO, GD 247/59/Q/1, William Cunninghame to John Turner, 18 July, 1774.
32. *Ibid.*, Cunninghame to J. Robinson, 13 August, 1774; Cunninghame to Thomas Gordon, 15 July, 1774; Forbes, *op. cit.*, 45–6.
33. See below, p. 128.
34. SRO, Oswald Papers, GD 213/53, John Anderson to Richard Oswald, 1 February, 1775; *Edinburgh Evening Courant*, 4 September, 1776.
35. *Ibid.*, John Anderson to Richard Oswald, 22 September, 1776, 4 October, 1776.
36. *Edinburgh Evening Courant*, 20 November, 1776.
37. Price, *op. cit.*, 646.
38. *Ibid.*, 683.
39. M. L. Robertson, 'Scottish Commerce and the American War of Independence', *Econ. Hist. Rev.*, 2nd. ser., IX (1956), 123.
40. SRO, CE 60/1/9, Account of Quantities of tobacco in the hands of each importer, 5 August, 1776.
41. SRO, Oswald Papers, GD 213/53, John Anderson to Richard Oswald, 18 February, 1777.
42. *Edinburgh Evening Courant*, 30 August, 1777.
43. SRO, CE 60/1/10, Account of tobacco remaining in merchant's hands at Greenock and Port Glasgow, 4 February, 1778.
44. William Lee Letterbooks, 1769–1795 (In private hands, London), William Lee to Donald, Scott and Co., Glasgow, 18 March, 1776.
45. NLS, MS 8759, Alexander Houston and Co.'s Home Letter Book H, A. Houston and Co. to John Turris (Dunkirk), 9 December, 1777.
46. SRO, CE 60/1/10, Collector, Port Glasgow and Greenock to H.M. Board of Customs, 3 November, 1777.
47. *Caledonian Mercury*, 9 June, 1777.
48. SRO, Customs Accounts, Port Glasgow, E.504/28/28.
49. 17 July, 1776.
50. SL, CSP 190/13, Answers by Speirs, French and Co. . . . 2; GCA, Speirs Papers, TD 131/4, Ledger B; TD 131/5, Ledger C.
51. SRO, GD 247/59/Q/1, William Cunninghame to James Robinson, 27 May, 4 August, 1775; SL, CSP 190/13, G. Sherriff to Speirs, French and Co., 3 June, 1775.
52. See above, p. 107.
53. SRO, Customs Accounts, Port Glasgow and Greenock, E.504/28/27–8; E.504/15/27–8.
54. SRO, CE 60/1/9, An Account of the quantities of Tobacco imported at this port remaining in the possession of each importer at 5th August, 1776.
55. See above, pp. 59–60.
56. A. Hamilton (ed.), *Works of Thomas Reid*, I, 43; ML, Bogle MSS, XC1, John Brown's Recollections, I, 112–13.

57. BM, Add. MS 33030/32-35.
58. See above, pp. 59-60.
59. SRO, GD 247/59, William Cunninghame to James Robinson, 2 April, 1772; SRO, GD 247/58/S, Cunninghame to Robinson, 14 August, 1774.
60. *Ibid*.
61. GCA, Dunlop Papers, additional Observations for James Dougal against Elizabeth and Barbara Cunninghame . . . 2.
62. BM, Add. MS, 33030/32.
63. PRO, AO 12/56/188; SL, CSP, Information for Messrs. Thomas, Peter and William Bogle, 15 Oct., 1769.
64. Quoted in A. J. Voke, 'Accounting Methods of Colonial Merchants in Virginia', *Journ. of Accoutancy*, XLII (1926), 5.
65. PRO, AO 13/30/130, Letter of Ben Toter, 15 April, 1775.
66. SRO, UP Currie Dal Misc. 20/4, J. Lawson to Messrs. Thomas Phillips and Co., September, 1774; to Nancy Semple, 1 April, 1774.
67. EUL, Mercantile Accounts, Virginia and Maryland, John Hamilton to John Brown and Co., 28 May, 1774.
68. ML, Bogle MSS, Bundle 59, John Gray to George Brown, 22 June, 1809.
69. Soltow, *loc. cit.*, 96.
70. NLS, Charles Steuart Papers, MS 5028, James Parker to Charles Steuart, 14 August, 1774.
71. *Ibid.*, 29 September, 1774; 17 May, 1774. See also *Caledonian Mercury*, 31 May, 1775; *Edinburgh Evening Courant*, 10 November, 1777.
72. PRO, AO 12/56/288.
73. LC, James Dunlop Family Papers, James Ritchie and Co. to Messrs. McCoull, Anderson, Montgomerie and Dunlop, 5 February, 1785.
74. GCA, Dunlop Papers, State of James Dunlop's subjects, 1793.
75. SRO, GD 247/151/3, State of the Funds of Neil Jamieson.
76. *Ibid.*, State of Robert Dunmore's Subjects; GCA, Journal of Baird, Hay and Co.
77. GCA, Speirs Papers, TD 131/13, Sederunt Book of Alexander Speirs's Trustees, 5; TD 131/5, Ledger C, 28; P. J. Ford (ed.), *The Writings of Thomas Jefferson* (New York, 1892-9), IV, 348.
78. James Denholm, *A History of Glasgow* (Glasgow, 1804), 407; John Knox, *A View of the British Empire more especially Scotland* (London, 1785), I, 102, 171; Robert Reid, *Old Glasgow and its Environs* (Glasgow, 1864), 175; George Stewart, *Progress of Glasgow* (Glasgow, 1883).
79. Reid, *op. cit.*, 173.
80. *Glasgow Mercury*, 25 July, 1787; SRO, GRS 415/45; PRS (Glasgow), 28/337.
81. See below, p. 131.
82. Senex (J. M. Reid), III, 280; SRO, Customs Accounts, Port Glasgow and Greenock, E.504/28/34-6; E.504/15/33-5; GCA, B.10/15/8140.
83. Matriculation Albums, Glasgow University, Matric. No. 1420; PRO, AO 12/9/59-61.
84. For details and source material see T. M. Devine, *Glasgow Merchants in Colonial Trade* (Strathclyde Ph.D. Thesis, 1971), II, 557-61. James Pagan, *Sketch of the History of Glasgow* (Glasgow, 1847), 80 listed 46 firms involved in the tobacco trade in 1774. The discrepancy may have occurred because Pagan occasionally lists as units individuals who were merely registering cargoes for their respective companies.
85. SRO, Currie Dal Seq. B1/1, Buchanan, Hastie and Co. (1777).
86. Senex, *op. cit.*, II, 369; Gourlay, *op. cit.*, 64.
87. GCA, Council Minute Book, C1/1/36, 5 January, 1780; C1/1/37, 24 June, 1784.
88. Gourlay, *op. cit.*, 65.
89. ML, Bogle MSS, XCL, John Brown's Recollections, I, December, 1777, 54.
90. It should be remembered too that the company failed in December, 1777 and British property was not sequestrated in Virginia until March, 1778.
91. See, for example, SRO, Reg. of Deeds, 231/903 DAL; 218/783 DAL; 222/1104 MACK; 231/1/614; GCA, Reg. of Deeds, B.10/15/8045, 8075, 8080, 8091, 8079.
92. SRO, Currie Dal Seq. B/1/1, Buchanan, Hastie and Co. (1777).

93. NLS, MS 8793, Letterbook E of Alexander Houston and Co., Houstons to David Macfarlane, 30 November, 1777; to Thomas Townsend, 8 December, 1777; to Messrs. Turner and Paul, 30 December, 1777.
94. SRO, UP 1 Currie Dal B5/8, Thomas Buchanan versus Bogle and Somervell (1778).
95. ML. Bogle MSS, XCL, John Brown's Recollections, I, 54–5..
96. GCA, Council Minute Book, C1/1/37, 28 November, 1782, 138.
97. GCA, Mitchell Johnston Collection, Lawsuit of John Mackenzie.
98. LC, James Dunlop Family Papers, Henry Ritchie to James Dunlop, 2 November, 1781.
99. *Ibid.*, 31 May, 1787; GCA, B.10/15/8440, Settlement of Hugh Wylie.
100. GCA, Journal of Baird, Hay and Co.; Reg. of Deeds, B.10/15/8339, Disposition by Archibald Grahame as factor on the sequestrated estate of Messrs. Smellies, 6 July, 1781.
101. There is much evidence of the difficulties caused by this new factor. In July, 1778, William Cunninghame observed that the borrowing of money could previously be done 'very easily' in London and Glasgow but 'now no person will do it at least such as have the smallest confidence in government security where they at present draw from 6–10 per cent per annum' [SRO, GD 247/59/Q/2, Cunninghame to Robert Dunmore, 27 July, 1778]. There were similar comments in 1779 and 1781 [NLS, MS 8797, A. Houston and Co. to Messrs. Turner and Paul, 1 December, 1778; to Fergus Paterson, 20 March, 1781].
102. SRO, GD 247/59/Q/2, W. Cunninghame to Robert Dunmore, 25 July, 1778; NLS, MS 8794, Letterbook E of Alexander Houston and Co., Houstons to Houston, Paterson and Co., 20 July, 1778.
103. Robert Dunmore and Co. in 1778 was squeezed between interruption in remittances and a temporary fall in sugar prices but were saved by a major £10,000 loan from the tobacco lord, William Cunninghame [SRO, GD 247/59/Q/2, W. Cunninghame to R. Dunmore, 25 July, 1778].
104. See below, p. 129.
105. See, for example, LC, James Dunlop Family Papers, correspondence of Henry Ritchie and James Dunlop.

8

The Opportunities of Trade During the American War

IN the first year of the American War the intention of the tobacco traders of Glasgow was to retain direct contact with Virginia and Maryland despite their state of open rebellion. Scots factors petitioned the Virginia Convention in the summer of 1775, declaring their willingness to contribute to the common cause and to abide by all commercial restrictions if they were excused from bearing arms. The Convention received this request favourably and permitted them to remain in the colony as neutrals if they agreed to swear on oath not to infringe the interests of the Patriots.[1] At the same time various companies in Glasgow subscribed a petition to Parliament demanding a more generous government policy towards the colonists[2] and, in addition, in late 1775, the tobacco merchants opposed an attempt by the Magistrates and Council of the Town to send a petition of loyalty to the King, 'in the midst of this present rebellion'.[3] The proceedings were disturbed by 'several American merchants' who remonstrated in very strong terms against such a course. They had their way; Glasgow was the only burgh in Scotland not to convey the customary loyal greetings to the monarch.[4]

The survival of this rather tortuous policy of neutrality depended upon the time taken to resolve the conflict in America. If hostilities endured for more than a matter of months, the Glasgow traders were likely to increasingly experience opprobrium at home and hostility in the colonies. In December, 1775, for example, the inhabitants of Lunenberg County in Virginia addressed the State Convention, stated that the Scots were abusing their privileges of neutrality and asked for a test whereby 'the friends of America may be distinguished from those who are inimical'. In response the Convention, conscious of the fact that most Scots factors were drifting towards loyalism through natural sympathy, resolved that all able-bodied men should do militia duty or leave the state.[5] The adoption of this policy was probably inevitable anyway since, as has been seen, the Scots were one of the least trusted groups in colonial society and well fitted to play the role of scapegoats.[6]

However, the legislation of December, 1775 was still only an oblique attack on their position. A year later came the decisive blow when the Virginia House of Delegates formally expelled 'foreign merchants'; all were to leave the state forty days after the order became law and any who remained were to be confined as enemies.[7] Before this legislation most employees of Glasgow firms seem to have remained in Virginia because of 'the general belief that peace would be restored in the course of a year at the most two years'.[8] From late 1776, however, a general withdrawal began.

The 'young men' in the Cunninghame stores were given 'annual discharges' and sent home.[9] A number of factors purchased a ship, the *Albion*, and set sail for Scotland in June, 1777, only to be detained by a British man-of-war on suspicion of being rebels![10] Most of the principal agents of the Glasgow companies were directed to British-held ports, such as New York, Philadelphia and Charlestown, where trade could still be continued in prize goods, in supplying the needs of the army and in illicit commerce with the rebels.[11] Recent research has shown that 112 Scottish 'merchants' opened stores in Philadelphia when British troops occupied the city and that that port was very much involved in the revival of the Chesapeake tobacco trade during the war.[12] Thomas Reid, factor in Northumberland County for McCall, Dennistoun and Co., received notice of his expulsion in December, 1777; he then reduced his dealings in as clear a fashion as possible, taking bills, bonds and notes in settlement. Reid then placed the company's papers 'in an old box in an old house' and left for New York where he set himself up as a purchaser of prize tobacco for the firm.[13]

Neil Jamieson of Glassfords was solicited to pledge his support for Congress but 'remained steady to his principles, to what they called a Tory'. Yet his company, while allowing Jamieson the luxury of standing by his political ideals, instructed another of their representatives to proclaim himself 'a loyal American' and by so doing 'did save a great deal of property belonging to the Company'.[14] Jamieson himself escaped on board a Royal Navy ship and proceeded to New York where he offered to help finance the purchase of provisions for British troops and seamen. When this was accepted he drew on his parent concern via the house of Edward and Rene Payne in London for more than £30,000. There were clearly other routes to speculative gain in 1775-7 in addition to selling tobacco at inflated prices. So crucial apparently was Glassford capital to the British war effort that the rebels tried to dissuade Jamieson from providing his support by promising him that his losses in Virginia would be made good. However, he knew where his economic and political interests lay: 'no earthly consideration could induce him to become an enemy to his King and Country'.[15]

Other Scots merchants retreated into the 'back country'. Neil McColl, an employee of James Ritchie and Co., retired to a plantation ten miles from Fredericksburg and was unable to communicate with his firm until early 1782.[16] There is evidence too that despite the official opposition to their presence a handful of Glasgow traders remained resident in Richmond and Petersburg, Virginia throughout the war. Some took an oath to Congress; others returned under flags of truce or after having assumed a position of neutrality by adopting Danish citizenship.[17] However, as the costs of war and problems of commerce both pressed on Virginia's impoverished exchequer, covetous eyes began to be cast on the properties of Glasgow companies. These could rightly be regarded as belonging to the enemy and so offered an attractive target for spoliation. Thus by an act of the Virginia Assembly in March, 1778 all 'lands, slaves, stocks and implements—together with crops now on hand' owned by British subjects were sequestrated into the hands of a Commission to be appointed by the Governor and Council of the State. This was to have the power to remit all accruals from this property to boost the war fund of Virginia.[18] In 1780 these sequestrated assets were sold by public auction because of 'the great losses and damage' suffered by the colonials at the hands of British arms and to help pay for the increasing burden of war expenses.[19] In that year, the stores of Neil Jamieson, John Brown and John Ballantyne were sold at Norfolk.[20] Dinwiddie, Crawford and Co. and William Cunninghame and Co. were the main sufferers in February-March, 1780 when property in Mecklenburg County was auctioned for £29,000.[21]

The state government itself took over several of the stores owned by Glasgow firms and used them as official buildings. The property of John McDowall and Co. was employed as the auditor's office, that of Speirs, Bowman and Co. for the use of the Treasurer. Until the state capital was completed in 1789 the Virginia Assembly met in a house which formerly belonged to the Cunninghames. Four hundred and twelve acres in Prince Edward County, owned by Speirs, Bowman and Co., were awarded to Hampden and Sydney College.[22] Some firms lost considerable assets. Of eighteen which petitioned Government for compensation in 1786, ten estimated their property losses during the war at over £2000, three at over £5000 and two at over £10,000.[23]

The departure of most of the colonial personnel of the Glasgow companies and the confiscation of their stores and other properties meant that no *direct* trade was possible with Virginia and Maryland during hostilities. British prohibition against imports from the rebellious colonies and congressional bans on commerce with the enemy further reduced the possibilities of open trade. However, a complete rupture of commercial relationships did not take place. Virginia and Maryland were specialist primary-producing areas dependent for consumer goods on external sources. Only by marketing tobacco—their most valuable crop—could they pay for war materials. In addition, the non-importation agreements of 1774-5 meant that European goods had become scarce even before the conflict began. One Virginia merchant in March, 1775 observed how:

We have little or no trade here for some time past occasioned by the extreme scarcity of all kinds of coarse goods and I am at a loss to see how the poorer sort of people and negroes are to be provided with Cloathing and Linen in future, when what they at present have is worn out.[24]

Throughout the Revolution imported goods cost many times more in terms of tobacco than they did in pre-war years. For example, before 1775 salt in Virginia normally sold for about 2/- per bushel or the price of twelve pounds of tobacco. Normal exchange during hostilities was one bushel of salt for one hundred pounds of tobacco.[25] Similarly, tobacco prices in Europe reached inflated heights. Because of war-time difficulties it has been estimated that the crop production of Virginia and Maryland averaged between one-half and one-third of pre-war levels.[26] At the same time demand for North American tobacco proved inelastic and only partially vulnerable to competition from European substitutes. James Ritchie and Co. estimated that profit in 1779 in this commercial context would be between 150 and 200 per cent. In 1780, Virginia tobacco sold for between 14d and 21d; a year later for between 2/5d and 2/10d per lb.[28] These prices are to be compared with those of the early 1770s of $2\frac{1}{2}$d per lb.

The opportunity to achieve speculative gains enticed most merchant houses to continue to prosecute American trade by circuitous routes despite the higher costs of such methods. In early 1775, non-importation arrangements among several of the American states had encouraged Glasgow firms to utilise other channels of supply. One journal noted:

Several of the most considerable merchants and manufacturers, have by the last packet boat from America received large orders from the provinces of Quebec, Nova Scotia, Georgia, East Florida and West Florida; all of which provinces have dissented from the resolution of the American Congress; and their merchants are resolved, if possible, to profit by the large quantity of all sorts of British goods, which they expect to smuggle into the other provinces. On which account they are all busy at work; and there are no less than sixteen ships lying to load for the single province of Georgia at present.[29]

In the first few years of war, until about 1779, this continued to be the geographical pattern of the export trade to North America. Some Glasgow houses, such as Colin Dunlop and Sons, had already established links with Canada before 1775 and a thriving commerce had been built up between the Clyde ports and the Canadian provinces in timber, potash and fish.[30] From the outbreak of hostilities, however, this region developed to a new prominence. Scottish exports to Canada rose from £4,742 in 1774 to £12,882 in 1775 and to £28,215 in 1777; Nova Scotia, of little account before the war, took goods to the value of £126,136 in 1777.[31] The imbalance of trade in favour of Scottish exports with these regions during this phase of the war, illustrates that Canada was being used to supply the rebel colonies to the south.[32]

However, the Clyde Customs Accounts reveal that after an initial period in which Canada was the preferred intermediate market, there was a trend subsequently to send goods to American ports in British hands which were closer to the tobacco colonies and where exiled factors of Glasgow firms resided. Of the ten ships freighting for North America in the period January, 1776 to April, 1777, seven sailed for Nova Scotia and two for Quebec. A year later a more complex pattern had evolved with Newfoundland and Nova Scotia together attracting seven vessels and New York and Philadelphia following behind with four and two ships respectively. By 1779 Canada had lost its former pre-eminence; during January-April of that year only two vessels sailed for Nova Scotia while six freighted for American ports.[33]

This movement to the south was a reflection of the revival, albeit on a very limited scale, of the Scottish tobacco trade from New York, Charlestown and Philadelphia. Tobacco cargoes were available there from prizes taken by naval vessels and privateers, and from collusive captures. Charlestown was the source of foreign goods for a large territory to the northward, reaching at times as far as New Jersey while Philadelphia was the principal

TABLE XXIV
Clyde Tobacco Imports, 1778–82

Year	Imports (Hogsheads)
1778	1,195
1779	3,051
1780	Customs Accounts incomplete
1781	1,013
1782	2,597

Source—SRO, E.504/15/29-37; E.504/28/28-35.

supplier of consumer commodities to Virginia at this time.[34] Thus from 1777 Glasgow houses began to switch their export trade to these centres. In December, 1777, for example, James Ritchie and Co. dispatched two ships (one, the *Albion*, with a cargo valued at between £7–8000) to Philadelphia with orders that the goods be disposed of for ready money.[35] Their chief agent, James Dunlop, had settled in New York with orders to buy tobacco as prices, the market situation and political circumstances justified. To do so he was permitted to draw on Ritchies for up to £5000.[36]

The Glasgow houses were able to re-establish themselves because American and European merchants had been unable to organise a transatlantic trade in tobacco and goods. The blockade of the Royal Navy, the unfamiliarity of foreign sea captains with the Chesapeake and high insurance premiums effectively diminished the chances of success. In 1778 a Marseilles merchant remarked that 'risk has become so very great that few or no Houses here care to adventure in that commerce'.[37] Indeed, the only influx of French merchants and ships in Virginia came in that year, shortly after the negotiation of the alliance between France and the Americans, but most were disillusioned by the effects of the depreciation of the paper currency in which they had to take most of their profits and did not return.[38]

An added problem was that foreign merchants seem not to have been able to provide the range of consumer goods in demand in the colonies. Some thought the French adventurers were if anything even more disliked than their Scottish predecessors. As one French sea captain wrote in 1778 of his fellow countrymen in Virginia, 'they are detested by the people, whom they impose upon, they are a thousand per cent more Jewish than the Jews of Europe'.[39]

The failure of the many attempts to develop a direct transatlantic trade between America and Europe meant that long before the war ended control had begun to slip back into the hands of British merchant firms. Yet because of the difficulties involved in supplying tobacco to the Continent in British

TABLE XXV
Source of Tobacco Imports, 1778–83, Greenock and Port Glasgow

Source	1778	1779	1781	1782	1783
New York	795	2309	106	829	784
West Indies	346	575	432	1768	526
Charlestown	—	52	475	—	—
Quebec	1	—	—	—	—
Prizes	53	—	—	—	—
Bermuda	—	—	—	—	156
TOTAL	1195	2936	1013	2597	1466

Source—SRO, E.504/15/29–37; E.504/28/28–35.

vessels after France entered the war in 1778, company representatives in America were instructed to gear their purchasing mainly, though not exclusively, to the needs of the British consumer.[40] As a result of this and the absolute fall in tobacco production in Virginia and Maryland, Clyde imports fell to a very low level and never reached more than a modest proportion of pre-war shipments.

Merchants based their calculations on the presumption that only limited supplies would become available for purchase at New York. In 1779, the price in Britain would only keep up if a maximum of 300 hogsheads were acquired between January and April; 'if more is brought in, sales may become heavy and prices may fail'.[41] An annual importation of 8–10,000 hogsheads would overstock the market.[42] Until French entry into the war in 1778, merchants had an additional reason for being wary of large purchases. Given the fluidity of the political and military situation, peace could be re-established with little warning and tobacco retail prices in Britain fall in anticipation of the re-opening of trade. Firms would thus be left with large stocks acquired at high prices. Only from 1779 did instructions to factors in New York advise that since an early end to hostilities was not now likely, purchases might be increased substantially.[43] Importation to the Clyde that year was nearly three times the level of 1778.

From that date too there was a significant change in the source of tobacco supplies. The Caribbean, rather than New York, became the major entrepot for the sale of Virginia and Maryland tobacco.

The new importance of the West Indies was partly a result of congressional trade policy. War conditions tended to accentuate the economic and political significance of tobacco. Of the major American export crops it lent itself most readily to development of trade with neutral powers, affording great possibilities of financing military operations and obtaining much needed manufactured goods. Dutch and Danish islands in the Caribbean were well suited to serve as centres of exchange between the Americans and European (including British) merchants. Virginia, Maryland and North Carolina maintained a regular correspondence with the mercantile firm of Harrison and Van Bibber in the West Indies. State authorities chartered ships, bought flour, tobacco and other commodities and consigned the cargoes to their West Indian representatives from whom in turn they obtained shipments of military stores, salt etc.[44] Small vessels of 40-50 tons and swift blockade runners were used to avoid the attentions of the Royal Navy.

The principal centres of this clandestine commerce were the Dutch island of St. Eustatius and later, when Holland entered the war, the Danish islands of St. Thomas and St. Croix. The British, despite the fact that they were the 'enemy', were the main customers and suppliers of the Americans. When Rodney captured St. Eustatius in 1781, John Adams, the American patriot saw the irony:

> There was found in that island a greater quantity of property belonging to the British themselves than to the French, Dutch or Americans. They have broken up a trade which was more advantageous to them than any of their enemies as it was a channel through which British manufactures were conveyed to North America.[45]

From 1780 Parliament legalised the trade in American tobacco from foreign West Indian islands and imposed a special additional duty on it.[46]

Glasgow firms were well equipped to enter this trade in a vigorous fashion. The Caribbean was not unfamiliar territory. Some Clyde merchants had always been more interested in sugar from the West Indies than tobacco from Virginia. Even specialist tobacco importers made 'adventures' to the Caribbean when sugar prices merited it or when the tobacco market was depressed. Moreover, American traders had to keep correspondents there in order to satisfy the requirements of their stores for West Indian commodities. Merchants with less experience made use of their contacts in Glasgow to extend their links in the Caribbean.[47]

From 1779-80, then, some Glasgow houses began to embark heavily in the West Indian clandestine tobacco trade. James Ritchie and Co. informed their New York agent in December, 1779 that 'very large quantities are now conveyed to St. Eustatius where it is sold at reasonable prices'. Dunlop, their factor, was advised to get a correspondent there 'as on these things the state of market in Europe will in great measure depend'.[48] In spring the company dispatched James Anderson to the West Indies and gave him 'unlimited credit' to purchase for them 'either prize tobacco, sugar, rum and even land and slaves if a very great bargain offered'. In addition, Anderson obtained a power of attorney from several other Glasgow merchants to acquire tobacco on their behalf to the amount of £4000.[49]

Through investment in this sector it was possible not only to tap fruitful supplies of American tobacco but also to re-establish contact with European markets. Speirs, French and Co. endeavoured between 1780-2 to develop a major trade directly between continental ports and the West Indies. Their representative in the Caribbean, Robert Burton, was instructed to lay out as much as £50,000 sterling 'in such commodities and to ship them to such ports in Europe as will bring the best price'.[50] He sent his tobacco to Hamburg, Ostend and Amsterdam in neutral vessels on which insurance premiums were low. Agents of Speirs in these centres marketed the cargoes and sent back European manufactures to Burton in the Caribbean.[51]

It is clear from the discussion so far that the Glasgow tobacco trade survived in attenuated form during the war and continued to be a source of profit for those firms with the liquid resources to endure the high operating and credits costs of wartime commerce. Yet war offered further opportunities for gain in addition to returns from 'normal' trade. The strategic necessity to dispatch a large army to North America and latterly to send troops to the West Indies encouraged merchants to charter their vessels as transports. By so doing the merchant could be sure that his investment would be well protected as transports always sailed under heavy naval escort. In addition, owners were cushioned from the rising shipping costs of wartime by the fact that Government itself paid wages and offered compensation for damage and loss. On the other hand, earnings would probably be much less than in ordinary commerce although they would certainly be more stable.[52] Indeed one firm in 1776 thought that chartering vessels as transports would pay the costs of the outward voyage to the colonies and enable ships to take advantage of the re-opening of ports when the rebellion was crushed:

... it was our principal or rather our only motive, for hiring our ships to the Government, to have them in America at the time the ports are opened, and upon that event that they should quit the service instantly and run to Virginia and bring home a cargo of tobacco, by which we expect to make a good deal of money.[53]

In 1776-7 Clyde shipowners were in a particularly good position to satisfy government needs. The disruption of American commerce left 'many vessels out of employ' and available for hire to the Navy Board.[54] An added advantage was that Greenock was the most obvious port of embarkation for the Highland regiments. So in January, 1776 government representatives arrived in Glasgow to contract for 7000 tons of shipping. Patrick Colquohoun, a leading tobacco merchant and future Lord Provost, was appointed agent to the contractors for victualling the transports. By early February the required tonnage had been hired and nine Glasgow-owned vessels entered government service. At the end of the month some sailed from Greenock carrying the 31st Regiment and were followed in April by the remainder which embarked the 42nd and 71st Regiments of Highlanders, consisting of 3,466 officers and men. When France entered the war in 1778, a second substantial exodus of over 6500 men left the Clyde.[55]

This pattern of employment illustrated one of the drawbacks of government service as far as the shipowner was concerned. Utilisation of vessels was only for limited periods at specified times. Transportation of troops from the U.K. took place only on a considerable scale in 1776 and 1778. Possibly a more common role for merchantmen, therefore, was to assist in the carriage of provisions to the armies fighting in North America and the West Indies. By so doing traders were able to partially solve one of the traditional problems of Caribbean commerce. Shipping capacity on the outward voyage to the West Indian islands was always under-utilised because exports to that area did not require as much cargo space as bulk imports of sugar, tobacco and cotton. When supplies of foodstuffs from America to the Caribbean were interrupted, Ireland became the source of provisions for British garrisons and since Glasgow merchantmen used the Irish port of Cork as a convoy assembly point during the war it became possible to contract vessels for the victualling service as a complementary function to their normal trading activities. One Clyde firm, Robert Dunmore and Co. approached 'the Contractor for the Jamaica troops' in early 1778 and established an association with an Irish corn agent in Cork who 'will at all times fill up our ships with bread for Antigua having at this time no less than 6000 men to supply with provisions daily'.[56]

In the popular imagination privateering is perhaps regarded as the easiest and quickest route to fortune in the wars of this period. The reality, however, was quite different. Owners of privateers experienced high costs and an often elusive return on capital. More than any other wartime activity, privateering was a gamble. Alderman Creighton of London argued that the expense of outfitting made it unprofitable because 'a prize was as much a matter of chance as the obtainment of a ten or twenty thousand pounds prize in the lottery'.[57] A 'letter of marque' for a privateer, giving official powers to act against enemy merchantmen, required payment to the Admiralty of £3000 as bail and security if it carried over 150 men and £1500 if under that complement. Again an expensive armament would have to be fitted if the privateer was to be capable of taking the richer prizes which were themselves usually well-protected. Provisions necessary for such a ship exceeded those for the ordinary merchantman bound for a certain destination on a specific time schedule. While the need to cruise at sea for as long as possible compelled the privateer's store intake to be above the norm, extra hands had also to be hired if the vessel was to be transformed into an efficient fighting ship. This happened too during a war when labour costs rose very significantly.[58]

Moreover, even if luck was in and a ship was taken not all profit accrued to the owner. One quarter of the prize money was traditionally distributed among the crew and the Crown took a further one-sixth.[59] Returns had to be sufficient to cover high operating costs but the owner of a privateer was as much at the mercy of market forces in the speedy and profitable sale of captured produce as the merchant engaged in normal commerce. Thus Speirs, French and Co. complained in the autumn of 1781 that although the *Enterprise* had taken two prizes worth 'at least £1200' no profit would be made because of the state of the market and rising costs.[60] A further problem was that most enemy vessels during the American War were protected by convoy and those which were not were normally fast 'running ships' able to match for speed all but the most efficient privateers.[61]

It is clear therefore that there were many obstacles to successful privateering. The great attraction, however, was precisely that of the gamble—the chance to make gains of many hundreds per cent on outlay by taking a valuable cargo when market conditions seemed favourable for its sale. The Scottish press in November, 1778 was filled with the dramatic news that the *Cochrane*, belonging to William Cunninghame and Co., had taken a French East Indiaman with its holds full of silks and spices reputed to be worth £100,000.[62] This was the kind of dazzling success which enticed others to venture into privateering. Even low-cost investments could prove lucky. The *Endeavour* mounted only ten three-pounders but managed to take a French merchantman en route from the Caribbean:

> She (the *Endeavour*) was bound for the West Indies but ordered by the owners to cruise a few days in a certain latitude, where she had the good fortune to meet with the West Indiaman which struck in the dark, not knowing the size of the schooner.[63]

Almost certainly more common, however, than these colourful episodes, always reported in detail in the press, were the unsuccessful voyages which showed as net losses in the merchant's accounts. During the American War, there were thirty-seven vessels owned by Glasgow, Greenock and Port Glasgow interests and sailing under a 'letter of marque'. Throughout the period of hostilities forty-seven enemy ships were taken. This suggests an average figure of less than two prizes per Clyde privateer captured during the seven years of war.[64]

In the first phase of the conflict little effort appears to have been made to equip privateers. The expense of doing so would have been ruinous when early victory seemed so certain and when rebel vessels with valuable cargoes were few and far between. Only when France became a combatant did substantial investment commence. Like Britain, France had a transatlantic commercial empire connected by long sea-lanes within which vessels loaded with silks, spices, sugar and other lucrative cargoes might be attacked. In the years 1775-7 the Clyde Customs Accounts only refer to three privateers freighting outwards.[65] However, in September, 1778, the press talked of a 'privateering spirit' which prevailed at Greenock:

> This preserved us from being dejected by the gloomy aspect of the times; we shall have, in three weeks, a most capital armament ready for sea.[66]

The Customs Accounts fully substantiate this comment. Between August and October, 1778, five privateers were outfitted with 'a Letter of Marque and Reprisal and bound on a cruise against the American rebels and for the apprehending and Taking the Ships, vessels and goods belonging to the French king'.[67] A further five were ready for action before the end of the year.[68]

Some merchant houses seem to have developed a major investment in privateering. Robert Dunmore and Co. owned five, William Cunninghame and Co., three and Alexander Houston and Co., four.[69] Firms such as these could hope to strike gold (if not literally!) with at least one of their vessels. Some did record outstanding success runs. The *Cochrane* belonging to Cunninghames took three American ships between January and April, 1778. The *Elizabeth*, one of the Houston privateers, captured two French West Indiamen a few days after being commissioned; *La Victoire* and the *Beauvoisin* contained cargoes of sugar and coffee valued at over £12,000.[70] Other companies, however, conscious of the high costs and risks of privateering, preferred to play for safety by acquiring a 'letter of marque' for their ships, fitting them with a few additional cannon and freighting them also for trade. This hybrid type of vessel was an attempt to cut down the element of gambling in privateering. A cargo would cover operating costs and if luck was in a capture might also be made.

On the other hand, the gains from this form of investment were probably more theoretical than real. Captains of such merchantmen were always faced with a dilemma—the decision whether to aim for the dependable freight or the more elusive but much more profitable prize. It was difficult to have the best of both worlds. As Capt. James Laurie of the brig *Hasard* pointed out to his employers, if the ship was bent on trade with the West Indies, the outward freight from the Clyde would not allow her to sail 'sufficiently fast to afford hope of success as a privateer'.[71] Another master, Capt. Smith of the *Sally*, was fortunate enough in 1777 to take a prize off St. Kitts but two days afterwards encountered an American privateer. He had to scuttle the prize and make off because with the holds of his own ship already crammed with sugar and rum, his mobility was limited.[72]

REFERENCES

1. *The Proceedings of the Convention of Delegates... of Virginia* (Richmond, 1816), July, 1775, 24.
2. *Edinburgh Evening Courant*, 1 February, 1775.
3. *Caldonian Mercury*, 11 October, 1775.
4. SRO, GD 213/53, John Anderson to Richard Oswald, 3 November, 1775.
5. *Proceedings of Virginia Convention*, 67-8.
6. See above, pp. 103-4.
7. Henning, *Statutes of Virginia*.
8. PRO, AO 12/56/285-6.
9. SRO, GD 247/59/Q/1, Walter Colquohoun to James Robinson, 7 June, 1776.
10. 'The Journal of Ebenezer Hazard in Virginia, 1777' *Virginia Magazine of History and Biography*, Vol. 62 (1954), 418.
11. See above, pp. 127-31.
12. W. H. Siebert, 'The Loyalists in Pennsylvania', *Ohio State University Bulletin*, XXIV, 23-45.
13. Harrell, *op. cit.*, 72.
14. PRO, AO 12/55/46; AO 12/9/35.
15. PRO, AO 12/55/47-55.
16. Library of Congress, Washington, James Dunlop Family Papers, Box 1, Neil McColl to James Dunlop, 27 February, 1782. [This material is used from transcripts taken by Mr. Stuart Butler of the University of St. Andrews. I am very grateful to Mr. Butler for allowing me to see and use these important papers].
17. Samuel Mordecai, *Richmond in Bygone Days*, Ch. II; PRO, AO 12/9/49; Coulter, *op. cit.*
18. *Edinburgh Evening Courant*, 13 June, 1778, Reprint of an 'Act for sequestering British property'.
19. *Scots Magazine*, XLIV (1781), 651-53.
20. *Ibid.*, XLII (1780), 634.
21. Harrell, *op. cit.*, 95.
22. *Ibid.*, 95-100.
23. PRO, AO 12-13, *passim*.
24. W. Allason to T. Martin, 10 March, 1775 in *Richmond College Historical Papers*, II, 164.
25. Coakley, *op. cit.*, 380.
26. *Ibid.*
27. LC, James Dunlop Family Papers, Box 1, Hugh Wylie to James Dunlop, 27 August, 1779.
28. *Ibid.*, James Ritchie and Co. to James Dunlop, 28 April, 1780; Henry Ritchie to James Dunlop, 2 November, 1781; GCA, Speirs Papers, TD 131/9, Alexander Speirs to J. G. Martens, 11 October, 1781.
29. *Caledonian Mercury*, 11 January, 1775.
30. D. S. Macmillan, "The 'New Men' in Action: Scottish Mercantile and Shipping Operations in the North American Colonies 1760-1825", in D. S. Macmillan (ed.), *Canadian Business History: Selected Studies, 1497-1971* (Toronto, 1972), 44-103.
31. PRO, Customs 14/1B, 14/2.
32. Chamber of Commerce, Glasgow, Abstract of the General Customs of Scotland 1755-1801.
33. SRO, Customs Accounts, Port Glasgow and Greenock, E.504/28/29-35; E.504/15/28-37.
34. Gray. *op. cit.*, II, 581; Coakley, *op. cit.*, 294.
35. LC, James Dunlop Family Papers, James Ritchie and Co. to William Woodrop and James Dunlop, 12 December, 1777.
26. *Ibid.*, J. Ritchie and Co. to James Dunlop, 26 December, 1778.
37. Quoted in Coakley, *op cit.*, 166.
38. *Ibid.*, 167.
39. *Ibid.*, 335.

40. LC, James Dunlop Family Papers, James Ritchie and Co. to James Dunlop, 29 January, 1779. The last tobacco was exported from Port Glasgow in the third quarter of 1777 (230 hogsheads for Havre de Grace by Glassford, Gordon and Co.). Re-export trade was not revived until April–June, 1783.
41. *Ibid*.
42. *Ibid*., 2 July, 1779.
43. *Ibid*.,
44. Gray, *op. cit*., II, 578; Macpherson, *op. cit*., III, 719–20.
45. Quoted in Coulter, *op. cit*., 152.
46. 20 Geo. III, C.39.
47. SL, CSP 190/13, Speirs, French and Co. to Robert Burton, 10 March, 1779.
48. LC, James Dunlop Family Papers, Hugh Wylie to James Dunlop, 22 December, 1779.
49. *Ibid*., James Anderson to James Dunlop, 15 March, 1780.
50. GCA, Speirs Papers, TD 131/9, Letterbook of Alexander Speirs, Speirs to Robert Burton, 28 February, 1782.
51. *Ibid*., to Thomas Eden, 3 January, 1782; to J. G. Martins, 3 January, 1782; to George Lindsay, 26 January, 1782.
52. Davis, *op. cit*., 330; David Syrett, *Shipping and the American War, 1775–83* (London, 1970), 79–80; 'The West India Merchants and the Conveyance of the King's Troops to the Caribbean', *Journ. Soc. for Army Hist. Research*, XLV (1967), 109.
53. LC, James Dunlop Family Papers, James Ritchie and Co. to Capt. James Chalmers, 20 Jan., 1777.
54. *Scots Magazine*, June, 1776.
55. *Edinburgh Evening Courant*, 22, 27 January, 10, 24 February, 1776; SRO, CE 60/1/10, Collector, Greenock and Port Glasgow to H.M. Board of Customs, 13 May, 1778; Syrett, *op. cit*., 103–5; 201–2.
56. SRO, GD 247/59/Q/2, William Cunninghame to Robert Dunmore and Co., 13, 18 August, 1778.
57. Quoted in M. K. Barritt, 'The Navy and the Clyde in the American War, 1777–83', *Mariners Mirror*, 55 (1969), 35.
58. See below, pp. 146–7. The average complement of Glasgow privateers during the war seems to have been between 40–50. This was substantially larger than the ordinary merchantman.
59. A typical division was as follows:

	Shares
Captain	16
First Mate	8
Second Mate	4
Boatswain	2
Carpenter	2
Gunner	2
Each seaman's share (suppose 25)	25
Each landsman or half seaman (suppose 5)	2½
Each apprentice	1½
	63

NLS, MS 8759, Alex, Houston and Co. to Capt. A. McKinlay, 3 April, 1778.
60. GCA, TD 131/9, Alexander Speirs to J. G. Martens, 25 October, 1781; for a similar case see SRO, UP Inglis 5/4/22, Speirs, Murdoch and Co. versus Campbell, Ingram and Co. (1784).
61. Davis, *op. cit*., 333.
62. *Edinburgh Evening Courant*, 7 November, 1778.
63. *Ibid*., SRO, E.504/15/31.

64. This generalisation is based on examination of the Scottish press, 1775–83 and of the Port Glasgow and Greenock Customs Accounts.
65. SRO, E.504/15/25–30; E.504/28/24–30.
66. *Edinburgh Evening Courant*, 22 August, 1778.
67. SRO, E.504/15/30–1.
68. *Edinburgh Evening Courant*, 22 December, 1778.
69. SRO, GD/247/59/Q/2; E.504/28/30, 32; NLS, MS 8794, Alexander Houston and Co. to Capt. Alex. Mackenzie, 5 March, 1779; to Capt. W. Buchanan, 8 March, 1779; to Capt. J. McGregor, 11 March, 1779.
70. *Glasgow Mercury*, 17 January, 19 March, 9 April, 1778; SRO, E.504/28/29, 31.
71. SRO, GD 247/58/P/2, Henry King and Co. to Robert Dunmore and Co., 7 August, 1779.
72. NLS, MS 8793, A. Houston and Co. to Messrs. Turner and Paul, 27 September, 1777.

9

The Difficulties of Trade During the American War

IN the public eye perhaps the most striking of the problems which faced merchant houses was the seeming ubiquity of American privateers in the years 1776–7 and the attentions of their French allies in the years after 1778. Danger to their shipping from enemy attack was a relatively novel experience for Glasgow colonial merchants. Daniel Defoe pointed out how in the early 1700s, Clyde vessels were relatively safe in this regard,

> The Glasgow vessels are no sooner out of the Firth of Clyde, but they stretch away to the north-west, are out of the road of the privateers immediately, and are often at the capes of Virginia before the London ships get clear of the Channel.[1]

Professor Price has noted how it was not until the latter stages of the Seven Years War, in the early 1760s that French privateers penetrated the northern sea-lanes in force.[2] Glasgow's commerce had developed immeasurably from that period and the American rebels would have personal knowledge of the rich pickings to be made from it. As early as September-October, 1775 the colonials began to fit out privateers (always the weapon of the weaker power in time of war) at Philadelphia, Boston and other ports.[3] In 1776–7 such activities continued and a Scottish newspaper in May, 1777 reported with some alarm that on the twenty-fifth of that month, twenty-one privateers, carrying 388 guns and 846 men had left Boston.[4] One calculation estimated that in the first two years of hostilities the Americans had over 170 such vessels at sea of varying sizes and capabilities.[5] No time was wasted in deploying them in the main sea-lanes of the Atlantic and 'very soon they swarmed round every one of the West Indian islands'.[6]

The convoy system was set up to protect merchant shipping, but apart from the imperfections of the system itself,[7] Glasgow ships were vulnerable and almost unprotected by naval escort in two critical areas—in the Clyde Estuary and in the Irish Sea and around the islands of the West Indies. The harbour of Cork was at once the main assembly point for out-going convoys and also an attraction to Glasgow West India vessels since from the beginning of the war it had acted as a major provisions base for the Caribbean.[8] From 1776 until the winter of 1778 no official naval escort was supplied for the voyage from the Clyde to this port.[9] In 1776-7 the necessity of transporting an army to North America and provisioning it once there had left only ten frigates in home waters, of which six at that time were under repair.[10] In addition, the Admiralty's traditional desire for financial retrenchment during years of peace meant that trade tended to be hit severely in the early years of war and in these economy drives the smaller ships, the type well adapted for convoy duty, were the main sufferers.[11]

In the 1760s and 1770s the problem was likely to be particularly serious. The Seven Years War, ending in 1763, had left the country £112 millions in debt and thus the tendency to pennypinching commenced from that date until 1775. Of the eighty ships of the line required during wartime, none was in service in the months before 1776.[12] The petitions of Glasgow Town Council and the Conventions of Royal Burghs in 1777 for Admiralty assistance against 'the alarming depredations made by rebel privateers' were unlikely to shift the Royal Navy's concentration on its major role of supplying and transporting the army, a task which exhausted most of the energies of a service notoriously dilatory in awakening from its peacetime somnolence.[13] The only crumb of comfort for the city's commercial interests came in July, 1777 when HMS *Arethusa* proceeded north and began to cruise between the Mull of Kintyre and Belfast Lough.[10] Yet the specific request for an escort (or escorts) for 'the trade of Glasgow' was refused: 'it would be impossible for their lordships to station a ship for the protection of each port, more especially while so great a part of the fleet is stationed in America and the Indies'.[15]

More promising were developments in March, 1778 when two out of the eight armed ships fitted out for coastal protection arrived in the Clyde.[16] Such generous support was likely to be short-lived, however, as with the entry of France into the war, Government had to find ships to contain the enemy Channel squadrons and to conduct operations in what was developing into a global conflict.[17] Thus the Clyde was left with a single 'armed ship', HMS *Satisfaction*, one of the two arrivals of March, 1778. This vessel unfortunately belied her name: she had originally been built as a collier, sailed heavily and, it was alleged, could hardly keep up with a loaded merchantman. Hugh Wylie, Lord Provost of Glasgow and himself extensively involved in colonial trade, complained to the Admiralty how although the Clyde estuary was 'very much infested with privateers' they had escaped with impunity due to the demonstrable inadequacies of the Clyde's 'guardship'.[18] However, the Clyde was even stripped of this protection and the *Satisfaction* sailed for London in December, 1780. A request for a standing convoy for the shipping of Greenock and Port Glasgow had already been turned down in August, 1778; it would be supplied, 'as soon as the various services which have claim to their Lordships' attention will admit of it'.[19]

Efforts were redoubled with the departure of the *Satisfaction* and in April, 1781, the frigate HMS *Seaford* was despatched to the Clyde.[20] This was the first direct protection of any value afforded Glasgow shipping by the Royal Navy from the outbreak of war. Even then the situation was not wholly satisfactory. Glasgow's Lord Provost complained about insufficient liaison between the commander of the vessel and the merchants of the town. The former was to be under complete Admiralty control and because of this, the *Seaford*,

> ... can be of little service to the Trade of this river for unless the Chief Magistrate have it in his power to order a convoy to Cork or out to the North Channel or to cruise as the circumstances of the times may require, she will do us very little service.[21]

Protection of some sort was clearly necessary during the war whether it was supplied by government or by local initiative. In 1776–7, American privateers were allowed to rampage almost at will in the two narrow channels of the Firth of Clyde—the North and St. George's. Five appeared off Ireland in November, 1776, and rumour rapidly spread up the West Coast that, to use a contemporary euphemism, they intended to 'visit' Greenock and Port Glasgow.[22] Three more appeared in the spring of 1777—the *Reprisal* (18 guns and 130 men), the *Lexington* (16 guns and 110 men) and the *Dolphin* (10 guns and 64 men). They 'intended visiting Clyde very soon and could tell directly what troops and ships there were there and how many were expected in the next West Indies fleet'.[23] Throughout July and early August, the Clyde ports and the West Coast were in a state of panic. It seems likely that the Americans previously concentrating their activities on the wider stretches of open sea 'especially the tracts to and from the West Indies',[24] were now adopting a new and more effective strategy. They were attempting to bottle up enemy commerce in its home ports, attack it on the outward or inward voyage and so take full advantage of the inadequacies in Royal Naval resources. Fears were even expressed that landings might be made by the rebels: at Ayr, in response to these fears, the good citizens of the town hastened to remove their 'valuable furniture' further inland in July, 1777.[25]

Loss of merchant vessels reached a dangerously high level during the summer of 1777. In June fourteen merchantmen were taken by the Americans and in the following July, between the fifth and the fourteenth of the month, nine vessels were lost.[26] Although this year was perhaps the worst period for Glasgow shipping, basically because of the unprepared nature of its defences,[27] the years 1780–1 approached it in the intensity of enemy attacks. Hugh Wylie warned Captain Christian of HMS *Seaford* in April, 1781 how 'many vessels have been captured of late years in and about the North Channel and there is but too much reason to fear that more enemys will infest those seas than hitherto . . .'.[28] Sailing in company was no guarantee of protection. On 23rd June, 1780, the *Catherine*, bound for Jamaica, the *Venus* and the *London* for Georgia, and the *Margaret* for New York 'all belonging to Clyde' were taken after a day's sail from Port Glasgow by a French man o' war of 64 guns.[29] John Knox thought that the Clyde lost 313 vessels 'of various sizes' during the American War.[30] Although he almost certainly exaggerated, it is equally clear that losses were on a considerable scale.

Because of governmental impotence for long stretches of the war, local initiative tried to fill the gap. The most effective means of ensuring at least a modicum of protection for merchant vessels was by arming them. It is very probable that the refusal to undertake this expensive fitting out of merchantmen in 1775-7 explains the extreme vulnerability of Glasgow shipping for much of that period. Advertisements for outgoing ships in the *Glasgow Mercury* only begin to indicate that most vessels have been armed in the autumn of 1777 and more especially in the summer of 1778.[31] Even a wealthy firm

TABLE XXVI

Armament of A. Houston and Co.'s Ships, 1778-83

Sally	10 Carriage Guns
	6 Swivel Guns
Juno	10 Six Pounders
	4 Cohorns
Jupiter	18 Carriage Guns
	6 Nine Pounders
	6 Swivels
Castlesemple	12 Six Pounders
	2 Cohorns
Robert	8 Carriage Guns

Source—NLS, MS, 8793-4; 8759.

like Alexander Houston and Co. only began to realise, with the entry of France into the conflict in 1778 that the war was likely to be lengthy and thus proceeded to arm their ships.

Most vessels were fitted with Carron Company's famous product, the carronade. A Company advertisement in 1779 pointed out that 'the spirit of enterprise . . . of the mercantile gentlemen of the city of Glasgow never appeared with greater lustre than in their exertions for the security of their commerce by arming with these guns'.[32] Unlike heavy cannon they did not reduce a ship's speed markedly. The gun was 'so extremely light that the smallest ship can carry almost any weight of shot without being attended with the inconvenience imputed generally to light guns'.[33] Merchant skippers testified to the capabilities of the weapon. Captain John Hastie pointed out that 'our carronades were of great service' in an engagement with a French privateer in August, 1778.[34] Similar praise was given by another master after a skirmish with a large French ship, *La Nymphe*.[35] The captain of the *Sharp* of Glasgow attributed his escape from an American privateer near

Cape Clear to the efficiency of his carronades and he 'intended never to arm with anything else in the future'.[36]

Another method of protection attempted was by means of mercantile co-operation. The merchants of Port Glasgow, Greenock and Glasgow agreed to subscribe £3000 for the fitting out of three armed ships in the crisis period of June-July, 1777[37] so that, wrote a contemporary:

> We hope soon to be able to protect our trade without the assistance of government, who it seems, cannot spare us any frigates at present.[38]

So urgently was some form of defence required that the sum was subscribed in a day;[39] seamen were easily hired because of 'the stop to the American trade leaving half of them idle';[40] 100 men were enlisted, 600 stand of arms was brought down from Dumbarton and stores and ammunition were made ready.[41] There was a spirit of adventure among the members of the expedition: the *Scots Magazine* reported that 'the sailors are so keen . . . that in case of calm weather they are taking plenty of oars on board'.[42]

Whatever the psychological benefits which might be derived from showing the flag the first sortie of the squadron arguably did more harm than good. The picturesquely named *Charming Fanny* had to put back to port while the *Katie* and *Ulysses* set out for an eight day cruise against the American marauders. The *Katie* sighted a merchant vessel and a brig but did not follow; the *Ulysses* had the embarrassing task of escorting an English ship into Greenock. The latter's master had taken the *Ulysses* to be an enemy privateer and thrown his papers overboard. Indeed, the one concrete result seems to have been to make confusion worse confounded in the Irish Sea: 'several other brigs, sloops and boats were greatly frightened and almost went ashore to keep from them'.[43] The dénouement of the farce came when the two vessels put into Belfast for information:

> The Mayor and aldermen held a council to take the Captain and the principle [sic] officers into custody, under suspicion of their being American privateers, but on finding they were fitted out to protect the trade of Clyde, they desisted from their purpose. On the other hand when their real designs were made public a mob, instigated by a native of America, had nearly arose to maltreat them . . .[44]

A third means of defence was the construction of shore batteries: these, at least, would safeguard the anchorages. In addition, financial compensation by government was likely to be forthcoming since such a venture fitted in with military strategy for the defence of the west coast. Sir Adolphous Oughton, Commander-in-Chief, Scotland, had in fact written to the Lord Provost of Glasgow in September, 1778, noting that there was 'ground of belief' an invasion might be attempted on the west coast and desiring the Town Council to commission some cannon from Carron Co. for fortifying Greenock.[45] A few weeks later, Lord Frederick Campbell, Commander of the Western Fencibles, quartered in Greenock, was authorised by the Town Councils of Glasgow and Greenock to erect a battery 'for the defence of shipping belonging to the River Clyde and West Coast'.[46] Twelve cannon were delivered from Carron and when work was completed the two towns were compensated for their expenditure by the Government.[47]

At the other end of the merchant's voyage—the islands of the Caribbean—problems were just as likely to exist. The nature of the inter-island sea routes was such that the enemy privateer was invulnerable to control by the Royal Navy. Line-of-battle ships were almost useless for everyday cruising among the numerous islands: privateers could escape into refuges where the more unwieldy men o' war found it impossible to follow.[48] The observations of one Dominican planter must have been fairly typical of the time. He reported that in June, 1777 there were operating near the island several American privateers of thirty-six guns and 'an innumerable number of smaller ones, which', he indicated, 'it is very difficult to get hold of, as our ships upon the station are too large and too dull sailors to come up with them'.[49] In addition, it may be questioned whether the Navy had any real heart for pursuing privateers in this area. Few were large or heavily armed and the capture of one would mean meagre prize money for officers and men in relation to the trouble involved.[50]

Efforts were certainly made to set up local island-to-island convoys on an *ad hoc* basis but the nature of Caribbean commerce proved a decided obstacle to their success.[51] The fact that supercargoes often had specific instructions on the length of stay in a particular port and the need to obtain a full freight speedily because of steeply rising running expenses,[52] tended to erode their effectiveness. One gains the impression that Glasgow merchants, some of them fresh to the trade, especially after 1779, would be at a particular disadvantage.[53] Several were still in the process of making regular contact with the West Indian islands and could not therefore predict a full freight of sugar, tobacco, cotton or rum awaiting them when their ships put into a particular port.[54] This situation could mean 'ships swarming about the seas scuttling imprudently from island to island in pursuit of the last halfpenny of profit',[55] and this in turn rendered them easy prey for the lurking privateer. Once the convoy assembly point was reached—the Jamaica fleet rendezvoused at Bluefields Bay—the merchant ship was comparatively secure. There were, however, exceptions to this general rule. The perennial storms of the Caribbean could scatter a convoyed fleet, inadequate liaison between escorting captain and merchant skipper might have unfortunate results and, after 1778, anticipation of fleet engagements between the French and Royal Navies could mean that merchantmen were stripped of their escort.[56]

The perils of wartime commerce were represented in the merchant's accounting by the expense of insurance premiums. During the war these rose rapidly but for most sectors of commerce the ensuing costs were probably bearable. After all increases in premiums must be set against the inflated prices of imported commodities which often (but not always) compensated the merchant for his outlay. The defeats on the North American mainland, the entry of more powerful enemies into the fray after 1778 and persistent shipping losses all gave a boost to premiums as the war progressed. For instance, rates for voyages from the Clyde to the West Indies shot up from 13 guineas per cent in June, 1777 to 25 guineas per cent the following year. On less dangerous routes, such as New York–Clyde, the figure was 20 per cent.[57] Yet, since half the sum was always returnable if merchantmen travelled with convoy, even these rates were not prohibitive.

Indeed it was probably not so much high premium rates as the operation of the insurance system itself which caused difficulties for ship-owners. Rumour of heavy losses might discourage underwriters from guaranteeing vessels and cargoes. In the summer of 1777 it was reported that most of the Glasgow underwriters had 'given up the trade' and that it was 'difficult to get a large sum done even at London'.[58] Almost certainly this extreme reaction was a temporary response to the very heavy series of losses in that period. However, certain areas were always unattractive to underwriters. The inter-island trade in the Caribbean was one of these. Insurers were 'very shy of West India risks' and in 1778 they refused to underwrite craft plying between St. Kitts and St. Croix.[59] Persons with surplus funds were perhaps more likely in the latter stages of war to invest in government stock, a more secure method of obtaining returns. Bankruptcies among insurers posed a further problem. In 1778-9 these were extensive in London to whose underwriters Glasgow merchants were increasingly turning for insurance cover. As a result, one Glasgow house, Alexander Houston and Co., recovered nothing from the loss of two of their ships.[60]

Moreover, the underwriting system, though doubtless satisfactory in general, did not always guarantee speedy compensation. The complex nature of many policies could lead to endless legal debate whether a ship-owner was entitled to the insured sum or whether he had in some way failed to conform to regulations.[61] In war conditions underwriters were entitled to demand that shipowners arm their ships satisfactorily and engage an adequate crew. All this raised costs. Henry Clarke, Robert Dunmore and Co.'s London correspondent tried to arrange a policy for the *Janet Laurie* to sail 'in company with a number of arm'd West India men . . .'. But he later reported:

> It was with much difficulty I effected this as our underwriters are very shy of West India risques unless really intended to go with convoy or of considerable force; besides the number of men is also as material as the guns.[62]

The considerable difference in the cost of premiums with and without convoy ensured that most vessels sailed under escort. However, despite its obvious advantages the system had many drawbacks. It was a necessary evil. Delay was in the logic of any convoy. The speed was that of the slowest vessel in the fleet and days were sometimes spent awaiting latecomers and the arrival of the naval escort.[63] The system imposed on British commodity markets recurrent cycles of shortages and gluts with their accompanying price fluctuations. In other words, it was yet another element encouraging volatility in wartime trade.[64]

Given the limitations and problems associated with the convoy system merchants were understandably anxious to circumvent it. One alternative was to fit out a fast armed vessel to sail unescorted. *Theoretically* such 'running ships' had considerable attractions: they were at once able to reach market earlier than convoyed merchantmen and possibly even gain from the inflexibility of the convoy system itself.

Yet investment in such a vessel was hardly less of a gamble than any other form of wartime commerce. The reluctance of underwriters to insure unescorted vessels even if armed and sailing in company with other armed ships has already been noted.[65] This obstacle would inevitably be a disincentive to many who wished to operate 'running ships'. Again, the time of arrival of such a vessel in the Clyde would be a major factor in determining the profitability of a voyage. If the arrival of the convoyed fleet was not far distant, buyers and brokers were likely to refrain from hasty purchases. Thus the Leith Sugar House Co. refused to buy the cargo of the 'running ship' *Hanover* in the summer of 1778, their manager pointing out that the main West India fleet was expected soon and that therefore prices would plummet.[66] In a sense, therefore, this type of merchantman was just as much at the mercy of the wartime commodity cycle, though in a less direct fashion, as the ordinary vessel sailing with convoy. In addition, the expenses of a 'running ship' were formidable. It demanded a higher complement than the normal trading vessel if it was to be turned into a reasonably effective fighting ship—this too when, after the early surplus of 1776-7, war was putting up demand for both experienced and inexperienced shipping labour and also creating considerable distortion in the market for such labour.[67] A more sophisticated armament was necessary at a time when iron prices were also moving upwards. The result of these rising costs was that such vessels had to obtain a good freight if adequate remuneration was to be had by the owners. Alexander Houston and Co. owners of the 'running ship' *Britannia* described:

> the very heavy expenses we have been at outfitting the ship and that without the greatest dispatch, frugality and care together with a full freight home, we must sink money by her.[68]

Even if ships were armed and speedy, merchants often advised their captains to sail with convoy so great was the saving in premium.[69] These instructions were particularly common on the return voyage from the Caribbean or North America when holds were bulging with colonial produce.[70] Indeed, the conclusion must be that even if armed, 'running it' was very much a last resort, to be reserved for particular supply and demand situations. If on rendezvous at the convoy assembly point, it was found that the fleet had already sailed, then skippers of 'running ships' were usually ordered to proceed without escort.[71] Even then it was preferable to sail in the company of other armed ships. One Glasgow captain found himself waiting at Cork with no prospect of a convoy; with his colleagues he formed 'a small fleet of five sail' to cross the ocean. All were equally armed with ten–twelve cannon apiece.[72] Almost certainly the 'running ship', sailing alone without escort or company, was not as common a sight as one might at first suppose from a recognition of its ostensible advantages.

The most important single element in the operating expenses of the shipowner was labour costs and all the evidence suggests that they rose substantially throughout the period of hostilities. The basic problem during most eighteenth century wars was scarcity of seamen caused by impressment by the Royal Navy from the merchant service. Indeed by the time of the American War, the Senior Service could only function at full strength by 'recruiting' more than eighty per cent of all British merchant seamen.[73] In the light of this statistic it is indeed very possible that the press gang rather than the enemy privateer posed the biggest single threat to the merchant's business. If government had not relaxed the clauses of the Navigation Acts—by allowing merchantmen to carry foreign seamen to the extent of three-quarters of their complement—little overseas trade would have been conducted from British ports.[74]

Initially the press was not very active in Scottish waters and shipowners had little difficulty in attracting labour of sufficient quality and quantity; 'the stop to the American trade', it was stated in the summer of 1777 had left 'half the seamen idle'.[75] In the spring of 1778, however, with mobilisation of the Navy in anticipation of war with France, the first inroads into the Clyde's supply of seamen took place. A Greenock merchant noted in March how 'they were almost all press'd below—not a vessel can be got out for want of hands'.[76] The consequent scarcity of labour pushed up wages and in the following year Alexander Houston and Co. complained that labour expenses 'attending all our ships' were so 'monstrous' that 'unless they get great dispatch and much higher freights than last year we must sink a great deal of money by them'.[77] The entry of Holland into the war in 1780 and the maritime nature of much of the fighting exacerbated the problem and Houstons loudly lamented the 'costs of navigation' which threatened to drive them to bankruptcy.[78]

Such statements must be accepted with a good deal of caution. Exaggerated pessimism is the hallmark of most mercantile correspondence at this time. Nevertheless, such objective evidence as does exist confirms the impression of considerable wage inflation in the shipping industry. Although no precise or continuous rates are available for the colonial trades, wages in the Clyde herring fishery, for instance, quadrupled between 1775 and 1783.[79] One merchant house also reckoned that its total outlay on labour was likely to be substantially greater than in peacetime because the quality of seamen deteriorated (the most experienced having been pressed) and so an overall increase in numbers was necessary to compensate for this.[80]

THE DIFFICULTIES OF TRADE DURING THE AMERICAN WAR 147

The war in addition tended to create an artificial scarcity of seamen. In order to escape the press they often lived in areas while ashore where not only the regulating officer but also the shipowner found difficulty in gaining access. The experience of one firm's foray into Ayrshire in search of labour is worth quoting in full to illustrate this. Two representatives of Robert Dunmore and Co. were scouring the county for seamen in September, 1778. From their base in Largs, they wrote that their journey to Irvine on the 21st of the month had proved 'a very troublesome and unsuccessful expedition'. Only five men had agreed to accept their terms and only two of these had been formally engaged although the ship which they were to crew was already clear to sail. The following week brought little change in their luck. One of the men already hired at Irvine sent back his advance pay, having obtained promise of higher earnings for his services elsewhere. Captain McCauslan went to Irvine, Saltcoats and Ayr but 'could not get one man' and his colleague, Thomas Crawford complained:

Is it not very surprising that in Beith, Irvine and Saltcoats, where there are so many sailors, there should be such difficulty in getting so few as we want.[81]

During the American War the Atlantic trades, being largely carried on by convoyed vessels were so geared to time schedules that impressment and fear of the press, by interfering with a ship's timetable, could easily render a voyage unprofitable. Even delaying a ship in order to obtain a full complement could be self-defeating as those numbers of the crew already hired might desert for fear of a visit from the press.[82] Because of this merchants took as much care as possible to ensure immunity for their seamen. It was possible to acquire, with sufficient money and influence, 'protections' from the Admiralty which 'guaranteed' a shipowner from the press. Yet their effectiveness often depended on the whim of the individual naval commander and, in the Caribbean and North America, the distance from the control of central authority encouraged infringement. Even in the Clyde, protections were not absolute guarantees of immunity, especially in such periods of rapid mobilisation as 1778.[83]

Some Glasgow merchants therefore ran their own system of unofficial exemption. Ships returning from the West Indies or America were directed to anchor off Fairlie on the Ayrshire coast and most of the crew (except the captain, first mate, ship's carpenter, apprentices and boys who were all exempt from pressing) boarded longboats and headed for the mainland. Once there they congregated in the Beith area; an understanding apparently existed between the farmers and smugglers of Ayrshire and the captains of incoming vessels which allowed for warnings to be given when the press-gang was in the vicinity.[80] Even this ingenious and enterprising technique was by no means foolproof. The navy was quite ruthless in pursuit of its ends! On one occasion an escort vessel pressed the merchantmen it had convoyed before they entered the Firth of Clyde and there were several other instances of pressing off Ireland on the outward voyage.

REFERENCES

1. Quoted in McCure, *op. cit.*, 313.
2. Price, *loc. cit.*, 305.
3. Gomer Williams, *History of the Liverpool Privateers and Letters of Marque with an Account of the Liverpool Slave Trade* (1897, new imp., London, 1966), 181.
4. *Edinburgh Evening Courant*, 21 July, 1777.
5. Williams, *op. cit.*, 181.
6. *Ibid.*
7. See above, p. 144.
8. Ireland gradually replaced the American colonies as the source for West India provisions during the war. Restrictions on trade with the West Indies from Ireland were removed in 1778 by 18 Geo. III c.55, continued from 1780 by 20 Geo. III c.10; Glasgow merchants left agents in Cork who maintained close links with provision contractors, SRO, GD 247/59/Q/2, W. Crawford to R. Dunmore and Co., 18 August, 1778. Cork was also the major depot for shipment of army provisions; Syrett, *op. cit.*, 44.
9. *Glasgow Mercury*, 22 September, 1778.
10. M. K. Barritt, 'The Navy and the Clyde in the American War, 1777-83', *The Mariner's Mirror*, 55 (1969), 33.
11. Sir Herbert Richmond, 'The Navy', in A. S. Turberville (ed.), *Johnson's England, An Account of the Life and Manners of his Age* (Oxford, 1933), I, 40-1.
12. *Ibid.*
13. For these petitions see GCA, Council Minute Book, C1/1/36/97, 9 Sept., 1778; *Edinburgh Evening Courant*, 5, 26 July, 1777; *Caldonian Mercury*, 2 July, 1777.
14. *Edinburgh Evening Courant*, 2 July, 1777.
15. *Ibid.*, 26 July, 1777, (Copy), Phillip Stephens, Secretary to the Admiralty to the Magistrates and Council of Glasgow.
16. *Glasgow Mercury*, 12 March, 1778.
17. For naval strategy during this period see Sir W. L. Clowes, *The Royal Navy from the Earliest Times to the Present* (London, 1897-1903), III, 21 ff.
18. Hugh Wylie and John Campbell to Phillip Stephens, 15 December, 1780; Wylie to John Crawford, 1 December, 1780 in *SHR* XVI (1919).
19. *Glasgow Mercury*, 22 September, 1778.
20. GCA, Town Council Minute Book, C1/1/36/444.
21. H. Wylie to John Crawford, 11 April, 1781 in *SHR* XVI (1919).
22. *Edinburgh Evening Courant*, 23 November, 1776.
23. *Ibid.*, 5 July, 1777; *Caledonian Mercury*, 30 June, 1777.
24. NLS, MS 8793, Alex. Houston and Co. to Rev. Hugh Knox, 14 October, 1776; to Captain Daniel Graham, 4 January, 1777.
25. *Edinburgh Evening Courant*, 12 July, 19 July, 1777; *Scots Magazine*, June, 1777.
26. *Ibid.*, July 19, 1777; *Caledonian Mercury*, 30 June, 1777.
27. See below.
28. H. Wylie to Captain B. Christian, 18 April in *SHR* XVI (1919).
29. *Glasgow Mercury*, 6 July, 1780. For other captures see *ibid.*, 10 August, 1780; 28 June, 1781.
30. Knox, *op. cit.*, II, 533-4.
31. See *Glasgow Mercury*, 1775-August, 1777, *passim*.
32. Quoted in R. H. Campbell, *Carron Company* (Edinburgh, 1961), 191.
33. SRO, GD 247/59/P/2, Advertisement on carronades published by Robert Dunmore and Co.
34. *Glasgow Mercury*, 22 September, 1778.
35. *Ibid.*, 21 October, 1779.
36. Campbell, *Carron Company*, 191.
37. *Scots Magazine*, June, 1777.
38. *Edinburgh Evening Courant*, 16 July, 1777.
39. *Scots Magazine*, June, 1777.
40. Quoted in Barritt, *loc. cit.*, 34.
41. *Scots Magazine*, June, 1777.

42. *Ibid.*
43. *Edinburgh Evening Courant*, 26 July, 1777.
44. *Ibid.*
45. GCA, Council Minute Book, C1/1/36/97, 9 September, 1778.
46. *Ibid.*; George Williamson, *Old Greenock* (Paisley, 1880), 168.
47. GCA, Council Minute Book, C1/1/37/463.
48. Richard Pares, *War and Trade in the West Indies, 1739–63*, (Oxford, 1936), 293.
49. *Edinburgh Evening Courant*, 9 August, 1777; Extract of a letter from a gentleman at Dominica to his friend at Edinburgh, dated 11 June, 1777.
50. *Ibid.*, 20 August, 1777, Extract of a letter from St. Vincents, 10 June, 1777.
51. NLS, MS 8793, A. H. and Co. to Messrs. Turner and Paul, 6 March, 1777.
52. See above, pp. 146–7.
53. See above, pp. 130–1.
54. *Ibid.*
55. Pares, *op. cit.*, 258.
56. For examples of the above see SRO, GD 247/140, Petition of Robert Dunmore and Co. to Lords and Council of Session, 17 Jan., 1786; NLS, Charles Steuart Letterbooks, MS 5031, Thomas Riddoach to Charles Steuart, 20 July, 1779; SRO, GD 247/59/Q/2, W. Cunninghame to R. Dunmore and Co., 2 July, 1778.
57. NLS, MSS 8793–4; 8759; SRO, GD 241/1, Insurance Notes, 1779; LC, James Dunlop Family Papers, James Ritchie and Co. to James Dunlop, 2 July, 1779.
58. NLS, MS 8793, Alex. Houston and Co. to Messrs. Houston and Paterson, 5 June, 1777.
59. SRO, GD 247/59/Q/2, Henry Clarke to R. Dunmore and Co., 17 February, 1778.
60. NLS, MS 8759, Home Letterbook H of A. Houston and Co., A. Houston and Co. to W. Crichton, 12 June, 1778.
61. For one example of the kind of tortuous wrangle which could ensue see SRO, GD 247/140, Petition of R. Dunmore and Co. . . . 17 January, 1780
62. SRO, GD 247/59/Q/2, Henry Clarke to Robert Dunmore and Co., 17 February, 1778.
63. For an instance of one captain's frustration at the convoy system see SRO, GD 247/58/P/2, Extracts from the Journal of Capt. Wright of the ship *Clyde* on her voyage from Jamaica to the Clyde in 1778 and 1779.
64. NLS, MS 8793–4, Foreign Letterbooks of Alex. Houston and Co., *passim*; SRO, GD 247/59/Q/2, Cunninghame-Dunmore correspondence.
65. See above.
66. SRO, GD 247/59/Q/2, Charles Cowan to R. Dunmore and Co., 9 July, 1778.
67. GCA, Thomas Houston Law Papers, A, Grieve to Messrs. T. Houston and Co., 14 March, 1779.
68. NLS, MS 8793, A. Houston and Co. to David Scott, 12 February, 1777.
69. For examples of such instructions see NLS, MS 8794, Alex Houston and Co. to Messrs. Turner and Paul, 1 Dec., 1778; to Capt. David Scott, 24 February, 1779; to Capt. Daniel Graham, 7 December, 1778; to Capt. Daniel Graham, 28 January, 1778.
70. *Ibid.*
71. *Ibid.*, A. Houston and Co. to Capt. John McGregor, 17 February, 1777; to Captains David Scott, Buchanan, Barbour and Park, 10 February, 1780.
72. *Caledonian Mercury*, 27 November, 1776.
73. Davis, *op. cit.*, 323.
74. 16 Geo. III, c.20 (1776); renewed 18 Geo. III, c.6 (1778); 9 Geo. III, c.14 (1779) and 21 Geo. III, c.11 (1781).
75. *Caledonian Mercury*, 13 July, 1777.
76. NLS, MS 5030, John Maclean to Charles Stewart, 31 March, 1778
77. NLS, MS 8794, A. Houston and Co. to Robert Houston, 20 April, 1779.
78. *Ibid.*, to Messrs. Houston and Paterson, 15 January, 1781.
79. Macpherson, *op. cit.*, III, 634.
80. GCA, Thomas Houston Law Papers, ? to Thomas Houston and Co. 14 October, 1779.
81. SRO, GD 247/59/Q/2, Thomas Crawford to Robert Dunmore and Co., 22, 26 September, 1778.
82. For an example of this see NLS, MS 8794, A. Houston and Co. to Messrs. Akers and Houston, 14 October, 1779.

83. Dora M. Clark, 'The Impressment of Seamen in the American Colonies', in *Essays in Colonial History presented to Charles Maclean Andrews* (Newhaven, 1931), 203.
84. Senex, *op. cit.*, II, 139.
85. 'Chips from an Old Glasgow Ship's Log, 1777–1823', *Old Glasgow Club Transactions* III, 102; *Edinburgh Evening Courant*, 9 August, 1777; NLS, MS 8795, Home Letterbook H of A. Houston and Co., to Mr. Milliken, 19 September, 1778; to William McDowall, 1 October, 1778.

Part IV
THE AFTERMATH OF THE AMERICAN WAR

10

The Problem of Glasgow's Pre-War Debts

AS peace between America, Britain and France became imminent in 1782, Glasgow houses trading to the former colonies turned their attention to a matter of central concern to their interests. The re-establishment of 'normal' relations with Virginia and Maryland inevitably raised the issue of the large debts owed Scottish merchants by planters in these states which had remained uncollected when hostilities broke out in 1775. The legal situation which confronted Glasgow was the declaration of the Virginia Council in 1778 suspending debt actions in which British subjects appeared as plaintiffs until further direction by the legislature. This obstacle was strengthened by a series of political and economic problems in the areas concerned which made debt-collection extremely difficult.[1] However, despite these, merchants quickly mounted a planned campaign to recover the sums owed them. On the one hand, political pressure was exerted on the British Government by Glasgow Town Council, Chamber of Commerce and the Committee of American merchants to ensure that the city's financial interests were protected during negotiations leading to a definitive peace treaty. At the same time factors and agents were dispatched to North America with instructions to begin the actual business of debt collection when hostilities ceased.

With rumours of an early peace in the air in early 1782, Patrick Colquohoun, the city's provost, wrote to John Crawford, Member of Parliament for the Glasgow burghs, urging him to ensure that at any peace conference, British representatives would not neglect 'securing the very large sums that are owing them (i.e. Glasgow merchants) by the inhabitants of Virginia, Maryland and Carolina'. As spokesman for these interests, Colquohoun hoped that as their debts were 'immense', no treaty would be signed in haste before they had an opportunity to state their case to the contracting parties. Crawford was to ascertain when negotiations were to begin and at what stage a delegation from Glasgow might be sent to confer with relevant government representatives.[2] Crawford, on the other hand, was sceptical about the possibilities of peace, '. . . it is a million to one that the present minister will not be the person we will trust with America'. He thus thought it improper to speak to government about Glasgow's debts at that stage but assured Colquohoun that they would be 'a principal object of the treaty'.[3]

Notwithstanding Crawford's sanguinity, however, the city's merchants were determined to declare their concern to the responsible minister and a month after Colquohoun's letter, sixty-nine firms in Glasgow signed a memorial and conveyed it to Lord Shelbourne. After reiterating the huge debts owed them (which they calculated as around £1,300,000) they pointed out how none of this had been recoverable since 1775 and so they welcomed the prospect of peace. Shelbourne was asked to receive a deputation from the city who would give him further details on their problems.[4]

Despite these early initiatives, preliminary peace negotiations revealed that the claims of Glasgow and other British creditors were likely to be ignored amid the exigencies of international diplomacy. As a result of a cabinet meeting in August, 1782, the British plenipotentiary in Paris, Richard Oswald (himself a member of an important Glasgow merchant family) was instructed that the British government was prepared to waive the rights of merchants whose debts had been incurred before 1775. The same directive agreed to renounce the vast area between the Ohio and the Great Lakes and the claims for compensation of refugees and loyalists.[5]

Luckily, however, it was this trio of concessions which prevented the question of Glasgow's debts being summarily rejected at the conference table. A Treaty which perpetuated American competition with a truncated empire, surrendered huge areas of territory and made no provision for the much-favoured loyalists was likely to have been politically unacceptable. It would have encouraged a combination of hostile interests which, in the prevailing mood of political uncertainty, would have broken both Treaty and Government. Thus, as negotiations dragged on it soon became accepted that without some recognition of the validity of the debts and the necessity for compensating those who had lost property, the clamour in Shelbourne's own words 'will scarcely be able to be withstood'.[6] Thus in November, 1782 the British Cabinet reversed their policy and decided that any treaty must include an explicit declaration that British merchants be enabled to institute proceedings for the recovery of *bona fide* debts due them before 1775. As a result, that declaration was incorporated as Article IV of the Preliminary Articles of Peace signed between Britain and the United States. Yet, as Glasgow traders were to discover in subsequent years, this was very much a paper victory. There were still massive, and possibly insurmountable obstacles confronting their debt collectors during this initial phase of peace.

In the latter months of 1782 most Glasgow firms with American connections were beginning to actively plan their strategy to liquidate the sums owed them by tobacco planters. There was an atmosphere of urgency about the operation; 1782 had seen a fall in tobacco prices and further pressure on credit. Several companies therefore looked to debt collection as the means to solvency.[7] Perhaps because of this some of them were rather too optimistic concerning the possibilities of success. James Ritchie and Co. thought that:

> ... two years will put them [the planters] in such a train that anybody may collect what remains—for the people in general must be in better circumstances now than they were eight years ago by the increase of their slaves and by the advanced price of these and land...[8]

Ritchies dispatched four of their factors to Virginia to re-open stores in the areas in which they formerly traded:

> ... our chief motive in opening stores... is to facilitate the payment of our old debt by having it in our power to supply our old Debtors with necessaries.[9]

Acknowledging the difficulty which some would have in making immediate repayment and aware of the hostility generated by the recent war, planters were to be allowed to liquidate their advances over a period of four years.[10] Other firms followed similar strategies. In December, 1782, four of the most reliable employees of Speirs, French and Co. in the West Indies were ordered to the former colonies and directed 'to follow a plan for the collections of their large subjects there'.[11] Another major enterprise, John Glassford and Co., was said to have been 'employed assiduously in endeavouring to recover their property... and this by means of an agent sent out'.[12]

Doubtless most companies made equally hopeful forays at this time into Virginia and Maryland. Yet, for the following few years, the efforts of even the most energetic debt-collectors were unsuccessful. Some were violently rejected by the planters; John Riddell of Glassfords was driven from Virginia by an infuriated mob when he tried to carry out his firm's instructions.[13] William Cunninghame's agent left just as hastily.[14] The wounds left by British depredations in the state during the war were not easily healed. Alexander Hamilton, a representative of one of the largest Scottish houses, told his Glasgow office in 1784 that 'collecting debts in this world was at all times a very fatiguing as well as a disagreeable business, it is now greatly more so'. Four years later Hamilton had nothing better to report:

> The debts come in very slow and grow dayly worse... the Sums thus lost are very considerable and unless something is done... there is no knowing to what extent [more debts] will arise.[15]

Alexander McCall, agent for George Kippen and Co. informed Thomas Jefferson as late as August, 1788 that only three out of the large number of 'prominent Virginians' indebted to his firm had declared their willingness to make payment. Similar complaints came from other Glasgow companies.[16]

It was quite clear that the relatively weak American Confederation was powerless to restrain individual states from passing legislation which conflicted with decisions made by the central government in the international sphere. Before the adoption of the Constitution in 1787, there was no Supreme Court to declare unconstitutional such particularist actions. It followed therefore that Glasgow creditors were initially thrown upon the tender mercies of the Virginia, Maryland and Carolina State legislatures and the directives of the local Assemblies. These bodies quickly showed the tenor of their attitude. The May Assembly of Virginia in response to popular clamour passed a law which provided that no debt due a British merchant should be recoverable in any court in the state. In South Carolina, by an ordinance accepted by the State Assembly in March, 1784, no suit could be instituted for a debt incurred previous to 1782 until 1 January, 1786.[17] The Congress of the United States ratified the Treaty of Paris in early 1784 and, in compliance with the obligations of Article IV of that document, each state was recommended to repeal all existing laws against loyalists and recovery of debt. Virginia and Maryland refused to do so.

Behind this official recalcitrance lay serious economic and political problems. Even if the state legislatures had been more acquiescent it is doubtful whether debt recovery would have taken place any more rapidly. The United States in general and the former tobacco colonies in particular suffered from an acute balance of payments problem after 1783 and the economy was incapable of producing the liquid funds necessary for repayment purposes. The sharp increase in the importations of British goods after the war coupled with the fall in tobacco prices from 1785 immensely exacerbated existing difficulties caused by war expenditure and trading malaise during hostilities. Long before peace was signed the scale of depreciation of paper money in Virginia in 1780 had reached the phenomenal level of 1000 per cent. The net result was that specie flowed out of the country leaving unpaid balances behind. Furthermore, as will be shown in the next chapter, British merchants once again began to take control of the market and were thus in a position to force down tobacco prices as the balance of trade now worked in their favour. Yet, ironically, sagging tobacco prices inevitably postponed Virginians' ability to pay pre-war debts.[18]

The depreciation in paper money during the war had been so spectacular that in July, 1781 it ceased to be legal tender. Holders of this paper were allowed to redeem it the following year for certificates valued at 1000 to 1 and carrying 6 per cent interest. This action was accompanied by heavy taxation as the state attempted to repay its war debt.[19] This was to add to the combination of factors slowly depriving the country of almost all its circulating medium. Thomas Jefferson put the matter bluntly, '. . . in truth, the Virginia planters were bankrupt'.[20] In a letter to a Glasgow merchant, Alexander McCall, he argued, there:

> are two circumstances of difficulty in the paiment of these debts. To speak of the particular state with which you and I are best acquainted, we know that it's debt is ten times the amount of it's circulating cash. To pay that debt at once then is a physical impossibility. Time is requisite. Were all the creditors to rush to judgement together, a mass of two millions of property would be brought to market where there is but the tenth of that sum of money in circulation to purchase it. Both debtor and creditor would be ruined, as debts would be thus rendered desperate which are in themselves good.[21]

Moreover, Glasgow houses increasingly found themselves in a dilemma over the debt question. If trade was to be re-established on the old basis, planters would be likely to expect the customary liberal grants of credit which had almost been their prerogative in pre-war days. Yet it could be argued that to fulfil planter desires in this respect would be to add yet another debt burden to the existing one and possibly to further postpone the date of repayment. Virginia debtors also had a 'moral' basis for their opposition. Many were outraged at British plunder of the state and were especially angered by the refusal of the Army commander, Sir Guy Carleton, to return slaves carried away during the war. This violation of the preliminary peace treaty made it easy to argue that, if the British were not willing to comply with its provisions, neither would the Virginians.[22] Planters could also contend that they had already transferred at least part of their liability to the state. A Virginia State Loan Office had been established in 1777 to borrow war finance. The sequestration law of the same year provided that debts due British subjects could be paid into this office and the debtor would be given a certificate of payment discharging him from all future obligations to the creditor.[23] Many such debts were inevitably liquidated in paper money which was depreciating rapidly. On the one hand, therefore, debtors argued that they had honoured their obligations; yet on the other, the sum actually remaining in the Loan Office in 1783 was a derisory £12,035 sterling (£273,554..13..7 Virginia currency) and was hardly sufficient to pay even the interest on bonded debts.[24]

As a result of all these short and long term problems, Glasgow merchants had to adopt a more accommodating and flexible policy towards debt recovery. In October, 1784, 54 tobacco merchants sent a communication to the Virginia Assembly stating their willingness to accept payment for debts due them from Virginia in annual instalments.[25] A bill providing for the payment of debts in seven annual instalments, without interest from 1775-83, did pass the House but failed to be accepted by the Senate.[26] Pressure was thus once again directed towards the U.K. and U.S.A. Governments. Merchants of Glasgow, Liverpool, Bristol, Whitehaven and London interested in the pre-1775 American trades joined forces in 1785 to plead their case before ministers.[27] At the same time in May, 1785, a leading American, John Adams, arrived in London and the committee appointed by the various trading interests secured a meeting with him. They met Adams at his Piccadilly hotel on 9 June.[28] At this and at subsequent meetings the justice of the contention that the planters were not able to make immediate payment was admitted. It was therefore agreed that debts should be paid in five annual instalments, with the merchants eventually and reluctantly renouncing their claim to interest during the war.[29]

The U.K. Government was also able to hold out some hope. Lord Carmarthen, Secretary of State, expressed his desire 'to procure every possible relief for so respectable body of men whose case certainly deserved and would meet with every possible attention'.[30] Henry Dundas and Viscount Sydney gave equally warm promises of support and it was suggested that a British Minister would now go to North America to see what could be done.[31] The Committee considered that the 1785 negotiations 'promise better success than at any period since the war'.[32] Certainly the legislative prospect for debt recovery did brighten; New York agreed to pay debts in yearly instalments,[33] and even Virginia in October, 1787 nearly agreed to repeal all Acts which had up to that point prohibited the payment of British debts.[34] However, there was an important qualification to this decision: the implementation of the Act was to be suspended until:

> The Governor, with the advice of Council shall by his Proclamation notify to this state that Great Britain hath delivered up to the United States the posts therein occupied by British troops ... and is also taking measures for the further fulfilment of the said treaty by delivering up the negroes belonging to the citizens of this state taken away contrary to this seventh article of the treaty.[35]

Knowledgeable Virginians realised that this simply meant a continuation of the *status quo*. Relations between the U.S.A. and the U.K., particularly over the Americans' exclusion from the West Indies carrying trade, were not cordial at this juncture and progress towards agreement over military posts and negroes was unlikely.[36]

The result was that by the end of 1787, matters were at a stand. The Glasgow Chamber of Commerce pronounced regretfully that 'hitherto any negotiations upon that subject had been ineffectual'.[37] The only noteworthy development had been that Government was appointing Consuls to each of the states to act as on-the-spot representatives.[38] The U.K.Government was prepared to make compensation for fixed property lost by loyalists; Commissioners sat in London to hear claims and an office was opened to issue certificates of reimbursement.[39] Yet Government could not afford to tackle the debt problem in this fashion because of the size of the sum involved and to the petitions of Glasgow the Lord Advocate could only reply that 'there was little probability of early accommodation about American debts through the medium of Government'.[40]

In the event, progress came through constitutional change and economic advance in the United States which were the only practical bases for debt recovery. The establishment of a new national government was followed by the creation of a federal court system which proved more amenable to the point of view of British creditors. Yet although the United States Court, Virginia District began operation in 1790 and several Glasgow houses immediately filed suits in it, problems remained. The federal court had jurisdiction only over debts of more than $500 and most of the individual sums owed Glasgow merchants were smaller than this. Inevitably therefore most creditors had to plead their cause before district and county courts still governed by the law of 1782 preventing the recovery of British debts. Nevertheless, as recent research on the federal court records has shown,

Scottish creditors were increasingly successful in debt actions brought before it. In 1793, out of sixty-eight cases, fifty-two were decided in favour of the plaintiff; in 1794, 65 out of 91; in 1795, 98 out of 118. In that year too advertisements for sale of land because of court decisions favourable to merchants began to appear in Virginia newspapers.[41]

Two developments in 1795 and 1796 were also of immense importance. In the former year 'Jay's Treaty' between the United States and Great Britain settled the controversial slave issue to the satisfaction of both parties. In 1796 too the U.S. Supreme Court annulled all state legislation which was contrary to the Treaty of Paris. In effect, this dismantled all the legal defences Virginians had erected to avoid payment. The district and county courts were now the scene of most activity and, although the representative of one Glasgow firm alleged that they were filled with judges who had 'violent prejudices against the payment of British Debts', creditors, by 1797, were certainly winning most of the cases they fought in them.[42] Furthermore, merchants who were owed pre-war debts were to have an additional recourse. A Convention of 1802 provided that the United States should pay Britain £600,000 in compensation to be distributed among those who still had outstanding claims.[43] The British Government, by authority of Act of Parliament, appointed a Board of Commissioners to confer in London on these and to send agents to the colonies to investigate their validity. After nine years labour this body finally reported in 1811. By that date it had awarded £415,921 to those creditors who had proven their cases satisfactorily. In Glasgow the distribution was greeted with predictable complaints about the smallness of the sum and the 'peculiar hardships' of the claimants.[44] Yet, on balance, it can be reasonably assumed that almost thirty years after the signing of the peace treaty, a large part of Glasgow's pre-war debts had been recovered by a combination of private endeavour in the courts and diplomatic effort in international negotiations.[45]

REFERENCES

1. See above, pp. 156–7.
2. ML, Chamber of Commerce MSS, Bundle 4, Patrick Colquohoun to John Crawford, 11 March, 1782.
3. *Ibid.*, John Crawford to P. Colquohoun, 18 March, 1782.
4. BM, Shelbourne MSS, v.87/8, A Memorial of the Merchants of Glasgow interested in the North America trade previous to the year 1776, dated 30 May, 1782.
5. Vincent T. Harlow, *The Founding of the Second British Empire* (London, 1952), I, 274–5.
6. *Ibid.*, 290.
7. LC, James Dunlop Family Papers, Henry Ritchie to James Dunlop, 28 August, 1783.

8. *Ibid.*, 28 November, 1783.
9. *Ibid.*, Box 6, Instructions from Messrs. James Ritchie and Co. of Glasgow to Messrs. James Anderson etc. 31 March, 1784.
10. *Ibid.*
11. GCA, Speirs Papers, TD 131/13, Sederunt Book of the Trustees of Alexander Speirs of Elderslie, 8–9.
12. PRO, AO 12/9/35.
13. *Ibid.*
14. PRO, AO 12/56/286.
15. Alexander Hamilton to James Brown and Co., 10 March, 1784; 5 April, 1788 quoted in M. L. Rich, 'Speculations on the Significance of Debt, Virginia, 1781–89', *Virginia Magazine of History and Biography*, 76 (1968).
16. P. F. Ford (ed.), *The Writings of Thomas Jefferson* (New York, 1892–99), V. 151. See also GCA, Speirs Papers, TD 131/9, Archibald Speirs to Mr. Robert, 15 February, 1787; LC, James Dunlop Family Papers, Thomas Montgomerie to James Dunlop, 14 July, 1784. Any success in this sphere was apparently worthy of wide publicity. The *Scots Magazine* thought fit to bring it to national attention in 1787 that one merchant had actually received a remittance from Virginia for a debt contracted before the war. *Scots Magazine*, XLIX (1787), 361.
17. *Statutes of Virginia*, X, 471; *Glasgow Mercury*, 14 September, 1786.
18. Rich, *loc. cit.*, 301–317.
19. Emory G. Evans, 'Private Indebtedness and the Revolution in Virginia, 1776–1796', *William and Mary Quarterly*, Third Ser., XXVIII (1971), 362.
20. *Writings of Jefferson*, VI, 148.
21. T. Jefferson to Alexander McCall, 19 April, 1786 in *Jefferson Papers*, IX, 388–90.
22. Evans, *loc. cit.*, 360–61.
23. *Edinburgh Evening Courant*, 13 June, 1778.
24. Bemis, *op. cit.*, 80; *Glasgow Mercury*, 14 September, 1786.
25. *Glasgow Mercury*, 23 March, 1786.
26. *Glasgow Mercury*, 22 July, 1784; 14 September, 1796.
27. UOS, Minutes of Glasgow Chamber of Commerce (Xerox copies), 1783–9, I, 144.
28. *Ibid.*,
29. *Ibid.*, 145; Harrell, *op. cit.*, 149–50.
30. UOS, Chamber of Commerce Minutes, I, 144–5.
31. *Ibid.*
32. *Ibid.*
33. *Glasgow Mercury*, 6 June, 1787.
34. SRO, GD 247/140, Acts passed at a General Assembly of the Commonwealth of Virginia, 15 October, 1787.
35. *Ibid.*
36. See Bemis, *op. cit.*, *passim*.
37. UOS, Chamber of Commerce Minutes, I, 258.
38. *Ibid.*
39. PRO, AO 12/56; SL, CSP 369/13, Appendix I–III.
40. ML, Chamber of Commerce MSS, Bundle 16, Lord Advocate to Gilbert Hamilton, 20 April, 1787.
41. Evans, *loc. cit.*, 371–2.
42. *Ibid.*, 373.
43. J. B. Moore, *History and Digest of International Arbitrations to which the United States has been a party*, 270.
44. ML, Bogle MSS, Bundle 59, Gilbert Hamilton to Robert Bogle, 7 March, 1809; GCA, Minute Book of the Merchants House of Glasgow, 30 January, 1812.
45. See, for example, *Glasgow Herald*, 14 June, 21 June, 29 July, 1811, for notice of distribution of funds to creditors of Glasgow firms which had become insolvent during the American War leaving uncollected debts in the colonies.

11

The Renewal of Trade with North America After 1783

THE supremacy of Glasgow and other British ports in the American trades before 1775 seemed to be based on the restrictions imposed by the Navigation Acts. If government policy had not dictated that some 'enumerated' commodities should first be brought to the United Kingdom before later sale, it appeared natural to assume that merchants would have preferred to freight directly to Europe and so avoid additional port, transhipment and

TABLE XXVII
Scottish Tobacco Imports (lbs.), 1770–1800

Year	Amount
1770	38,708,809
1775	45,863,154
1780	5,022,149
1785	9,158,971
1790	10,615,535
1795	2,731,091
1800	4,074,919

Source—PRO, Customs, 14.

customs charges. Certainly after 1783 tobacco imports to the Clyde did not show any substantial recovery.

Figures of ships entering Port Glasgow and Greenock from North America in 1785 and 1791 also indicate that most tobacco en route for Europe bypassed Glasgow. In 1785 the number of vessels from the United States had fallen to less than half that of 1772 (67 compared with 136) and represented some sixteen per cent instead of twenty-eight per cent of the total number of incoming merchantmen. There had been some recovery by 1791 when the number inwards from North America had risen to 84 but this was partly caused by a substantial increase in trade with British Canada rather than with the United States.[1] Although Port Glasgow, the main tobacco shipping point was affected by this fall in the importation of American produce, Greenock was sustained by an expansion of her existing Caribbean and Irish trades, a rise in commerce with Canada and a significant increase in the exportation of the manufactured products of the industrialising areas of west-central Scotland.

In the former colonies the prospect of revived tobacco exportation after 1783 seemed at first equally bleak. During British raids in 1779–81 and Cornwallis's invasion of 1781 many slaves—the labour force of the plantations—had escaped or been taken by the army. A further blow was the burning of tobacco warehouses in a series of campaigns in Virginia. The end result of these depredations was to stoke up anti-British feeling which culminated in the legislation of 1781–3 prohibiting the return of loyalist merchants who had left the state at the beginning of war. Despite this initial phase of difficulty, however, European prices for American tobacco in 1783 were so attractive in relation to pre-war levels that re-settlement of tobacco lands and revival in production soon began.

Four years after peace was signed tobacco again accounted for eighty-four per cent of Virginia's exports and although Maryland's share did decline, this was more than compensated for by vigorous expansion in North and South Carolina. By 1786 total American tobacco exports had reached the levels prevailing before 1775 and remained there until the start of the European wars in 1792–3.[2]

Although, as we have seen, only a minor proportion of these new crops were shipped directly to Scottish ports, Glasgow merchants managed to maintain a substantial financial and organisational role in the American tobacco trade to Europe. Just as importantly, the tobacco lords continued temporarily to dominate the export trade from Scotland to Virginia in manufactured articles. Although only careful statistical research on incomplete sources can tell us exactly how far the Glasgow firms managed to re-establish their pre-eminence, the indications that they did so on a considerable scale are abundant.

In 1785, Patrick Henry, the American patriot, complained to Thomas Jefferson that independence had not successfully broken the power of the British merchants in Virginia:

> We are much disappointed in our Expectations of French and Dutch Traders rivalling the British here. The latter engross the greatest share of our trade, and was it not that the Irish bid up for our produce, the Scotch would soon be on their former Footing. I see no way to place our Commerce in a better State, but discriminating by Taxes between our own and foreign Vessels and goods.[3]

The Glasgow traders four years later confirmed Henry's assessment. In answer to a government enquiry in 1789, they described how the American tobacco trade employed 200–250 ships of all nations. About three-quarters of these were British (not including those British vessels which had taken out American papers). Significantly, however, about two-thirds of the tobacco cargoes carried in British bottoms were transported direct to European markets and so were not documented in U.K. customs records.[4]

The trading routes of Glasgow vessels after 1783 reflect this pattern. While in 1772, more ships entered Greenock and Port Glasgow from North America than left for that region, the reverse was the case in 1785 and 1791. In those later years a number of vessels taking manufactured goods to the plantations brought the tobacco not to the Clyde but to Europe, whence they returned direct to Scotland.[5] Indeed, as Table XXVIII illustrates, the export trade of the Clyde ports to the independent United States continued unabated after the war. While the total number of vessels from

TABLE XXVIII

Ships Inwards and Outwards, North America—Port Glasgow—Greenock, 1772 and 1791

1772	In	Out
Port Glasgow	87	57
Greenock	49	46
TOTAL	136	103
1791		
Port Glasgow	42	39
Greenock	42	56
TOTAL	84	95

Source—Crispin, *loc. cit.*, 133 based on SRO, Customs Accounts, Greenock and Port Glasgow, 1772, 1791.

America fell from 136 to 84 (a drop of 38 per cent) between 1772 and 1779, the number freighting for that region from Port Glasgow and Greenock only diminished from 103 to 95 (a drop of only 11 per cent).

The great Glasgow firms quickly moved back to the Chesapeake when the laws against émigré loyalists were rescinded. In March, 1783 several ships were being advertised as loading in Port Glasgow for Virginia.[6] Contemporaries were optimistic that despite independence the old commercial ties would be renewed. The captain of the first American merchantman to put into the Clyde after the peace reported that 'the people in America were very glad of peace and wished much to have their trade as formerly with Great Britain'.[7] The skipper of the Glasgow-owned *Success* gave the same assurance:

... The trading people (in the United States) speak with certainty of Britain having the principal share of the commerce with America.[8]

One merchant suggested in the spring of 1783 that 'a great many people will go from this (Glasgow) to America this summer'[9] and mercantile correspondence for the following few years abounds with references of the re-establishment of stores in old sites, movement into fresh tobacco areas and renewal of links with planters.

By the middle of 1784, on one estimate, there were about eighty stores in Petersburg and as many in Richmond.[10] In Georgetown there were seventeen or eighteen, mainly run by Scots factors.[11] Throughout Virginia, the major Glasgow companies were once again beginning to control purchasing. In Petersburg it was said that:

> Messrs. Donalds have been grasping all the trade . . . and they as well as some [   ] fallen on a most destructive plan to buy the planters tobo upon credit, to give some interest and the rise.[12]

It was hardly surprising that David Buchanan found 'the Glas. goods continue still to be much liked . . . and Glasgow may yet have a great share of the trade'.[13] In April, 1784, a factor of James Ritchie and Co. described in some astonishment the rapid nature of the development:

> A ship, the *Terry*, has arrived freighted by French, Crawford and Co. Mr. Green has bought a store for James McCoull. Mr. Somervell for David Russell opens in Petersburg. D. Buchanan has £200 worth of goods just arrived in the *Albany*—he has bought a storehouse and retails. Mr. Hart is still here and has hired a store house—expects £10,000 cargo in 3 parcels for wholesale (not retail). Leitch is going to follow up debts of Russell, Corbett and Hay. John and Roger Stewart in Greenock have just sent a ship with £2800 stg. in cargo. Andrew and Geo. Buchanan are concerned with Mr. Leitch and they are owners of the *Albany* . . . These gentlemen seem to drive with spirit.[14]

Both long-established and new organisations based in Glasgow were involved in this revival. The three most famous 'lords' of an earlier generation, Alexander Speirs, John Glassford and William Cunninghame had all disappeared from the scene. Cunninghame seems to have retired from active participation in trade although he remained a sleeping partner in Robert Dunmore and Co.;[15] both Speirs and Glassford had died before peace was signed. Yet the three syndicates formerly headed by these men continued to play a major role in Chesapeake trade after the war. Robert Findlay, Cunninghame's kinsman and protégé, became associated with the Hopkirks and a branch of the Buchanan family to form Findlay, Hopkirks and Co.[16] The Speirs and the Glassford companies continued under the leadership of men long-experienced in the tobacco trade before 1775.[17]

In 1785, these three organisations, together with Colin Dunlop and Sons and a new enterprise, Corbett, Russell and Co., shipped more than ninety per cent of Port Glasgow's tobacco imports.[18] However, these firms and their smaller rivals traded in the main directly to France and Holland. After 1783 the French Farmers General were still dependent on American sources of tobacco. During the early years of peace their buying agency switched from Britain to the United States. Yet purchasing was restored to the control of the Alexander family, bankers of Edinburgh. William Alexander was sent to the Chesapeake to buy tobacco on French account and was succeeded in 1787 by Alexander Donald, scion of a well known family of Glasgow merchants.[19]

The Scots firms seem once again to have begun to cater for French demand. As before the war persistent references to the 'French price' and the purchasing tactics of the French agent predominated in merchant correspondence.[20] The Glasgow men also shipped to Liverpool, Bristol, London and Holland. Clearly, the cargoes actually imported into the Clyde after 1783 represented only a fraction of Glasgow interest in the trade.

There were probably two reasons for this dramatic revival in commercial fortunes. Because of their continuing commitment to agriculture, Virginians failed to develop a powerful indigenous merchant class during the years of war. Recovery from the losses sustained then and expansion into virgin territory in the future demanded capital and credit. For this planters once again turned to their traditional suppliers, the Scots storekeepers.[21] In addition, foreign competitors, notably the French, were unable to satisfy the consumer tastes of the planter class at satisfactory prices. Only the Glasgow houses and other British merchants had the experience and the contacts with industrial suppliers to cater for their tastes. Significantly, tobacco ships delivering cargoes to Europe loaded up with manufactured goods for the return voyage in British ports and not at continental centres. Foreign merchants found difficulty because of the insistence of the Americans on the kinds of commodities to which they had become long accustomed.[22] Seven years after independence was granted the colonies, a native of Philadelphia argued that their commercial dependency continued:

> ... there are not imported into all the United States from Europe, five thousand pounds value of manufactures but what comes from Britain; the French and the Dutch are quite drove out of the trade by the superior quality and cheapness of British articles.[23]

Because of the assumption that the Glasgow tobacco trade 'collapsed' in 1775, previous writers on the subject were concerned to explain how merchants involved in it recovered by diversifying into other sectors. The most popular suggestions were that 'former' tobacco lords had switched their interests to the Caribbean and the importation of sugar and cotton or had begun to invest in the new industrial developments of the later eighteenth century.[24] However, the record shows that there was no dramatic dispersal of merchant resources into new areas. Although tobacco firms were heavily involved in Caribbean commerce during the war this was primarily as a means to re-establish the interrupted tobacco trade by circuitous routes.[25] After 1783 sugar and cotton importation from there, although growing markedly, continued to be handled by established Glasgow houses experienced in trade to the West Indies before 1775 or by newcomers with no previous interests in tobacco commerce.[26] There was no comprehensive movement of tobacco companies away from American trade into the Caribbean. The link between the two was through the more subtle mechanism of movement by individual 'Virginia merchants', such as William Cunninghame, Arthur Connell and the Somervells into West India partnerships, and by the existing diversified nature of the business community which allowed men to have interests, long before 1775, in firms which operated in both sectors.

Neither is there any indication of a dramatic increase in the injection of funds into the domestic economy. American merchants were primarily concerned to renew their links with the plantations and not to commit themselves to speculative industrial investment. These traders continued to put *some* of their money into manufacturing and extractive industry but this was a traditional practice long-established before 1775.[27]

The American War cannot therefore be regarded as a watershed in Scottish economic history. The operation of a series of complex factors within the domestic economy rather than re-deployment of capital by a few powerful merchants was the factor responsible for accelerated growth. Yet although they were not directly involved in the considerable industrial expansion which characterised these decades, the tobacco lords could not remain immune from it. Their position of social and economic dominance had depended to a considerable degree on the absence of competing groups in Glasgow business society. Not only had they controlled foreign trade but they had also financed most of the city's important industries in the early eighteenth century. Later this monopoly began to weaken. As the West India trade expanded so too did new fortunes begin to be made in manufacturing industry. The *Glasgow Courier*, after an analysis of the city's population between 1712 and 1790, commented in 1791 how 'we have become a manufacturing instead of a mercantile town'.[28] Glasgow was a much greater and more complicated organism in 1800 than it had been a few decades before. Single groups, no matter how powerful, would have much less opportunity to dominate a city of 77,385 persons—total population in 1801—than a town of 28,300—total population in 1763.[29]

This new complexity was reflected in the recruitment of merchant burgesses. Between 1766-70 about 158 men had become merchant burgesses of Glasgow. This figure more than doubled between 1786-90 to 381. As the total number of merchants grew so the proportion of American and West India traders declined. Between 1766-70 they had formed 10.1 per cent of those gaining burgess-ships. In the four years 1801-5 the figure had dropped to 2.1 per cent and fell again between 1811-15 to 0.4 per cent.[30] Equally symbolic of their diminishing, though still important, role in local affairs was a decline in their political power. In the 1770s and 1780s the tobacco and West India interest had controlled the merchant rank on Glasgow Town Council.[31] In 1790 ten of the thirteen members of council belonged to this group although the majority traded to the Caribbean rather than to North America. In the later years of that decade their representation alternated between four in 1797 and seven in 1798. However, by the turn of the century the downward trend had become even more explicit; by then their numbers had dropped from nine in 1800 to five in 1801 and thereafter to two in every successive year until 1806.[32]

Of importance too in the erosion of the influence of the old mercantile aristocracy was the emergence of functional specialisation. One of the bases of the overseas merchant's supremacy at an earlier period had been that he, almost alone, had the wealth and motivation required to perform a series of functions necessary for the health of domestic industry and internal trade as well as of foreign commerce. He was a combination of insurer, banker, builder and provider of industrial capital. Gradually, however, these several functions were fragmented and undertaken by specialists, a trend which was indicative of the new wealth in society and of the more complex needs of a rapidly growing economy. For example, in the construction boom of the 1780s specialised building companies such as William Harley and Co., which developed Blythswood Square and the surrounding area, and Jack, Paterson and Co. usurped the role of the merchant speculators of a previous generation.[33] From the 1790s too it is possible to speak of a steady decline in the extent of merchant investment in industry. Between 1795 and 1816 they took up shares in only nine partnerships according to the sources consulted; four of these, however, were simply renewals of existing contracts. These figures can be contrasted with the twenty-one industrial partnerships in which tobacco and sugar importers had interests between 1780-95.[34] Previously most ventures in Glasgow which had needed anything more than a very modest financial provision had required their support. Now domestic industry seems to have become capable of producing its own resources for future expansion.

REFERENCES

1. B. Crispin, 'Clyde Shipping and the American War', *SHR* 41 (1962), 128; Macmillan, *loc. cit., passim.*
2. Price, *op. cit.*, 728-31; Gray, *op. cit.*, II, 597; W. A. Low, 'Merchant and Planter Relations in Post-Revolutionary Virginia, 1783-1789', *Virginia Magazine of History and Biography*, Vol. 61 (1953), 308-17.
3. Patrick Henry to Thomas Jefferson, 10 September, 1785 in *Jefferson Papers*, VII, 509.
4. PRO, BT 6/20, Answers to the several Questions respecting the Commerce and Shipping between Great Britain and the United States of America, 16 December, 1789.
5. Crispin, *loc. cit.*, 129.
6. LC, James Dunlop Family Papers, James Anderson to James Dunlop, 15 March, 1783.
7. *Glasgow Mercury*, 7 August, 1783.
8. *Ibid.*, 11 December, 1783.
9. LC, James Dunlop Family Papers, James Anderson to James Dunlop, 15 March, 1783.

168   THE AFTERMATH OF THE AMERICAN WAR

10. *Ibid.*, James Dunlop sen. to James Dunlop, 20 July, 1784.
11. *Ibid.*, Thomas Montgomerie to James Dunlop, 10 August, 1784.
12. *Ibid.*, James Dunlop sen. to James Dunlop, 16 September, 1784.
13. *Ibid.*, David Buchanan to James Dunlop, 5 April, 1784.
14. *Ibid.*, James Dunlop sen. to James Dunlop, 13 April, 1784.
15. SRO, GD 247/140 (Copy) Memorial and Queries for the Trustees of the late Mr. Cunninghame.
16. SRO, RH 15/2237, Contract of Findlay, Hopkirks and Co.
17. GCA, TD 131/3, Sederunt Book of the Trustees of Alexander Speirs of Elderslie, 1782–85, *passim*; *Glasgow Advertiser*, 22 January, 1790; *Glasgow Mercury*, 19 January, 1790.
18. SRO, E.504/28/38–40, Port Glasgow Customs Accounts, October, 1784–April, 1786.
19. Price, *op. cit.*, 742, 784.
20. See, for example, LC, James Dunlop Family Papers, James Dunlop sen. to James Dunlop, 23 December, 1784 'The French agent loads Andr. Johnsons ship the Elizabeth at City point. Archd. Dunlop buying for him at Cabin Point at 31/- all money has got about 100 hhds. The Agent has also freighted 2 ships of Messrs. Speirs building in Maryland and will soon be ready to load these two in Potomack. Their ships with the Hamboroughman will carry nearly 3000 hhds. tobo'. There are many other references in this collection to French buying from Glasgow factors.
21. PRO, BT 6/20, Answers to the Several Questions respecting the Commerce and Shipping between Great Britain and the United States of America, 16 December, 1789.
22. Gray, *op. cit.*, II, 599.
23. *Glasgow Advertiser*, 8 January, 1790, Extract of a letter from Philadelphia, 10 October, 1789.
24. For this thesis which has had a long pedigree see William Fullarton, *General View of the Agriculture of the County of Ayr* (1793), 130; Denholm, *op. cit.*, 408; Macpherson, *op. cit.*, III, 593; H. Hamilton, *The Industrial Revolution in Scotland* (Oxford, 1932), 121; L. J. Saunders, *Scottish Democracy 1815–40* (Edinburgh, 1950), 98; J. Cunnison and J. B. S. Gilfillan (eds.), *Third Statistical Account of Scotland: Glasgow Region* (Glasgow, 1958), 103; Hamilton, *op. cit.*, 168; Robertson, *loc. cit.*, 130.
25. See above, pp. 130–1.
26. See the list of West India firms and merchants in ML, Abstract of Minute Books of the Glasgow West India Association, Individual Subscriptions, 6 and Clyde port books for the period.
27. See above, pp. 43–6 for a detailed criticism of the 'transfer of capital' thesis.
28. *Glasgow Courier*, 8 September, 1791.
29. *Transactions of the Glasgow and Clydesdale Statistical Soc.* I: 'Population of Glasgow, 1755–1831'; GCA, Council Minute Book, C1/1/40/174, 9 August, 1792.
30. Calculations based on Glasgow Roll of Burgesses and GCA, Matriculation Book of the Merchants House of Glasgow.
31. See above, p. 11.
32. GCA, Council Minute Book, C1/1/41–47. Before the later eighteenth century tobacco merchants had monopolised the office of Provost of Glasgow. From the 1790s to 1815, however, their place was taken by Caribbean traders (John Hamilton, 1800–1. 1804–5 and 1810–11; James Black, 1808–9, 1816–17; James Mackenzie 1806–7) and the new manufacturing class (Kirkman Finlay, 1811–12; Henry Monteith, 1814–15). See Gourlay, *Provosts of Glasgow*, *passim*.
33. Senex (J. M. Reid), *op. cit.*, III, 320–21; J. R. Kellett, 'Property Speculators and the Building of Glasgow, 1783–1830', *SJPE*, VIII (1961).
34. These figures are primarily based on local and national registers of deeds, court of session data and Glasgow newspapers. However, relevant business records were also used. For a full list of sources see Bibliography.

CONCLUSION

CONCLUSION

Conclusion

IN the second half of the eighteenth century the tobacco merchants of Glasgow formed a small, tightly-knit group linked by partnership connection, marriage alliance and kinship loyalties. Within the community itself control was retained by an inner élite whose friends and relations provided the provosts, councillors and baillies who ruled the town throughout the period. Yet these merchants were not a self-perpetuating caste. Insolvency among established families and the very considerable rate of expansion in the colonial trades combined to loosen the bonds of any enduring monopoly and to offer openings to the ambitious. On the other hand, existing contacts within the community and a measure of wealth were normally vital if the aspirant was to achieve the desired goal of partnership status. Thus, newcomers tended to come from the 'middling' ranks of Lowland Scottish society. While none were scions of the aristocracy, only a mere handful were the sons of skilled craftsmen. Most were the offspring of merchants, lairds and professional families, the majority had reached a commendable level of educational achievement and most had access to sources of credit and capital among their kin.

The reward for the successful was wealth on a scale never before imagined in Scotland. Returns were not always dependent, however, on profit from tobacco importation. Although most traders probably did specialise in American commerce few did so to the exclusion of other interests. The Caribbean sugar trade, the wine and salt trades of Europe, marine insurance, banking, manufacturing and landholding were integral parts of the commercial régime of the great tobacco lords. One must conclude, therefore, that their opulence was not based on one activity alone but on the net return from a series of compatible and suitably inter-locking investments.

Such riches quickly changed the face of Glasgow. The merchants' town houses dominated the burgh while the rise of the luxury trades was another consequence of their achievements. Yet not all the benefits were retained and enjoyed by a minority. A whole variety of manufactories grew up in the Clyde towns parallel with the rise of the tobacco trade; urban expansion (partly financed by the merchants)[1] resulted from the ancillary employments so vital to the functioning of a great commercial centre; for the first time too the West of Scotland acquired a large-scale infrastructure of banks, warehouses, docks and marine insurance facilities which could be devoted to other, and equally successful, economic activities in later times; commercial contacts developed with areas as far apart as North America and Eastern Europe strengthened existing Scottish overseas links and were of major relevance to the nation's trade expansion in the nineteenth century. Moreover, since not only the merchants themselves, but also other moneyed elements in central Scotland had a financial stake in the tobacco companies (through the mechanism of bond-lending) some of the gains from the trade were likely to be diffused throughout a wide circle among the middle classes.

How far the tobacco trade was itself responsible for basic economic change in Scotland is more debatable. The complexity of the origins of mercantile profit was such that it is virtually impossible to measure precisely the share deriving from the American trade itself. Furthermore, there is no evidence of transfer of resources from commerce to industry in the critical two decades after c.1780. On the contrary, the *relative* importance of merchant investment in West of Scotland industry declined at this time, a pattern which suggests that domestic traders and manufacturers had, in the main, the financial capability to undertake the kind of new developments which were associated with the period. On the other hand, the role of the tobacco lords in an earlier era may have been more significant. They seem to have been one of the few groups in the western Lowlands with the motivation and resources to develop 'factory' industry at a time when production typically took place in the home and the farmstead. They, together with local landed proprietors, provided the capital for the Monkland Canal and also spent considerable sums on river improvement and maintenance.[2] According to the sources consulted they seem to have been purchasing most of their cargoes for America in Scotland itself. Although apparently this demand was not of major importance in *quantitative* terms, it may have been much more significant *qualitatively* by developing within the economy a series of novel consumer industries and thus strengthening the composition of Scottish exports.[3]

Perhaps, however, the single most common investment for the successful trader was in land. He bought estates for a variety of reasons and seems to have had little difficulty in securing them. Unlike the pattern in some English trading centres,[4] landownership was not incompatible with merchanting and few families gave up their interests in commerce when they acquired estates. In some ways, indeed, merchants regarded landownership as an extension of their commercial activities and did much to improve both the agrarian and industrial potential of their properties. Around Glasgow they seem to have had little difficulty in gaining acceptance by county society and several of them obtained positions of power in rural politics and administration.

The main basis of their material success was the supremacy of the tobacco firms in Atlantic trade. Building on existing geographical advantage, the Glasgow men evolved commercial methods which were remarkably well adapted to the needs of both clients in America and customers in Europe. The great Glasgow companies with their chains of stores in the colonies practised economies of scale, exploited the London capital market for financial assistance and developed sources of supply all over the European and American continents to feed their outlets. Only these firms (and a few competitors in Whitehaven and elsewhere) had the type of régime suited to the smaller planter of Virginia and Maryland on whose production mainly depended the extension of the eighteenth century tobacco trade; only they operated a system of bulk sales based on rapid turnover which commended itself to the French agents who bought for the biggest single market in Europe. Despite, however, those influences which favoured and helped them, it was the merchants themselves who were finally responsible for taking advantage of the opportunities which were presented. By any standards they were a remarkable breed, able to exploit developing situations, attempt, adapt and develop new techniques and, perhaps above all, take risks. Their capabilities in a critical situation were perhaps most apparent in the crisis of the American War period. The eight years of hostilities were successfully negotiated, bankruptcies were few, alternative markets and investments were strengthened and above all the Scottish firms successfully renewed their position in the United States after 1783.

REFERENCES

1. *Glasgow Journal*, 3 April, 1777; Stewart, *op. cit.*, 224; GCA, C1/1/35, Council Minute Book; James Muir, *Glasgow Streets and Places* (Glasgow and Edinburgh, 1899).
2. GCA, Register of Deeds, B.10/15/7368; SL, Court of Session Process, 441/62; G. Thomson, 'James Watt and the Monkland Canal', *SHR*, 39 (1950), 121.
3. For a similar effect in Bristol and Hull, see W. E. Minchinton, 'Bristol—Metropolis of the West in the Eighteenth Century', *Trans. R. Hist. Soc.*, 5th. ser., IV (1954); Gordon Jackson, *Hull in the Eighteenth Century* (Oxford, 1972), 179–199.
4. R. G. Wilson, 'Records for a study of the Leeds Woollen Merchants, 1700–1830', *Archives*, VIII (1967), 9–10.

Appendix I

THE TOBACCO MERCHANTS OF GLASGOW
c.1740–90

APPENDIX I

The Tobacco Merchants of Glasgow, c.1740–90

As far as possible all persons who either individually or collectively imported tobacco between c.1740–90 to the Clyde ports have been included in this list. There are only two exceptions:
(1) those who were not registered burgesses and guild brethren of the burgh of Glasgow;
(2) those who did not import tobacco on a regular basis.

The main sources have all been cited in the bibliography but, because of limitations on space, detailed references have not been given in this Appendix. The reader interested in source material used should examine the footnotes in the text, the bibliography and consult my 1971 Strathclyde Ph.D. thesis. In the early stages of selection and research on specific merchants I found 'Glasgow Copartneries, Joint Stock Companies and Ventures to 1775' (typescript in Glasgow City Archives, based on the burghal Register of Deeds) an invaluable aid.

Occasionally it has not always been possible to distinguish the interests of different individuals with the same name. Although every effort has been made to eliminate confusion, in certain cases ambiguity still remains. These instances have been marked with an asterisk. The 'biographies' are not intended to be exhaustive; for further detail consult the text.

Key
b = date when merchant registered as burgess and guild brother of the burgh of Glasgow.
U = matriculated at the University of Glasgow.
F = father's name and occupation if known.
I = shares in manufacturing and industrial ventures.

AITON, Andrew (1696–1772): b. 1728; F, Sir John Aiton of that Ilk; I, Broomley Printfield Co., Haarlem Linen and Dye Manufactory; Provost, 1738–9, 1739–40.
ALSTON, John (1743–1818): b. 1768; F. George Alston of Muirburn; U.
BAIRD, James sen.; b. 1736; F, unknown, obtained burgess-ship by purchase.
BAIRD, James jun.: b. 1769; F, James Baird (above), merchant in Glasgow; U.
BALLANTYNE, John: b. 1774; F, William Ballantyne, merchant in Glasgow.
BALLANTYNE, James: b. 1774; F, William Ballantyne, merchant in Glasgow.
BARNS, John (?–1791): b. 1740; F, Robert Barns, laird in Ayrshire.
BERRIE, James: b. 1738; F, unknown, obtained burgess-ship by marriage.
BERRIE, Robert: b. 1738; F. unknown, obtained burgess-ship by marriage.
BLACKBURN, Andrew: b. 1741; F, John Blackburn, merchant in Glasgow; I, Glasgow Ropework Co., Broomley Printfield Co.
BLACKBURN, Hugh: b. 1759; F, John Blackburn, merchant in Glasgow; I, Glasgow Ropework Co.
BLACKBURN, John: b. ?; F, Hugh Blackburn, merchant in Glasgow; I, Shotts Iron Co.; purchased estate of Killearn in Stirlingshire; U.

APPENDIX I

BOGLE, Archibald (1730–1812): b. 1755; F, Robert Bogle III of Shettleston, merchant in Glasgow.

BOGLE, George II (Daldowie) (1701–84): b. 1752; F, Robert Bogle of Daldowie, merchant in Glasgow; U, married Anne, daughter of Sir John Sinclair of Stevenston; Lord Rector of Glasgow University, 1737, 1743, 1747, 1757; I, Easter Sugar House, Glasgow Cudbear Works, Smithfield Iron Co.; inherited estates of Daldowie and Whiteinch acquired by his family in 1720 and 1731.

*BOGLE, Robert (Daldowie): b. ?; F, George Bogle II (above), merchant in Glasgow; U; inherited estates of Daldowie and Whiteinch, 1787.

*BOGLE, Robert (Shettleston): b. 1752; F, Robert Bogle, merchant in Glasgow; U; I, Glasgow Ironwork Co., Smithfield Iron Co., Muirkirk Iron Co., Spinningdale Cotton Co.; inherited estates of Shettleston, Barony of Glasgow, from his father.

BOGLE, William, b. 1754; F, John Bogle, writer in Glasgow; U; I, Anderston Brewery Co.

BOWMAN, John (1701–97): b. 1739; F, John Bowman, merchant in Glasgow; U; I, Bell's Tannery; purchased estates of Ashgrove and Mongreenan in Ayrshire, 1766 and 1778; Provost of Glasgow, 1764–5, 1765–6.

BOYD, Robert: b. 1714; F, Robert Boyd, merchant in Londonderry.

BROCK, Walter: b. 1740; F, Robert Brock, merchant in Glasgow; U; I, Tartan Manufactory.

BROWN, Andrew: b. 1775; F, unknown, obtained burgess-ship by marriage.

BROWN, Alexander (1738–1803): b. 1757; F, James Brown, merchant in Glasgow.

BROWN, Hugh: b. 1757; F, unknown, obtained burgess-ship by marriage to Helen Dunmore, daughter of Thomas, merchant in Glasgow.

BROWN, JAMES: b. 1756; F, unknown, obtained burgess-ship by marriage.

BROWN, John (1694–1757): b. ?; F, unknown; I, Port Glasgow Ropework Co.

BUCHANAN, Andrew I (Drumpellier) (1691–1759): b. 1716; F, George Buchanan, maltster in Glasgow; I, King Street Sugarhouse; purchased estate of Drumpellier in Lanarkshire in 1735; Provost of Glasgow, 1740–1.

BUCHANAN, Andrew II (1725–1783): b. 1754; F, George Buchanan, merchant in Glasgow; U; I, King St. Sugar House, Andrew Buchanan and Co., linen weavers; leading partner in Buchanan, Hastie and Co. which crashed in 1777; subsequently appointed City Chamberlain but sacked for embezzlement.

BUCHANAN, Andrew jun.: b. 1774; F, Archibald Buchanan, merchant in Glasgow; U; primarily involved in the Caribbean trades but also had shares in Speirs, Bowman and Co.; I, McBrayne, Stenhouse and Co., printers and linen manufacturers; purchased estate of Ardenconnal in Dumbartonshire in 1783 and two smaller properties in Lanarkshire in 1791 and 1793.

BUCHANAN, George (1728–1762): b. 1746; F, Andrew Buchanan of Drumpellier, merchant in Glasgow; U; I, Glasgow Bottleworks Co.; United Sugarhouse Co.; purchased estate of Mount Vernon in Lanarkshire and built the 'Virginia Mansion' in Virginia St.

BUCHANAN, James (?–1786): b. 1762; F, Andrew Buchanan of Drumpellier, merchant in Glasgow; U; Provost of Glasgow, 1768–9, 1769–70, 1774–5, 1775–6; I, King Street Sugar House; obtained estate of Drumpellier in Lanarkshire by inheritance and purchased Langloan in the same county; after bankruptcy of Buchanan, Hastie and Co. became Commissioner of Customs in Edinburgh.

*BUCHANAN, William: b. ?; F, John Buchanan, weaver in Glasgow (?); U.

CAMPBELL, Alexander: b. 1753; F, unknown, obtained burgess-ship by nomination.

CAMPBELL, John Coats (1721–1804): b. 1743; F, Archibald Coats, merchant in Glasgow; U; Provost of Glasgow, 1784–5; I, Kilmarnock Worset Factory, Bell's Tannery, Glasgow Tanwork Co., Greenock Sugarhouse, Pollockshaws Printfield Co., Inkle Factory, Duntocher Cotton Co., A. and J. Newbigging, textile manufacturers; acquired estate of Clathick by inheritance from his mother Jean Campbell.

CAMPBELL, John sen.: b. ?; F, Alexander Campbell, captain in the Black Watch and scion of Highland landed family; U; mainly involved in West Indian sugar and cotton trade (in his own firm, John Campbell sen. and Co.) but held shares also in John Glassford and Co.; purchased estate of Morriston in Lanarkshire in 1796.

CAMPBELL, John jun. (1743–1790): b. 1773; F, Archibald Campbell of Succoth; obtained burgess-ship by marriage to Elizabeth, daughter of Andrew Houston; Provost of Glasgow 1788–9.

CHRISTIE, Robert (1717–1780): b. 1737; F, James Christie, merchant in Glasgow; I, Glasgow Inkle Factory Co.; owned estate of Fairfield; Provost of Glasgow, 1756-7, 1757-8.

COATES, Archibald (?–1770): b. 1738, by apprenticeship; F, unknown; I, Glasgow Tanwork Co.; Father of John Coates Campbell (above) and William (below).

COATES, William: b. 1752; F, Archibald Coates (above), merchant in Glasgow; U; I, Glasgow Tanwork Co.

COCHRANE, Andrew (1693–1777): b. 1726, as married Janet, daughter of Peter Murdoch; F, David Cochrane, merchant in Ayr; I, Glasgow Tanwork Co., King Street Sugarhouse; New Glasgow Tanwork Co.; owned estate of Brighouse; founding partner of Cochrane, Murdoch and Co., bankers.

COLQUOHOUN, Patrick (1745–1820): b. 1781; F, Adam Colquohoun, sheriff substitute of Dumbartonshire; sent by relatives to Virginia in 1761, his father having died, returned to Glasgow, 1766; owned estate of Woodcroft; actively involved in the foundation and early development of Glasgow Chamber of Commerce; Provost of Glasgow, 1782-3, 1783-4; left for London in 1789 where he became distinguished as a police magistrate and municipal reformer.

CONNELL, Arthur (1717–1775): b. 1740; F, Rev. Matthew Connell, minister of the church at Kilbride; I, Rope Manufactory of Glasgow, Greenock Sugarhouse; owned estate of Enochbank; Provost of Glasgow, 1772-3, 1773-4.

CONNELL, James: b. 1752; F, Rev. Matthew Connell, minister at Kilbride.

CORBETT, Archibald: b. 1762; F, James Corbett, merchant in Glasgow; I, Glasgow Ropework Co.

CORBETT, Cunninghame: b. 1776; F, John Corbett of Tollcross, merchant in Glasgow; inherited estate of Tollcross.

CORBETT, James (1690–1754): b. 1727; F, James Corbett, merchant in Glasgow; I, Glasgow Ropework Co.; father of Archibald (above); owned estates of Kenmuir and Stockbriggs.

CORBETT, John (1729–1815): b. 1731 free and gratis; F, Thomas Corbett of Tollcross; owned estate of Tollcross; I, Glasgow Tanwork Co.

COULTER, James: b. 1740; F, John Coulter, merchant in Glasgow; I, Wester Sugarhouse Co., Stocking Manufactory.

CRAWFORD, George: b. 1773; F, ?; obtained burgess-ship by purchase; I, Port Glasgow Sugar House, Milton Print Works; owned estates in the barony of Houston, Renfrewshire.

*CRAWFORD, Robert: b. 1764; F, ?; obtained burgess-ship by purchase.

CRAWFORD, William: b. 1738; F, Matthew Crawford, merchant in Glasgow; I, Shuttlefield Factory Co.

CUNNINGHAME, William: b. 1763, as married Jean, daughter of Thomas Dunmore, merchant in Glasgow; F, ?; scion of a cadet branch of the Cunninghames of Caprington, lairds of Ayrshire; I, Port Glasgow Sugar House, Pollockshaws Printfield Co., Dalnottar Iron Co.; purchased estate of Lainshaw in Ayrshire, 1778 and other properties in the Stewartry of Kirkcudbright (Duchrae and Kilbucho); built mansion in Queen St. for £10,000.

DENNISTOUN, James sen.: b. 1743; F, James Dennistoun, laird of Colgrain, merchant in Glasgow; I, Glasgow Ropework Co., Sandyhills Coal Co., Smithfield Iron Co., Camlachie Coal Co., Dunmore Coal Co., Reynolds, Monteith and Co. (cotton spinners), John Monteath and Co. (cotton spinners); inherited, 1756, estate of Colgrain in Dumbartonshire.

DENNISTOUN, James jun. (1748–1816): b. 1774; F, James Dennistoun (above), merchant in Glasgow; I, Endrick Printfield Co., Reynolds, Monteith and Co., cotton spinners, Sandyhills Coal Co., Camlachie Coal Co., Dunmore Coal Co., John Monteath and Co. (cotton spinners).

DINWIDDIE, Lawrence (1696–1764): b. 1723; F, Robert Dinwiddie, merchant in Glasgow (who had come from Dumfriesshire to become a trader in the city in 1691); U; I, Bell's Tannery, Port Glasgow Ropework Co., Glasgow Tanwork Co., Delftfield Pottery Co.; purchased lands of Germiston and Balornock in 1748; Provost of Glasgow, 1742-3, 1743-4.

DINWIDDIE, Robert (?–1789): b. 1762; F, Lawrence Dinwiddie (above), merchant in Glasgow; U; I, Delfthouse Company of Glasgow; purchased estate of Whistleberry in Lanarkshire.

APPENDIX I

DONALD, Alexander (1742–?): b. 1774; F, James Donald, merchant in Glasgow.

DONALD, James (1713–1760): b. 1741; F, Thomas Donald of Lyleston, parish of Cardross, Dumbarton; obtained burgess-ship by marriage to daughter of Thomas Yuille of Darleith, merchant in Glasgow; owned estate of Geilston (Dumbartonshire) and other lands in and about Glasgow.

*DONALD, Robert (1724–1803): b. ?; F, Thomas Donald of Lyleston, landowner in the parish of Cardross, Dumbartonshire; Provost of Glasgow, 1776–7, 1777–8.

DONALD, Thomas (1745–1798): b. 1780; F, James Donald, merchant in Glasgow (above); I, Smithfield Iron Co., Glasgow Bottlework Co.; inherited estate of Geilston, Dumbartonshire from his father.

DREGHORN, Allan (?–1764): b. 1737; F, Robert Dreghorn, wright in Glasgow; I, Smithfield Iron Co.; built Dreghorn mansion in Clyde St. Owned estate of Ruchill.

DREGHORN, Robert: b. 1737; F. Robert Dreghorn, wright in Glasgow; owned estate of Blochairn.

DUNLOP, Colin (1706–1777): b. 1741; F, James Dunlop of Garnkirk, merchant in Glasgow; I, Rope Manufactory of Glasgow, Govan Coal Co., Knightswood Coal Co.; founder member of Dunlop, Houston and Co. (Glasgow Ship Bank); purchased estate of Carmyle in Lanarkshire; Provost of Glasgow, 1770–1, 1771–2.

DUNLOP, James (1741–1816): b. 1768; F, Colin Dunlop, merchant in Glasgow (above); I, Bell's Tannery, Ropework Manufactory of Glasgow, Glasgow Bottlework Co., Dumbarton Glasswork Co., Duntocher Cotton Co., Govan Coal Co., Knightswood Coal Co., Elderslie Coal Co., Fullarton Coal Co., Banknock Coal Co., Hamilton Farm Coal Co., Sandyhills Coal Co., Rutherglen Muir Coal Co., Camlachie Coal Co., Skaetrig Coal Co., McBrayne, Stenhouse and Co., linen printers and manufacturers; inherited estate of Carmyle in Lanarkshire, 1778, from his father, Colin; 1783 purchased Garnkirk from the agents of his uncle; 1783–1792, acquired a further fifteen mineral bearing properties in the barony of Glasgow and in Lanarkshire; partner and Glasgow agent of the Greenock Banking Co. Bankrupt in 1793.

DUNLOP, John (1744–1820): b. 1780; F, Colin Dunlop, merchant in Glasgow, younger brother of James (above); U; I, Duntocher Cotton Co.; purchased estate of Rosebank in Lanarkshire, 1791 and Carmylehill, barony of Glasgow, 1782; Collector of Customs at Bo'ness; Provost of Glasgow, 1794–5. Married Jessie, daughter of Sir Thomas Miller of Glencoe.

DUNLOP, Robert (1700–1762): b. 1734; F, James Dunlop of Garnkirk, merchant in Glasgow, brother of Colin (above); U; founding partner of Dunlop, Houston and Co., bankers in Glasgow; purchased estate of Househill, Renfrewshire.

DUNLOP, Thomas: b. 1738; F, James Dunlop of Garnkirk, merchant in Glasgow; I, Smithfield Iron Co.

DUNLOP, William: b. 1739; F, William Dunlop, merchant in Glasgow.

DUNMORE, Robert: b. 1773; F, Thomas Dunmore, merchant in Glasgow (below); U; I, Ropework Manufactory of Glasgow, Port Glasgow Sugar House, Glasgow Bottlework Co., Dalnottar Iron Co., Muirkirk Iron Co., Pollockshaws Printfield Co., Inkle Manufactory, Ballindalloch Cotton Co., Spinningdale Cotton Co., Endrick Printfield Co.; primarily involved in West Indies trade but one of his partnerships, Dunmore, Blackburn and Co., traded to Maryland; inherited estate of Kelvinside from his father; acquired various lands in Stirlingshire, 1785–92, subsequently consolidated into the barony of Ballindalloch. Bankrupt, 1797.

DUNMORE, Thomas (?–1790): b. ?; F, Robert Dunmore, merchant in Glasgow; Thomas was father of Robert, above; I, Shuttlefield Factory Co., Shoe Manufactory Co., Rope Manufactory of Glasgow, Dalnottar Iron Co., Pollockshaws Printfield Co.; purchased estate of Kelvinside (Bankhead), barony of Glasgow, 1749.

ELLIOT, David: b. 1779; F. ?; acquired burgess-ship by marriage to Sussanna Bogle, daughter of Robert.

FINDLAY, Robert (1748–1802): b. 1770; F, Rev. Robert Findlay, Professor of Divinity, University of Glasgow; nephew of William Cunninghame (see above); U; purchased estate of Easterhouse, barony of Glasgow, 1784.

FRENCH, William (1732–1802): b. 1755; F, James French, merchant in Glasgow; I, Easter Barrachney Coal Co.; purchased properties in Carmyle, barony of Glasgow; Provost, 1778–9, 1779–80. Bankrupt, 1786.

GLASSFORD, John (1715–83): b. 1737; F, James Glassford, merchant burgess of Paisley; U; began business originally as a manufacturer in textiles; I, Anderston Brewery Co., Pollockshaws Printfield Co., Graham, Liddell and Co., stocking weavers, Glasgow Cudbear Co., James McGregor and Co., linen dealers and bleachers, Prestonpans Vitriol Co., Glasgow Inkle Factory; purchased estate of Dougalston (Dumbarton), 1767, Netherwood (Stirlingshire) and Kilmanor and Whitehill (barony of Glasgow); married (2nd.) to fifth daughter of Earl of Cromarty.

GLASSFORD, Henry: b. 1795; F, John Glassford (above), merchant in Glasgow; inherited estates acquired by his father (see above).

GORDON, James: b. 1760, as served apprenticeship with John Glassford; F, uncertain, thought to be (Gourlay, *Glasgow Miscellany*, 47) a physician in Glasgow; I, Anderston Brewery Co., J. Hervey and Co., brewers in Paisley, Greenock Sugar House Co., Glasgow Bottleworks, Dalnottar Iron Co., Graham, Liddell and Co., stocking manufacturers, Glasgow Cudbear Co., Prestonpans Vitriol Co.

GORDON, William: b. 1718, by marriage; F, ?; I, King Street Sugarhouse, Bell's Tanwork Co.

GRAHAM, John: b. 1752; F, John Graham, merchant in Glasgow; I, Milngavie Factory Co.

GRAY, William: b. 1758; F, William Gray, merchant in Glasgow; I, Silvercraigs Weaving Factory Co.

GRINDLAY, Alexander: b. 1786; F, ?; obtained burgess-ship by marriage; I, Glasgow Inkle Factory.

HAMILTON, Archibald: b. 1733; F, ?; obtained burgess-ship by marriage.

HAMILTON, Archibald jun.: b. 1762; F, Archibald Hamilton, merchant in Glasgow, above; U; purchased estates of Woodside, barony of Glasgow.

*HAMILTON, John: b. 1756; F, Rev. John Hamilton, minister of the Church of Scotland; U; I, Glasgow Inkle Factory Co., Stocking Manufactory Co., Smithfield Iron Co.; purchased estate of Northpark, barony of Glasgow.

HASTIE, Robert: b. 1766; F, ?; obtained burgess-ship by purchase.

*HAY, John: b. 1785; F, John Hay, merchant in Paris.

HENDERSON, Archibald: b. 1766; F, Rev. Archibald Henderson, minister at Blantyre; purchased estate of Nether and Over Middleton, Renfrewshire.

HOPKIRK, James (1749–1836): b. 1785; F, Thomas Hopkirk, merchant in Glasgow; U; I, Anderston Brewery Co., J. Hervey and Co., brewers in Paisley, Glasgow Bottlework Co.; inherited estate of Dalbeth, 1781; purchased Easter Dalbeth, Glasgow, 1783.

*HOPKIRK, Thomas: b. 1774; F, Thomas Hopkirk, merchant in Glasgow; I, Anderston Brewery Co., Greenock Sugarhouse Co.

*HOPKIRK Thomas: b. 1734; F, Thomas Hopkirk, tailor in Glasgow; father of James and Thomas (above).

HOUSTON, Alexander: b. 1771; F, ?; scion of the Houstons, lairds of Calderhall; obtained burgess-ship by marriage to Lillias, daughter of Thomas Calder; primarily involved in West Indies trade but held shares also in William Cunninghame and Co.; I, Pollockshaws Printfield Co., Govan Coal Co., Knightswood Coal Co., Port Glasgow Ropework Co.; purchased estate of Jordanhill, Renfrew, 1750-52.

INGRAM, Archibald (1699–1770): b. 1729; F, ?; native of Dalserf (?), obtained burgess-ship by marriage; had shares in the Glasgow Arms Bank and the 'Painting Academy'; I, Pollockshaws Printfield Co., Inkle Manufactory, Graham, Liddell and Co., stocking Manufacturers; purchased estate of Cloberhill, parish of East Killpatrick; Provost of Glasgow, 1762-3, 1763-4.

INGRAM, James: b. 1762; F, Archibald Ingram, merchant in Glasgow; I, Pollockshaws Printfield Co., Inkle Factory.

JAMIESON, James: b. 1762; F, John Jamieson, merchant in Glasgow.

JAMIESON, John: b. 1759; F, ?; obtained burgess-ship by nomination.

KIPPEN, George (1737–1785): b. 1762; F, George Kippen, merchant in Glasgow; I, Dalnottar Iron Co.

LAWSON, James: b. ?; F, ?; involved in tobacco trade with his brother-in-law, John Semple, to Maryland and in iron manufacturing there.

LINDSAY, John: b. 1785; F, James Findlay, merchant in Glasgow: I, Duntocher Cotton Co.

APPENDIX I

Low, Alexander (?-1790): b. 1774; F, ?; obtained burgess-ship by purchase.
*McCall, Alexander: b. 1773; F, ?; obtained burgess-ship by purchase.
McCall, George: b. 1766; F, Samuel McCall, merchant in Glasgow; U.
*McCall, James (1726–1803): b. ?; F, Samuel McCall, merchant in Glasgow; U; purchased estate of Braehead, Lanarkshire.
*McCall, John I: b. ?; F, Samuel McCall, merchant in Glasgow; U; I, Anderston Brewery Co., John McGregor and Co., linen dealers and bleachers; purchased estate of Belvidere, barony of Glasgow.
*McCall, John II (1761–1819): b. 1783; F, Rev. John McCall, minister of Tron Church; U.
McCall, Samuel (1681–1759): b. 1708; F, ?; obtained burgess-ship by marriage and probably originated from Dumfriesshire. Father of George, James and John I (above).
McDowall, James: b. 1775; F, William McDowall II, merchant in Glasgow; U; mainly involved in West Indies trade (via his shares in Alexander Houston and Co.) but also a partner in T. and A. Donald and Co., tobacco importers; assets sequestrated at the bankruptcy of Alexander Houston and Co. in early nineteenth century; I, Walter Buchanan and Co., soap and candle manufacturers, Glasgow Ropework Co., South Sugar House, Dalnottar Iron Co., Muirkirk Iron Co., Milton Printworks, Duntocher Cotton Co., John Renfrew and Co., linen weavers. Inherited estate of Hagtonhill and others in Renfrewshire.
McDowall, John: b. 1773; F, ?; obtained burgess-ship by purchase.
McFie, Thomas: b. 1742; F, John McFie, merchant in Glasgow: I, Stocking Manufactory Co.
Mackie, Alexander: b. 1762; F, ?; obtained burgess-ship by purchase.
Mackay, Robert: b. 1774; F, ?; obtained burgess-ship by purchase; I, Glasgow Inkle Factory, Spinningdale Cotton Co.
McNair, Robert: b. 1765; F, Robert McNair, weaver in Glasgow.
Mackenzie, John: b. 1764; F, James Mackenzie, schoolmaster.
Miller, William jun.: b. 1751; F, William Miller, merchant in Glasgow.
Milliken, James: b. 1730; F, ?; obtained burgess-ship, 'free and gratis'.
Monro, John: b. 1756; F, ?; obtained burgess-ship by nomination.
Monteath, Walter: b. 1760; F, Walter Monteith, laird of Kepps; U; I, Glasgow Tanwork Co.; inherited estate of Kepps in Perthshire.
Munro, Alexander: b. 1750; F, Daniel Munro, tailor in Glasgow; U; purchased estate of north Woodside, barony of Glasgow; teller to the Glasgow Arms Bank.
Murdoch, George (1715–1795): b. 1737; F, James Murdoch, merchant in Glasgow: I, Dalnottar Iron Co., Glasgow Bottleworks Co., Glasgow Ropework Co.; purchased estate of Frisky Hall (Dumbartonshire); Comptroller of Customs at Port Glasgow and Greenock, 1771–84; Provost of Glasgow, 1754–5, 1755–6, 1766–7, 1767–8.
Murdoch, John: b. 1734; F, James Murdoch, merchant in Glasgow, brother of George (above); I, Argyllshire and Peebleshire Mineral Co.
Murdoch, Peter (1734–1817): b. 1756; F, Peter Murdoch, merchant in Glasgow; U; I, Muirkirk Iron Co., Anderston Brewery Co., Dalnottar Iron Co.; Glasgow Bottlework Co.; purchased, 1778, estate of Pirrotholm in Renfrewshire and inherited, 1776, 'lands in town and country' belonging to his uncle, George Murdoch.
Nisbet, Patrick: b. 1747; F, ?; obtained burgess-ship by serving apprenticeship; I, Delftfield Pottery Co.
Oswald, Alexander I (?-1768): b. 1720; F, Rev. James Oswald of Dunnett; I, Glasgow Bottleworks Co.
Oswald, Alexander II (1738–1813): b. 1775; F, Rev. Dr. George Oswald, minister in Caithness; I, South Sugar House, Linwood Cotton Co.; purchased, 1783, estate of Shieldhall in Lanarkshire.
Oswald, George (1735–1819): b. 1760, by purchase; F, Rev. Dr. George Oswald, minister in Caithness; I, South Sugar House, Smithfield Iron Co., Pollockshaws Printfield Co.; purchased estate of Langside, Renfrewshire, 1792; succeeded his cousin, Richard, at Scotstoun, 1766 and his uncle, Richard, at Auchencruive in Ayrshire, 1784; Rector of Glasgow University, 1797.
Oswald, James: b. 1766; F, ?; obtained burgess-ship by purchase.

OSWALD, Richard (1687–1766): b. 1724; F, Rev. James Oswald of Dunnett; involved in West Indies and Madeira trade as well as tobacco importation; built Oswald's land in Stockwell St., Glasgow; I, United Sugarhouse Co., Glasgow Bottleworks Co., Port Glasgow Ropework Co.; purchased estate of Scotstoun.

RAMSAY, Andrew I (1688–1754): b. 1717; F, ?; obtained burgess-ship by serving apprenticeship; Provost of Glasgow, 1734–5, 1735–6.

RAMSAY, Andrew II (1729–1775): b. 1757; F, Andrew Ramsay, merchant in Glasgow (above).

REID, Charles: b. ?; F, ?.

RIDDELL, Henry: b. 1781; F, John Riddell, Writer to the Signet; I, Prestonpans Vitriol Co.

RIDDELL, John (?–1794): b. 1780; F, ?; obtained burgess-ship by purchase.

RITCHIE, Henry (?–1792): b. 1762; F, John Ritchie, merchant in Glasgow; U; I, Greenock Ropework Co.

RITCHIE, James (1722–1799): b. 1748; F, John Ritchie, merchant in Glasgow; U; I, Greenock Ropework Co., Smithfield Iron Co.; inherited estates of Craigton (Lanarkshire) and Busby (Renfrewshire), 1783.

RITCHIE, John: b. 1722; F, John Ritchie, merchant in Glasgow; father of James and Henry, above; I, Silvercraigs Weaving Factory Co.

ROBERTSON, James: b. 1774; F, ?; obtained burgess-ship by marriage.

ROBERTSON, John: b. 1775; F, ?; obtained burgess-ship by purchase; I, Smithfield Iron Co., Muirkirk Iron Co., Spinningdale Cotton Co., Glasgow Cudbear Co.; purchased estate of Craigiehall (re-named Plantation) in barony of Glasgow, 1783.

ROWAN, James (?–1754): b. 1727; F, John Rowan of Teucharhill; obtain burgess-ship by marriage; inherited estate of Teucharhill from his father.

*ROWAN, John: b. ?; F, James Rowan (above), merchant in Glasgow.

RUSSELL, David (1747–?): b. 1779; F, James Russell, commissary clerk in Dunblain; I, James Finlay and Co., cotton spinners and merchants; purchased estate of Woodside, barony of Glasgow; later bought Torwoodhead and Hamilton Farm, 1801, in Stirlingshire.

SCOTT, Allan: b. 1766, F, James Scott, merchant in Glasgow; I, Smithfield Iron Co.

SCOTT, Joseph: b. 1728; F, ?; obtained burgess-ship by marriage.

SEMPLE, John: b. 1728; F, ?; obtained burgess-ship by purchase.

SIMSON, James: b. 1757; F, John Simson, Professor of Divinity, University of Glasgow.

SMELLIE, Archibald: b. 1737; F, John Smellie, merchant in Glasgow; purchased estate of Easterhill (barony of Glasgow), 1750; a bankrupt of the American War period when the assets of his firm, McCall, Smellie and Co., were sequestrated.

SMELLIE, Richard: b. 1769; F, Archibald Smellie, merchant in Glasgow.

SNODGRASS, William (?–1815): b. 1774; F, ?; obtained burgess-ship by purchase.

SOMERVELL, James (?–1791): b. 1770; F, William Somervell, writer in Glasgow; U; I, Rope Manufactory of Glasgow; purchased, 1781, estate of Hamilton Farm (Lanarkshire), parts of Scotstoun, 1787 (Lanarkshire) and later Sorn in Ayrshire.

SPEIRS, Alexander (1714–1782): b. 1753; F, John Speirs, burgess of Edinburgh; I, Bell's Tannery, Glasgow Tanwork Co., Wester Sugarhouse, Smithfield Iron Co., Port Glasgow Ropework, Hat Manufactory, Silk Shop, Pollockshaws Printfield Co., Inkle Manufactory; purchased series of estates in Renfrewshire, Stirlingshire and Lanarkshire between 1760 and 1782.

SPEIRS, Archibald: b. 1790; F, Alexander Speirs (above), merchant in Glasgow; as eldest living son inherited the bulk of his father's estates in Renfrewshire and Lanarkshire.

SPEIRS, Peter: b. 1785; F, Alexander Speirs (above), merchant in Glasgow; I, Culcreuch Cotton Spinning Co.; inherited estate of Culcreuch (Stirlingshire) from his father.

SPREULL, James (1699–1769): b. 1727; F, John Spreull, merchant in Glasgow.

STIRLING, Alexander: b. 1741; F, James Stirling, minister of the gospel, Barony parish; I, Tobacco Manufactory Co.

STIRLING, Walter: b. 1740; F, William Stirling, surgeon in Glasgow; I, Shuttlefield Factory Co.

SYM. Andrew: b. 1746; F, John Sym, writer in Glasgow; U.

THOMSON, Alexander: b. 1725; F, ?; obtained burgess-ship, 'free and gratis'.

THOMSON, Andrew: b. 1753; F, ?; obtained burgess-ship by nomination; U; I, Johnstone, Bannatyne and Co., stocking manufacturers; purchased estate of Faskine, Lanarkshire, 1763.

APPENDIX I

THOMSON, John: b. 1727; F, ?; obtained burgess-ship by marriage; I, South Sugarhouse Co., Dalquhurn Bleachfield.

WALLACE, Hugh: b. 1728; F, ?; brother of Sir Thomas Wallace of Craigie.

WALLACE, Thomas (?-1760): b. 1745; F, Thomas Wallace of Cairnhill; inherited estate of Cairnhill.

WALLACE, William: b. 1738; F, Michael Wallace, merchant in Glasgow.

WARDROP, James (?-1799): b. 1770; F, John Wardrop (below), merchant in Glasgow; U; inherited estate of Springbank, 1783, in the barony of Glasgow from his father.

WARDROP, John: b. 1746; F, ?; obtained burgess-ship, 'free and gratis'; came from Edinburgh; purchased estate of Springbank, barony of Glasgow; I, Stocking Manufactory Co., Holland Manufactory Co.

*WILSON, John (1693-1763) I: b. ?; F, ?; owned estate of Shieldhall, barony of Glasgow.

WILSON, John II: b. 1741; F, John Wilson I (above), merchant in Glasgow.

WYLIE, Hugh (?-1782); b. 1762; F, ?; obtained burgess-ship by marriage to Elizabeth, daughter of James Dunlop of Garnkirk, the elder; I, Francis Hamilton and Co., tanners in Glasgow, Rope Manufactory of Glasgow; purchased estate of Broomfield, barony of Glasgow; Provost, 1780-1, 1781-2; affairs in confusion as a result of the American War.

YUILLE, George: b. 1781; F, Thomas Yuille of Darleith, merchant in Glasgow.

Appendix II

PARTNERSHIP GROUPINGS IN THE GLASGOW TOBACCO TRADE, c.1765–1790

APPENDIX II

Partnership Groupings in the Glasgow Tobacco Trade, c.1765–1790

'CUNNINGHAME GROUP'

WILLIAM CUNNINGHAME AND CO.: William Cunninghame, Robert Bogle, Andrew Cochrane, Peter Murdoch, John Murdoch, James Robinson, William Reid, William Henderson, John Hamilton (the latter four, factors and storekeepers in America). [PRO, AO 12/56/292]

CUNNINGHAME, FINDLAY AND CO.: William Cunninghame, Robert Findlay, Robert Bogle, Alexander Houston, James Dougall, David Walker (the latter two, storekeepers in America). [PRO, AO 12/56/292]

CUNNINGHAME, BROWN AND CO.: William Cunninghame, Robert Findlay, James Brown. [PRO, AO 12/56/292]

'SPEIRS GROUP'

SPEIRS, BOWMAN AND CO.: Alexander Speirs, John Bowman, William French, Peter Murdoch, Andrew Buchanan (Ardenconnal), John Robertson. [GCA, Speirs Papers, TD 131/7, Ledger, 1785–88]

SPEIRS, FRENCH AND CO.: Alexander Speirs, William French, John Bowman, John Crawford, James Hopkirk, Archibald Moncrieff, Charles Cruickshanks (the latter two, factors in Maryland). [PRO, AO 12/9/55]

PATRICK COLQUOHOUN AND CO.: Patrick Colquohoun, Alexander Speirs, Alexander Ritchie, Joseph Scott, William Carmichael. [GCA, Speirs Papers, TD 131/19/54]

'GLASSFORD GROUP'

JOHN GLASSFORD AND CO.: John Glassford, James Gordon, John Campbell sen., John Campbell jun., Henry Riddell, Alexander Low, William Ingram. [PRO, AO 12/9/37]

GLASSFORD, GORDON, MONTEATH AND CO.: John Glassford, James Gordon, Walter Monteath, John Campbell jun., Neil Jamieson, Henry Riddell, Alexander Low, William Ingram. [*Glasgow Mercury*, 19 January, 1790]

HENDERSON, MCCALL AND CO.: Archibald Henderson, John Glassford, Alexander McCall, James Gordon, George Kippen, Arthur Connell, Neil Jamieson, John Lyle, William Shortridge. [SRO, CE 60/1/10]

GEORGE KIPPEN AND CO.: George Kippen, John Glassford, Alexander McCall, William Shortridge, Arthur Connell. [*Glasgow Advertiser*, 22 January, 1790]

'BUCHANAN–JAMIESON GROUP'

BUCHANAN, HASTIE AND CO.: Andrew Buchanan, Robert Hastie, James Jamieson, Walter Brock, William Buchanan, James Buchanan. [GCA, Probative Writs, B.10/12/4]

APPENDIX II

BOGLE, JAMIESON AND CO.: William Bogle, James Jamieson, Robert Hastie, John Buchanan. [GCA, Reg. of Deeds, B.10/15/8045]

JAMES JAMIESON AND CO.: James Jamieson, William Bogle, Andrew Buchanan, Robert Hastie, Walter Brock, William Buchanan, John Buchanan, Robert Lawson. [GCA, Reg. of Deeds, B.10/15/9593]

HASTIE, CORBETT AND CO.: Robert Hastie, Cunninghame Corbett, William Buchanan, James Somerville (former leading partner in Bogle, Jamieson and Co.), David Black. [GCA, Reg. of Deeds, B.10/15/7947; SRO, Reg. of Deeds, 231/516 MACK]

'THOMSON–McCALL GROUP'

THOMSON, SNODGRASS AND CO.: Andrew Thomson, William Snodgrass, George McCall, James and Samuel Crawford (Greenock), Archibald Bryce, John Snodgrass (Virginia). [GCA, Probative Writs, B.10/12/4]

GEORGE McCALL AND CO.: George McCall, Henry Mitchell, Andrew Thomson, Robert Pailjour. [GCA, Probative Writs, B.10/12/9]

McCALL, SMELLIE AND CO.: Archibald Smellie, Richard Smellie, George McCall, Henry Mitchell. [*Glasgow Courier*, 19 April, 1794]

'DONALD GROUP'

T. AND A. DONALD AND CO.: Thomas Donald, Alexander Donald, James McDowall, Walter Stirling [*Glasgow Courier*, 19 April, 1794]

THOMAS DONALD AND CO.: Thomas Donald, Robert Donald, Hugh Colquohoun, John McDowall. [*Glasgow Herald*, 7 February, 1812]

OTHER PARTNERSHIPS

PETER MURDOCH AND SONS: Peter Murdoch sen., Peter Murdoch, John Murdoch. [GCA, Reg. of Deeds, B.10/15/7628]

COLIN DUNLOP AND SONS: James Dunlop, Colin Dunlop, John Dunlop, John Lindsay. [GCA, Probative Writs, B.10/12/7]

GEORGE OSWALD AND CO.: George Oswald, Alexander Oswald, James Oswald (and others). [SRO, CE 60/1/8]

BAIRD, HAY AND CO.: James Baird, John Hay, Ninian Menzies, Peter Hay. [GCA, Journal of Baird, Hay and Co.]

JAMES BROWN AND CO.: Robert Dreghorn, James Brown, Matthew Orr, John Rowand, James Moore. [PRO, AO 12/9/59–61]

ARCHIBALD AND JOHN COATES AND CO.: John Coats Campbell, William Coats, John Riddell, James Scott, David McCulloch. [*Glasgow Courier*, 10 January, 1804]

CORBETT, RUSSELL AND CO.: Andrew Buchanan (Ardenconnal), David Russell, John Leitch, Cunninghame Corbett, Ross Corbett, Patrick Borthwick. [GCA, Probative Writs, B.10/12/9]

ALEXANDER CUNNINGHAME AND CO.: Alexander Cunninghame, William Cunninghame, Alexander Houston, Robert Bogle, James Dougal. [SRO, GD 247/58/P/1]

DUNMORE, BLACKBURN AND CO.: Thomas Dunmore, Robert Dunmore, Andrew Blackburn, Robert Gilmour, George Logan. [SRO, Reg. of Deeds, 251/704 MACK]

FINDLAY, HOPKIRKS AND CO.: George Buchanan, Andrew Buchanan jun., James Hopkirk, Robert Findlay, Thomas Hopkirk, J. Bannatyne, John Dunlop, Matthew Blair, John Campbell. [SRO, RH 15/2232]

JOHN McCALL AND CO.: John McCall, James Wardrop, Alexander Elliot, Allan Love. [GCA, Reg. of Deeds, B.10/15/8270]

ROBERT MACKAY AND CO.: Robert Mackay, James Gordon, John Riddell, William Robertson, John Robertson, John Spens Munro. [SRO. CC9/7/84/253]

BIBLIOGRAPHY

Bibliography

1. Manuscript Sources

LONDON

Public Record Office:
Customs, 14.
AO 12, 13, Petitions and Compensations of American Loyalists, 1785–89
T.79, Claims of Scottish firms for debts in America
B.T.6/20, Answers to the several questions respecting the Commerce and Shipping between Great Britain and the United States (1789)

British Museum:
Add MSS 33,080, v.160-2, 31-5.
Add MSS, 38, 388-90.
Shelbourne MSS, v.87/8.

EDINBURGH

Scottish Record Office:
Records of the Board of Customs and Excise:
    Collector to Board, CE 60/1/8–15.
    Collectors quarterly accounts, Port Glasgow, E.504/28.
    Collectors quarterly accounts, Greenock, E.504/15.
Old General Register of Sasines.
Particular Register of Sasines, 1770–1820, for Lanark, Renfrew, Barony of Glasgow, Dumbarton, Stirling, Ayr, Perth, Argyll.
Records of the Court of Session:
    (a) Unextracted Processes—
        1 Currie Dal C/11/9, Clyde Ironworks versus Colin Dunlop (1805)
        2 Inglis A.3/10, W. Allison versus John Campbell sen. and Co.
        1 Currie Dal B.11/20, Burns versus Houston, Burns and Co. (1806)
        Innes Durie L.8/1, Dennistoun, Buchanan and Co. versus Lillie etc. (1819)
        1 Currie Mack, Mc.4/7, Petition of Complaint of Laurence McDowall (1810)
        Inglis 5.4/22, Speirs, Murdoch and Co. versus Campbell, Ingram and Co. (1784)
        1 Currie Mack D.6/1, Ranking of the Creditors of James Dunlop (1797)
        1 Currie Mack D.5/14, Summons of James Dunlop's Trustee . . .
        1 Currie Mack, C.4/13, W. Cunninghame and Co. versus Craig (1777)
        Currie Dal Sequestrations, B.1/1, Buchanan, Hastie and Co. (1777)
        1 Currie Dal B.5/8, Thos. Buchanan versus Bogle and Somervell (1778)
        Innes Durie A.6/6, McNeill, Stewart and Co. versus Steel, Nisbet and Co. (1806)
        1 Adams Mack, 5.15/106, Trustees of W. McDowall versus W. McDowall (1818)

(b) Bill Chamber Processes—
   75756, James Dunlop and Co. versus W. McDowall (1801)
   44204, Robert Dunmore versus Howie and others
   65933, Bill of Advocation for Lord Blantyre and the Dalnottar Iron Co. (1809
   I, 29063, Bill of Advocation for Colin Dunlop and Sons (1776)
   I, 58514, A. Houston and Co. versus W. Campbell of Craigie (1806)
   II, 32506, Bill of Suspension, George Bogle and others (1786)
   II, 62556, Bill of Suspension, Robert Dennistoun and Co. versus F. Garden (1821)
   I, 60125, Arch. Speirs versus Martha Bogle (1785)
(c) Miscellaneous—
   Balance Books and other records of Dumbarton Glasswork Co. Misc. 22/ Adams Dal.
(d) RH 15 Series of Business Records extracted from Court of Session Records—
   RH 15/1179–1185, Letterbooks, accounts and legal papers of Lawson, Semple and Co. 1758–1772
   RH 15/407, Sequestration Papers, John Somerville and Co.
   RH 15/168, Sederunt Book of McCall, Riddell and Co.
   RH 15/232, Report in Process, Alex. Gordon versus Frances Cameron
   RH 15/1506, Ledger of Robertson, McKay and Co. 1797–1802
   RH 15/1925, Ledger of Omoa Ironworks
   RH 15/2232, Contract of Copartnery of Findlay, Hopkirks, and Co.
   RH 15/814, Sederunt Book of John Renfrew
Register of Deeds, 1760–1815
Commissariot of Glasgow Wills and Testaments
GD241/43/2, Thomson, Dickson and Shaw Papers
GD213/53, Oswald Papers
GD1/572/33, Dunlop Papers
GD64/247, Campbell of Jura Muniments
GD22/1/229, Cunninghame Graham Muniments
GD26/810, Leven and Melville Muniments
GD51/1, Melville Castle Muniments
GD237/139–63, McDowall of Garthland Papers
GD247/39, 58–9, 141, Letterbooks, Accounts and other Papers of William Cunninghame, 1768–1801
GD103/1/442, Society of Antiquaries Collection
GD1/40, Shipping and Trading Papers, West Indies, 1773–86
GD1/512, Papers of the Buchanans of Auchintorlie
GD1/523/1, Disposition of Partners of Glasgow Ropework

National Library of Scotland
   MS 5026–32, 5209, 6404, Charles Steuart Letterbooks
   MS 8759, 8793–4, Letterbooks of Alexander Houston and Co., 1775–81
   MS 8799, Sale Book of Alexander Houston and Co., 1775–9
   ACC 2346, Letterbook of Trust winding up the affairs of Alexander Houston and Co.
   ACC 3296, Speirs Papers
   MS 8800, Journal of William McDowall, 1729

Edinburgh University Library
   Microfilm M23, Mercantile accounts, Virginia and Maryland, 1753–1830, (Letters and accounts of James Brown and Co., Neil Jamieson and Co. and Glassford, Gordon and Co., originals in library of Congress, Washington).

GLASGOW

Glasgow City Archives:
   C.1/1, Town Council Minute Book
   B.10/15, Glasgow Burgh Court Register of Deeds

B.10/12, Glasgow Burgh Court Register of Probative Writs
Glasgow Burgh Register of Sasines
Records of Merchants House of Glasgow—Minute Books 1754–90, 1790–1826; Matriculation Book 1768–1830
Smith of Jordanhill Papers
Dunlop Legal Papers
Lockhart Family Papers (on microfilm 612)
Letterbook of John Brown Jun., 1772–85
Letterbook of Alex. Henderson, 1758–64 (xerox copy, original in C.G. Lee Collection, Alexandria Public Library, Virginia, U.S.A.)
Oswald Account Book
Letterbook of Hugh Wylie, 1781
Records of George Kippen, John Glassford and Co.
Alexander Hamilton Papers, 1760–70 (xerox copies, originals in possession of the Maryland Historical Society, Baltimore, Maryland, U.S.A.)
Neil Jamieson Correspondence (xerox copies, originals in possession of Library of Congress, Washington, U.S.A.)
Ritchie and Co., Legal Papers
Glasgow Southern Parliamentary Debating Association Collection
Law Papers of Messrs. Thos. Houston and Co., 1777–80
Law Papers of Dr. H. Mackelwraith, 1770–80
Sederunt Book of the Trust of George Oswald, 1818–28
Sederunt Book of James Somervell, 1791–97
Journal of Baird, Hay and Co., 1772–1816
Journal of John Leitch, 1798–1806
Decreet of Ranking of Creditors of Alexander Wilson of Shieldhall, 1781
Memorandum Book of Wiliiam Lockhart of Germiston
Ship Bank Balance Book, 1751–61
Ship Bank Ledger, Part I, 1769–1772
Thistle Bank Journal (xerox copies, originals in Bank of Scotland, Glasgow)

Mitchell Library
Bogle MSS
Campbell of Hallyards Papers
Glasgow Chamber of Commerce Correspondence, 1778–1812
Abstract of Minute Books of West India Association of Glasgow
Adam Montgomery Letterbook
MSS Notes on Family of Dunlop of Garnkirk

Baillie's Institution Library
Sederunt Book of Archibal Ingram
Alexander Houston and Co. Law Papers

Glasgow Chamber of Commerce
Minute Books of Glasgow Chamber of Commerce

LIBRARY OF CONGRESS, WASHINGTON, U.S.A.
James Dunlop Family Papers (here used from transcripts kindly supplied by Mr. Stuart Butler, University of St. Andrews)

IN PRIVATE HANDS
Finlay MSS (James Finlay and Co., Glasgow)
Speirs Papers (Major Crichton-Maitland, Houston House, Houston, Renfrewshire)

2. Printed Original Sources

A. Session Papers, Signet Library, Edinburgh:
   190/13, Messrs, Speirs, French and Co. (1780)

BIBLIOGRAPHY

309/3, Petition of Robert Dunmore (1797)
155/8, Information for Messrs. Bogle (1769)
180/7, Answers for Arch. Speirs of Elderslie (1779)
180/8, Answers for Miss Margaret N. Cranstoun (1800)
162/23, Information for Elizabeth and Barbara Cunninghame (1775)
438/18, Minutes in Process, Henry Riddell and others (1802)
422/53, Answers for John Geddes (1801)
413/27 Petition of James Allan (1800)
413/28, Petition of Andrew Thompson (1800)
608/41, Minutes of the Freeholders of Renfrewshire (1790)
374/5, Petition of Andrew Houston (1798)
406/21, Petition of James Dunlop (1799)
293/17, Information for H. and R. Baird (1814)

B. Newspapers and contemporary journals:
Glasgow Mercury
Glasgow Courier
Glasgow Herald and Advertiser
Glasgow Advertiser and Evening Intelligencer
Glasgow Journal
Glasgow Weekly Magazine
Glasgow Magazine and Review
Caledonian Mercury
Edinburgh Evening Courant
Edinburgh Advertiser
Scots Magazine

C. Official Papers:
W. J. Addison (ed), *The Matriculation Albums of the University of Glasgow, 1728–1858* (Glasgow 1913)
W. J. Addison (ed), *A Roll of Graduates of the University of Glasgow* (Glasgow, 1898)
J. R. Anderson (ed), *The Burgesses and Guild Brethren of Glasgow, 1573–1750* (Edinburgh 1925)
J. R. Anderson (ed), *The Burgesses and Guild Brethren of Glasgow, 1751–1846* (Edinburgh 1935)
J. B. Moore (ed), *History and Digest of the International Arbitrations to which the United States has been a Party.*
Anon., *The Proceedings of the Convention of Delegates ... of Virginia* (Richmond, 1816)
Anon., *Journal of the House of Delegates of the Commonwealth of Virginia* (Richmond, 1828)

D. Contemporary Writings and Business Records:
C. F. Adams (ed), *The Works of John Adams* (Boston, 1850)
P. F. Ford (ed), *The Writings of Thomas Jefferson* (New York, 1892–99)
Anon., (ed), *The Cochrane Correspondence concerning the Affairs of Glasgow*
I. Lettice, *Letters on a Tour through various parts of Scotland in the year 1792*
Glasgow Directories, 1787–1810
Glasgow Almanacks

3. Unpublished Theses

R. W. Coakley, 'Virginia Commerce during the American Revolution', University of Virginia, Ph.D. (1949)
C. B. Coulter, 'The Virginia Merchant', University of Princeton, Ph.D. (1944)
T. M. Devine, 'Glasgow Merchants in Colonial Trade, c.1770–1815' 2 vols., University of Strathclyde, Ph.D. (1971)
D. I. Fagerstrom, 'The American Revolutionary Movement in Scottish Opinion, 1763 to 1783', University of Edinburgh, Ph.D. (1951)

4. Secondary Sources

A. Articles:

Anon., 'The Rise of Glasgow's West Indian Trade, 1793-1818', *Three Banks Review*, 38 (1958)
Anon., 'Chips from an Old Glasgow Ship's Log, 1777-1823' *Old Glasgow Club Transactions*, III
Anon., 'The Dunlops of Garnkirk', *Proceedings of the Regality Club*, 2nd ser. (1893)
Anon., 'History of Buchanan St., and its Proprietors', *Old Glasgow Club Transactions* (1907-8)
B. L. Anderson, 'Provincial Aspects of the Financial Revolution of the Eighteenth Century', *Business History* xi (1969)
T. C. Barker, 'Smuggling in the Eighteenth Century: the evidence of the Scottish Tobacco Trade', *Virginia Magazine of History and Biography* (1954)
W. K. Barritt, 'The Navy and the Clyde in the American War, 1777-83', *Mariners Mirror*, 55 (1969)
K. Berrill, 'International Trade and the Rate of Economic Growth', *Econ. Hist. Rev.* 2nd ser., XII (1960)
H. C. Bell, 'The West India Trade before the American Revolution', *American Hist. Rev.* XXII (1917)
J. Butt, 'The Scottish Iron Industry before the Hot Blast', *Journal of West of Scotland Iron and Steel Inst.* XXIII, 6 (1965-6)
—'Glenbuck Iron Works', *Ayrshire Coll.*, 2nd ser., VIII (1967-9)
R. H. Campbell, 'An Economic History of Scotland in the Eighteenth Century', *SJPE* XI (1964)
—'The Anglo-Scottish Union of 1707: the Economic Consequences', *Econ. Hist. Rev.* 2nd ser., XVI (1964)
—'The Industrial Revolution in Scotland: a Revision Article', *SHR*, 46 (1968)
—'The Union and Economic Growth' in T. I. Rae (ed), *The Union of 1707: Its Impact on Scotland* (Glasgow, 1974)
Sydney D. Chapman, 'Fixed Capital Formation in the British Cotton Industry, 1770-1815', *Econ. Hist. Rev.* 2nd ser., XXIII (1970)
S. G. Checkland, 'Two Scottish West Indian Liquidations after 1793', *SJPE* IV (1957)
R. W. Coakley, 'The Two James Hunters of Fredericksburg', *The Virginia Magazine of History and Biography*, 56 (1948)
B. Crispin, 'Clyde Shipping and the American War', *SHR*, 41 (1962)
R. Davis, 'English Foreign Trade, 1700-1774', *Econ. Hist. Rev.*, 2nd ser., XV (1962)
Marc Engal and Joseph A. Ernst, 'An Economic Interpretation of the American Revolution', *William and Mary Quarterly*, 3rd ser., XXIX (1972)
Emory G. Evans, 'Planter Indebtedness and the Coming of the Revolution in Virginia', *William and Mary Quarterly*, 3rd ser., XIX (1962)
—'Private Indebtedness and the Revolution in Virginia', *William and Mary Quarterly*, 3rd ser., XXVIII (1971)
D. A. Farnie, 'The Commercial Empire of the Atlantic, 1607-1783', *Econ. Hist. Rev.* 2nd ser., XV (1962)
H. J. Habbakuk, 'English Landownership, 1680-1740', *Econ. Hist. Rev.* X (1940)
—'The English Land Market in the Eighteenth Century', in J. S. Bromley and E. H. Kossman (eds), *Britain and the Netherlands* (London, 1960)
H. Hamilton, 'Combination in the West of Scotland Coal Trade, 1790-1817', *Economic History*, II (1930)
—'The Founding of the Glasgow Chamber of Commerce in 1783', *SJPE*, I (1954)
—'The Failure of the Ayr Bank, 1772', *Econ. Hist. Rev.* 2nd ser., VIII (1967)
J. R. Hume and J. Butt, 'Muirkirk, 1786-1802', *SHR* XIV (1966)
Merrill Jensen, 'The American Revolution and American Agriculture', *Agricultural History* XLIII (1969)
A. H. John, 'The London Assurance Company and the Marine Insurance Market in the Eighteenth Century', *Economica*, new ser., XXV (1958)
J. R. Kellett, 'Property Speculators and the Building of Glasgow, 1783-1830', *SJPE* VIII (1961)

J. R. Kellett, 'The Private Incomes of Glasgow's Lord Provosts', *Accountants Magazine* (1968)

A. C. Land, 'Economic Base and Social Structure: The Northern Chesapeake in the Eighteenth Century', *Journ. Econ. Hist.* XXV (1965)

—'Economic Behaviour in a Planting Society', *Journ. Southern History* XXXIII (1967)

—'The Tobacco Staple and the Planter's Problems: Technology, Labour and Crops', *Agricultural History*, XLIII (1969)

W. A. Low, 'Merchant and Planter Relations in post-Revolutionary Virginia, 1783–89', *The Virginia Magazine of History and Biography*, 61 (1953)

T. Lugton, 'Social Life of Glasgow in the Eighteenth Century', *Old Glasgow Club Trans.* II (1911–12)

D. S. Macmillan, 'The "New Men" in Action: Scottish Mercantile and Shipping Operations in the North American Colonies' in D. S. Macmillan (ed), *Canadian Business History*, (Toronto, 1972)

W. H. Mathew, 'The Origins and Occupations of Glasgow Students' *Past and Present*, 33 (1966)

W. E. Minchinton, 'Bristol—Metropolis of the West in the Eighteenth Century', *Trans. R. Hist. Soc.* 5th ser., IV (1954)

—'The Merchants in England in the Eighteenth Century', *Explorations in Entrepreneurial History* X (1957)

Jacob M. Price, 'The Beginnings of Tobacco Manufacture in Virginia', *The Virginia Magazine of History and Biography*, 64 (1956)

—'The Rise of Glasgow in the Chesapeake Tobacco Trade, 1707–75', in P. L. Payne (ed), *Studies in Scottish Business History* (London, 1967)

—'The Economic Growth of the Chesapeake and the European Market', *Journ. Econ. Hist.* XXIV (1964)

—'Capital and Credit in the Chesapeake Tobacco Trade, 1750–1775', in V. B. Platt and D. C. Skaggs (eds), *Of Mother Country and Plantations, Proceedings of the 27th Conference in Early American History* (Bowling Green, 1971)

Myra L. Rich, 'Speculations on the Significance of Debt, Virginia, 1781–89', *Virginia Magazine of History and Biography*, 76 (1968)

M. L. Robertson, 'Scottish Commerce and the American War of Independence', *Econ. Hist. Rev.* 2nd ser., IX (1956)

W. St. Robinson jun., 'Richard Oswald the Peacemaker', *Ayrshire Collections*, 2nd ser., III (1959)

Andrew Scott, 'The History and Progress of the Four Leading Articles of Foreign Origin', *Trans. Glasgow Arch. Soc.* (1859)

Fred. Shelley (ed), 'The Journal of Ebenezer Hazard in Virginia, 1777', *The Virginia Magazine of History and Biography*, 62 (1954)

Richard Sheridan, 'The British Credit Crisis of 1772 and the American Colonies', *Journ. Econ. Hist.* XX (1960)

T. C. Smout, 'The Development and Enterprise of Glasgow, 1556–1707', *SJPE* VII (1960)

—'The Glasgow Merchant Community in the Seventeenth Century', *SHR*, 47 (1968)

—'Scottish Landowners and Economic Growth, 1650–1850', *SJPE* IX (1964)

J. H. Soltow, 'Scottish Traders in Virginia, 1750–75', *Econ. Hist. Rev.* 2nd ser., XII (1959)

—'The Role of Williamsburg in the Virginia Economy, 1750–75', *William and Mary Quarterly*, 3rd ser., XV (1958)

W. H. Siebert, 'The Loyalists in Pennsylvania', *Ohio State University Bulletin* XXIV

D. Syrett, 'The West India Merchants and the Conveyance of the King's Troops to the Caribbean, 1779–82', *Journ. of Society for Army Historical Research*, 45 (1967)

Thad W. Tate, 'The Coming of the Revolution in Virginia: Britain's Challenge to Virginia's Ruling Class, 1763–1776', *William and Mary Quarterly*, 3rd ser., XIX (1962)

E. E. B. Thomson, 'A Scottish Merchant in Felmouth in the Eighteenth Century', *The Virginia Magazine of History and Biography* XXXIX (1931)
G. Thomson, 'James Watt and the Monkland Canal', *SHR* XXIX (1950)
—'The Dalnottar Iron Company', *SHR* XXXV (1956)
R. P. Thomson, 'The Tobacco Export of the Upper James River Naval District, 1773-75', *William and Mary Quarterly*, 3rd ser., XVIII (1961)
A. J. Voke, 'Accounting Methods of Colonial Merchants in Virginia', *Journ. of Accountancy*, XLII (1926)
J. T. Ward, 'Ayrshire Landed Estates, 19th Century', *Ayrshire Collections*, 2nd ser., VIII (1967-9)
R. G. Wilson, 'Records for a study of the Leeds Woollen Merchants', *Archives*, VIII (1967)
—'The Denisons and Milneses: Eighteenth Century Merchant Landowners', in J. T. Ward and R. G. Wilson (eds), *Land and Industry* (Newton Abbot, 1971).

B. Books:

William Aiton, *General View of the Agriculture of the County of Ayr* (Glasgow, 1811)
Anon., *Lochwinnoch, An Ecclesiastical Sketch* (Paisley, 1878)
Anon., *The Constitution, Rules and History of the Royal Incorporation of Hutcheson's Hospital* (Glasgow, 1880)
Anon., *James Finlay & Co., Manufacturers and East India Merchants 1750-1950* (Glasgow, 1951)
Anon., *The Old Country Houses of the Old Glasgow Gentry* (Glasgow, 1870)
Anon., *A View of the Merchants House of Glasgow* (Glasgow, 1866)
Anon., *Old Glasgow Exhibition: Catalogue, Notes and Indexes* (Glasgow, 1894)
T. S. Ashton, *Economic Fluctuations in England* (Oxford, 1959)
Sir James Bell and James Paton, *Glasgow, its Municipal Organisation and Administration* (Glasgow, 1896)
C. W. Boase, *A Century of Banking in Dundee* (Dundee, 1864)
Henry Brougham, *An Enquiry into the Colonial Policy of the European Nations*, 2 vols. (London, 1803)
John Buchanan, *Banking in Glasgow during the Olden Time* (Glasgow, 1884)
R. M. Buchanan, *Notes on the Members of the Buchanan Society, 1725-1829* (Glasgow, 1931)
Andrew Brown, *History of Glasgow and of Paisley, Greenock and Port Glasgow* (Glasgow, 1795), 2 vols.
Burke's Landed Gentry (London, 1894 ed)
John Butt, *The Industrial Archaeology of Scotland* (Newton Abbot, 1967)
John Butt, (ed), *Robert Owen, Prince of Cotton Spinners* (Newton Abbot, 1971)
Rondo Cameron, *Banking in the early stages of Industrialisation* (Oxford, 1967)
Dugald Campbell, *Historical Sketch of the Town and Harbours of Greenock* (Greenock, 1879) vol. 1.
R. H. Campbell, *Carron Company* (Edinburgh, 1961)
—*Scotland since 1707, the Rise of an Industrial Society* (Oxford, 1965)
Alexander Carlyle, *Autobiography* (Edinburgh, 1861)
Robert Chambers, *The Picture of Scotland* (Edinburgh, 1827)
George Chalmers, *Estimate of the Comparative Strength of Great Britain* (London, 1794 ed)
Richard Champion, *Considerations on the Present Situation of Great Britain and the United States of America* (London, 1784)
James Cleland, *Statistical and Population Tables relative to the City of Glasgow* (Glasgow, 1829)
—*The Annals of Glasgow* (Glasgow, 1817)
Robert Chapman, *The Picture of Glasgow and Strangers' Guide with a Sketch of a Tour to Loch Lomond, Perth, Inveraray and the Falls of Clyde* (Glasgow, 1818)
James Cleland, *Historical Account of the Grammar School of Glasgow* (Glasgow, 1825)
Sir W. L. Clowes, *The Royal Navy from the Earliest Times to the Present* (London, 1897-1903), vol. III

BIBLIOGRAPHY

Henry Cockburn, *Memorials of His Time* (Edinburgh, 1909 ed)
David Craig, *Scottish Literature and the Scottish People, 1680–1830* (London, 1961)
Henry Cockburn, (ed), *Journal of Henry Cockburn, 1831–1854* (Edinburgh, 1874)
J. Cunnison and J. B. S. Gilfillan, *Third Statistical Account: Glasgow Region* (Glasgow, 1958)
Ralph Davis, *The Rise of the English Shipping Industry* (London, 1962)
Noel Deer, *The History of Sugar* (London, 1949) vol. II
Daniel Defoe, *The Complete English Tradesman* (London, 1745), 2 vols., Reprinted in *Works*, vols. 17–18 (Oxford, 1841)
G. D. Donald, *The Board of Green Cloth* (Glasgow, 1891)
B. F. Duckham, *History of the Scottish Coal Industry*, Vol. I (Newton Abbot, 1970)
Richard Duncan, *Notices and Documents illustrative of the Literary History of Glasgow during the greater part of last Century* (Glasgow, 1886)
J. Denholm, *History of Glasgow* (Glasgow, 1804)
Archibald Dunlop, *Memorabilia of the Family of Dunlop* (Privately Printed, N.D.)
George Eyre-Todd, *History of Glasgow* (Glasgow, 1934)
C. R. Fay, *English Economic History mainly since 1700* (Cambridge, 1948)
—*Adam Smith and the Scotland of his Day* (Cambridge, 1956)
William Ferguson, *Scotland, 1689 to the Present* (Edinburgh, and London, 1968)
James Coutts, *A History of The University of Glasgow, from its Foundations in 1451 to 1909* (Glasgow, 1909)
Thomas Ferguson, *The Dawn of Scottish Social Welfare* (London, 1948)
D. K. Fieldhouse, *The Colonial Empires* (London, 1966)
M. W. Flinn, *Origins of the Industrial Revolution* (London, 1968)
Sir William Forbes, *Memoirs of a Banking House* (London, 1860)
A. Forsyth, *The Beauties of Scotland* (Edinburgh, 1806)
William Fullarton, *General View of the Agriculture of the County of Ayr* (1783)
John Gibson, *The History of Glasgow from the Earliest Accounts to the Present Time* (Glasgow, 1777)
A. E. Gordon, *The History of Glasgow from the earliest times to the present time* (Glasgow, 1872) 2 vols.
James Gourlay, *A Glasgow Miscellany* (Privately Printed, N.D.)
James Gourlay, (ed), *The Provosts of Glasgow 1609–1832*
G. S. Graham, *Sea Power and British North America* (Cambridge, Mass., 1941)
H. G. Graham, *Social Life of Scotland in the Eighteenth Century* (Glasgow, 1899)
L. C. Gray, *History of Agriculture in the Southern United States to 1860* (Washington, 1933)
John Gunn and M. L. Newbiggin, (eds), *The City of Glasgow, its Origin, Growth and Development* (Edinburgh, 1921)
H. Hamilton, *The Industrial Revolution in Scotland* (Reprinted, London, 1966)
—*An Economic History of Scotland in the Eighteenth Century*, (Oxford, 1963)
V. T. Harlow, *The Founding of the Second British Empire* (London, 1952) vol. I
I. S. Harrell, *Loyalism in Virginia* (Durham, North Carolina, 1926)
J. P. P. Higgins and S. Pollard (eds), *Aspects of Capital Investment in Great Britain, 1750–1850* (London, 1971)
John M. Hutcheson, *Notes on the Sugar Industry of the United Kingdom* (Greenock, 1901)
J. R. Hutchinson, *The Press Gang Afloat and Ashore* (London, 1913)
Theodora Keith, *Commercial Relations of England and Scotland 1603–1707* (Cambridge, 1910)
A. W. Kerr, *History of Banking in Scotland* (Glasgow, 1926)
Joseph Irving, *The History of Dunbartonshire* (Dumbarton, 1857)
Joan Lindsay, *The Canals of Scotland* (Newton Abbot, 1968)
E. Lipson, *Economic History of England* (London, 1948) vol. III
David Loch, *Essays on the Trade, Manufactures and Fisheries of Scotland* (Edinburgh, 1778–79) 2 vols.
S. G. E. Lythe, *The Economy of Scotland in its European Setting, 1550–1625* (Edinburgh and London, 1960)

John Knox, *A View of the British Empire more especially Scotland* (3rd edition, London, 1785), 2 vols.
W. F. McArthur, *History of Port Glasgow* (Glasgow, 1932)
H. B. McCall, *Memoirs of My Ancestors* (Birmingham, 1884)
John McCure, *A View of the City of Glasgow* (Glasgow, 1736)
David Macpherson, *Annals of Commerce, Manufactures, Fisheries and Navigation* (London, 1805), vols. III–IV
Alexander Martin, *General View of the Agriculture of the County of Renfrew* (London, 1794)
W. H. Marwick, *Scotland in Modern Times* (London, 1964)
Peter Mathias, *The First Industrial Nation* (London, 1969)
A. P. Middleton, *Tobacco Coast: a Maritime History of Chesapeake Bay in the Colonial Era* (Newport News, 1953)
J. C. Millar, *The Origins of the American Revolution* (Revised edition, Oxford, 1959)
G. E. Mingay, *English Landed Society in the Eighteenth Century* (London, 1963)
J. O. Mitchell, *Old Glasgow Essays* (Glasgow, 1905)
—*Two Old Scottish Firms* (Glasgow, 1893)
James Muir, *Glasgow Streets and Places* (Glasgow and Edinburgh. 1892)
David Murray, *Memories of the Old College of Glasgow* (Glasgow, 1927)
—*Early Burgh Organisation in Scotland* (Glasgow, 1924)
John Naismith, *General View of the Agriculture of the County of Clydesdale* (Glasgow, 1798)
Sir Lewis Namier and John Brooke, *The History of Parliament: The House of Commons, 1754–90* (London, 1964)
New Statistical Account (Edinburgh, 1842)
J. U. Nef, *The Rise of the British Coal Industry* (London, 1932) vol. I
C. A. Oakley, *Connal and Co. Ltd., 1722–1946* (Glasgow, 1946)
James Pagan, *Sketches of the History of Glasgow* (Glasgow, 1847)
Richard Pares, *A West India Fortune* (London, 1950)
—*War and Trade in The West Indies 1739–63* (Oxford, 1936)
—*Yankees and Creoles* (Cambridge, Mass., 1956)
P. L. Payne (ed), *Studies in Scottish Business History* (London, 1967)
James Paterson, *History of the Counties of Ayr and Wigton* (Edinburgh, 1866), 4 vols.
Harold Perkin, *The Origins of Modern English Society* (London, 1969)
Sidney Pollard, *The Genesis of Modern Management* (London, 1965)
Jacob M. Price, *France and the Chesapeake* (Michigan, 1972) 2 vols.
G. S. Pryde, *Scotland from 1603 to the Present Day* (Edinburgh, 1962)
John Rae, *Life of Adam Smith* (London, 1895)
R. S. Rait, *History of the Union Bank of Scotland* (Glasgow, 1930)
Robert Reid, *Old Glasgow and its Environs* (Glasgow, 1864)
Sir H. W. Richmond, *The Navy in the War of 1739–48* (Cambridge, 1920)
William Robertson, *Historic Ayrshire* (Edinburgh, 1891) 2 vols.
L. J. Saunders, *Scottish Democracy, 1815–40, The Social and Intellectual Background* (Edinburgh, London, 1950)
P. A. Ramsay, *Views in Renfrewshire with Historical and Descriptive Notices* (Edinburgh, 1839)
W. R. Scott, *The Constitution of English, Scottish and Irish Joint-Stock Companies to 1720* (London, 1911)
W. R. Scott, *Adam Smith as Student and Professor* (Glasgow, 1937)
Senex (J. M. Reid), *Glasgow Past and Present* (Glasgow, 1884) 3 vols.
Seymour Shapiro, *Capital and the Cotton Industry in the Industrial Revolution* (New York, 1967)
B. C. Skinner, *The Crammond Company* (Edinburgh, 1965)
Sir John Sinclair (ed), *The Old Statistical Account* (Edinburgh, 1791–8) vols. 1–2, 5, 7–8, 12–14, 15, 17
T. C. Smout, *History of the Scottish People, 1550–1830* (London, 1969)
—*Scottish Trade on the Eve of Union* (Edinburgh and London, 1963)
George Stewart, *Progress of Glasgow* (Glasgow, 1883)

BIBLIOGRAPHY

—*Curiosities of Glasgow Citizenship* (Glasgow, 1881)
H. Stewart (ed), *Fasti Ecclesiae Scoticanae* (Edinburgh, 1920) vol. III
John Strang, *Glasgow and its Clubs* (Glasgow, 1864)
Helen J. Steven, *Sorn Parish: Its History and Associations* (Glasgow, 1898)
David Syrett, *Shipping and the American War, 1775–83* (London, 1970)
C. C. Thompson, *An Old Glasgow Family of Thomson* (Glasgow, 1903)
F. M. L. Thompson, *English landed Society in the 19th Century* (London, 1963)
A. S. Turberville (ed), *Johnson's England, An Account of the Life and Manners of his Age* (Oxford, 1953) vol. I
W. M. Wade, *The History of Glasgow, Ancient and Modern* (Paisley, 1821)
T. S. Willan, *The English Coasting Trade, 1600–1750* (New Ed., Manchester, 1967)
Eric Williams, *Capitalism and Slavery* (Chapel Hill, 1944)
Gomer Williams, *History of the Liverpool Privateers and Letters of Marque with an Account of the Liverpool Slave Trade* (1897, new imp., London, 1966)
Andrew Wight, *Present State of Husbandry in Scotland* (Edinburgh, 1778–84) 6. vols.
C. E. Wright and C. E. Fayle, *History of Lloyds* (London, 1928)

Index

Adams, John, 130, 157
Admiralty, 312, 139
Aiton, Andrew (1696–1772), 177
Allan, Alexander, iron merchant, 41
Allan, David, iron merchant, 41
Alexander, William, 67, 165
Alexander, William and Sons, 90, 165
Alexandria, Virginia, 107
Alston, John, jun., 21, 24, 25, 177
American Confederation, 155
American War of Independence, 4, 10, 20, 23, 43–4, 74, 97, 103–47, 166
Amsterdam, 131
Anderson, B. L., 14
Anderson, Messrs. Francis and John, iron merchants, 41
Anderson, James, factor, 131
Anderston Brewery Co., 83
Annandale, Marquis of, 96
Antigua, 62, 132
Argyll St., Glasgow, 11
Armaments (for merchant vessels), 41–2
Ashgrove estate, 28
Auchencruive estate, 32, n. 68
Ayr, 140, 147
Ayr Bank (Douglas, Heron and Co.), 20–1
Ayrshire, 5, 18, 19, 20, 21, 25, 28, 147

Baird, Hugh, iron merchant, 41
Baird, James, sen., 177, 188
Baird, James, jun., 177
Baird, John, iron merchant, 41
Baird, Robert, iron merchant, 41
Baird, Hay and Co., 76, 115, 116, 118, 188
Balgonie Iron Co., 41
Ballantyne, James, sen., 65
Ballantyne, James, jun., 65, 177
Ballantyne, John, 177
Ballantyne, J. and W. and Co., 111, 126
Ballandalloch Cotton Co., 45

Ballandalloch estate, 18
Banknock Coal Co., 43
Bankruptcies, *see under* Tobacco trade and Merchants
Bankruptcy Act, 1772, 98
Bank of Scotland, 95
Banking, 92–8; *see under also* Ayr Bank, Bank of Scotland, Glasgow Arms Bank, Greenock Banking Company, Renfrewshire Banking Company, Royal Bank of Scotland, Ship Bank, Thistle Bank.
Bannatyne, Neil, stocking manufacturer, 64
Barker, Prof. T. C., vi
Barns, John (?–1791), 177
Belfast, 139, 142
Bell's Tannery, 35, 38
Beith, Ayrshire, 147
Berkshire County, Maryland, 114
Berrie family, 73, 96
Berrie, James, 177
Berrie, Robert, 177
Bills of exchange, 89–91, 119
Black, Prof. Joseph, 8
Blackburn, Andrew, 177, 188
Blackburn, Hugh, 177
Blackburn, John, 41
Blackburn, John, West India merchant, 177
Blair, Matthew, merchant in Potomack, 77
Bluefields Bay, Jamaica, 143
Blythswood square, Glasgow, 167
Bogle family, 6, 7, 18, 24, 57, 64, 72, 82, 90
Bogle, Archibald (1730–1812), 178.
Bogle, George II [Daldowie] (1701–84), 3, 8, 13, 36, 40, 73, 91, 178
Bogle and Co., George, 79
Bogle, Matthew, 57
Bogle, Robert, 24, 25, 35, 45, 82, 91, 178
Bogle, Robert, jun., 23, 41, 178, 187, 188
Bogle, Susannah, 97
Bogle, William, 13, 75, 97, 178, 188

INDEX

Bogle, Jamieson and Co., 65, 76, 188
Bogle, Somervell and Co., 93, 95, 97, 109
Bogle MSS, 57
Bond-lending, 92–8
Bonnet lairds, 19
Bordeaux, 62
Borthwick, Patrick, factor, 188
Boston, 138
Bothwell, 23
Bowman family, 7
Bowman, John (1701–97), 28, 35, 72, 74, 178, 187
Boyd, Robert, 57, 178
Bristol, 65, 75, 90, 157, 165
Brock, Walter, 178, 187, 188
Brown, Alexander (1738–1803), 178
Brown, Andrew, 96, 178
Brown, Hugh, 178
Brown, James, 178
Brown, James and Co., 76, 104, 116, 126, 188
Brown, John (1694–1757), 178
Brown, John of Lanfine, Glasgow banker, 111
Brown, Carrick and Co., linen merchants, 39
Bryce, Archibald, factor
Buchanan family (of Drumpellier), 7, 18, 27, 29, 73, 74, 92.
Buchanan family (of Auchintorlie), 27
Buchanan, Andrew I, 178
Buchanan, Provost Andrew, 7, 36, 93, 178, 187, 188
Buchanan, Andrew, jun. (of Ardenconnal), 23, 24, 36, 164, 187, 188.
Buchanan, George (1728–1762), 178
Buchanan, George, jun., 37
Buchanan, James, 11, 36, 95–6, 178, 187
Buchanan, Thomas, 25
Buchanan, William, 77, 97, 179, 187, 188
Buchanan-Jamieson group, 74
Buchanan, Hastie and Co., 75, 76, 78, 95–6, 116–18, 187
Buchanan, Andrew and Co., linen merchants, 39
Buchanan, Archibald and Co., 7, 57, 72, 73
G. and A. Buchanan and Co., 75
Buchanan St., Glasgow, 11
Building (in Glasgow), 11, 167
Burns, James, iron merchant, 41
Burton, Robert, factor, 131
Busby estate, 18

Caithness, 6
Calder Ironworks, 41
Caledonian Mercury, 104, 111
Camlachie Coal Works, 42–3
Campbell, Alexander, 36, 51, 178
Campbell, Archibald, 27
Campbell, Lord Frederick, 142

Campbell, Islay of Succoth, 37
Campbell, James, 36
Campbell, John, jun. (1743–90), 178, 181
Campbell, John Coates (1721–1804), 9, 23, 35, 93, 178, 188
Campbell, John, merchant in Blandensburg, 77
Campbell, Neil, 10
Campbell, Prof. R. H., 62
Canada, 61, 120, 127, 128, 162
Canals, *see under*, Monkland Canal
Candleriggs, Glasgow, 11
Caribbean, *see under*, West Indies
Carleton, General Sir Guy, 157
Carlyle, Rev. Alexander, 8, 10, 45
Carmarthen, Lord, 157
Carmyle estate, 18
Carron Company, 141, 142, 143
Carronades, 141–2
Cape Clear, 142
Cape Finnisterre, 13
Capital, 75, 77–78, 89–98
Cash accompts, 96
Cathcart, Lord, 13
Charlestown, 125, 128
Chapman, Dr. S. D., 44
Chesapeake Bay, 56, 60, 66, 111, 125, 128, 163
Christian, Capt., 140
Christie, Robert (1717–80), 179
Clyde, river, v, 4, 7, 11, 13, 35–6, 66, 68, 72, 73, 107, 110, 116, 127, 128, 130, 131, 132, 134, 138, 139–41, 142, 143, 144, 146, 147, 161, 172
Clyde Iron Co., 41
Coal industry, 40–3
Coates, Archibald (?–1770), 179
Arch. and John Coates and Co., 188
Coates, George, 23
Coates, William, 179, 188
Coates, Campbell and Co., linen merchants, 39
Cockburn, Henry, 26
Cochrane, Andrew (1696–1777), 7, 9, 73, 74, 82, 93, 179, 187
Colquohoun, Hugh, 188
Colquohoun, Patrick (1745–1820), 11, 76, 132, 153, 179, 187
Commission system (or consignment system, in the tobacco trade), 55, 67
Committee of American Merchants, 153
Connell, Arthur (1717–75), 36, 166, 179, 187
Connell, James, 179
Consignment system (in the tobacco trade), 55, 67
Contracts of copartnery, 72, 76
Convention of Royal Burghs, 139
Convoys, 143, 144–5
Corbett, Archibald, 178

INDEX

Corbett, Cunninghame, 9, 25, 179, 188
Corbett, James (1690–1749), 37, 179
Corbett, John (1729–1815), 179
Corbett, Ross, 188
Corbett, James and Co. (the Rope Manufactory of Glasgow), 37
Corbett, Russell and Co., 164, 188
Cork, 132, 138, 146
Cotton industry, 43–6
Cotton trade, 13, 44, 143, 165
Coulter, James, 179
'Court price' (for tobacco), 61
Craig, John, storekeeper, 77, 83
Craigton estate, 18
Cramond Iron Co., 37, 41
Crawford, George, 21, 36, 92, 178
Crawford, John, Member of Parliament, 153
Crawford, Robert, 179
Crawford, Thomas, 147
Crawford, William, 36, 179
Creighton, Alderman, 132
Cross, Robert, 97
Cudbear Works, 39
Culcreuch Cotton Co., 45
Cullen, Prof. William, 8
Cumberland Factory Co., 39
Cunninghames of Caprington, lairds in Ayrshire, 6
Cunninghame, Alexander, 188
Cunninghame, Alexander and Co., 77, 188
Cunninghame, William, 4, 6, 7, 10, 11, 14, 20, 22, 25, 28, 37, 78, 82, 104, 105, 112, 155, 164, 166, 179, 187
Cunninghame, William and Co., 36, 60, 61, 65, 66, 68, 70, 73, 75, 76, 82–7, 115, 125, 126, 133, 134, 187
Cunninghame, Brown and Co., 74, 76, 82
Cunninghame, Findlay and Co., 65, 66, 73, 75, 76, 78, 82, 115, 187
Customs duties, 3, 15, n. 2

Dalbeth Coal Work, 40
Daldowie estate, 18, 40
Dalnottar Iron Co., 37, 41, 46, 83
Dalrymple, Col. William, 41
Deanston Mill Co., 45
Debt, 59–60, 64, 80, 111–15, 120, 153–9
Defoe, Daniel, 138
Dempster, George of Skibo, 45
Denholm, James, 115
Dennistoun family, 42
Dennistoun, James, sen., 25, 37, 45, 179
Dennistoun, James, jun. (1748–1816), 45, 179
Dennistoun, Richard, 36
Dennistoun, Robert, 36, 51
Devine, T. M., 20
Devon Ironworks, 41

Dinwiddie, Lawrence (1696–1764), 35, 179
Dinwiddie, Robert (?–1789), 179
Dinwiddie, Crawford and Co., 65, 68, 108, 111, 115, 126
Donald family, 4
Donald, Alexander (1742–?), 165, 180, 188
Donald, James (1713–60), 180
Donald, Robert (1724–1803), 180
Donald, Thomas (1745–98), 38, 76, 180, 188
Donald, T. and A. and Co., 61, 65, 74, 75, 76, 164, 188
Dougalston estate, 27
Downie, Patrick, merchant in Prestonpans, 40
Dreghorn, Allan (?–1764), 57, 93
Dreghorn, Robert, 57, 180, 188
Dreghorn, Murdoch and Co., 111
Drumpellier estate, 18
Dumbarton, 142
Dumbarton Brewery Co., 38
Dumbarton Glasswork Co., 38, 46
Dumbartonshire, 27, 29
Dumfries, Virginia, 105
Dumfriesshire, 7
Dundas, Henry, 158
Dundonald, Earl of, 13
Dunkirk, 110
Dunlop family, 4, 5, 26, 27, 29, 41, 42, 72
Dunlop, Colin (1706–77), 18, 29, 42, 65, 76, 91, 93, 180, 188
Dunlop, Colin and Sons, 109, 111, 115, 127, 164, 188
Dunlop, James (1741–1816), 7, 18, 21, 23, 24, 25, 35, 38, 42–3, 97, 180, 188
Dunlop, John (1744–1820), 91, 180, 188
Dunlop, Robert (1700–62), 93, 180
Dunlop, Thomas, 180
Dunlop, William, 180
Dunlop, Capt. William, 73
Dunmore, Francis, 26
Dunmore, Robert, 8, 10, 14, 18, 21, 36, 37, 45, 132, 134, 180, 188
Robert Dunmore and Co., 144, 147, 164
Dunmore, Thomas (?–1790), 180, 188
Dunmore, Blackburn and Co., 188
Dunmore, Gilmour and Co., 113
Dunmore Coal Co., 42
Dunn, William, cotton-spinner, 37

East Florida, 127
Easter Barrachney Coal Co., 42
Easter Sugar House, 36
Easterhill estate, 40
Edinburgh, 6, 13, 96
Edington, Thomas, ironmaster and coalmaster, 40
Education, *see under* Merchants
Elderslie Coal Co., 40, 43
Elliot, Alexander, 188

INDEX

Elliot, David, 180
Endrick Printfield Co., 39
Episcopalians, 8–9, 25, 97

Factors, *see under* Storekeepers
Faculty of Advocates, 96
Fairlie, Ayrshire, 147
Falmouth, Virginia, 61, 83
Farmers General of the French Customs, 66–7, 83, 90, 107, 109, 164
Farquar Court House, 84
Findlay, Robert (1748–1802), 9, 21, 25, 74, 78, 164, 180, 188
Findlay, Hopkirks and Co., 75, 77, 79, 164, 188
Finlay, James and Co., cotton-spinners and merchants, 44, 51
Fish trade, 13, 127
Flaxseed trade, 13
Fleming, W. and J., coppersmiths, 64
Florida, 127
Forbes, Sir William of Pitsligo, 24
Foulis Academy, 9
France, 62, 64–5, 67, 68, 110, 132, 133, 146, 164
Fredericksburg, Virginia, 61, 83, 125
French agents, *see under*, Farmers General of the French Customs
'French price', 65, 83, 165
French, William (1732–1802), 7, 23, 42, 74, 115, 180, 187
Fullarton Coal Work, 43
Fullarton, Col. William, 20

Gartshore, John, 57
Georgetown, 164
Georgia, 127, 140
German states, 62, 65
Gilmour, Robert, 188
Glasgow, 6, 8, 13, 14, 18, 19, 20, 22, 23, 24, 25, 26, 37, 38, 40, 42, 48, 55, 56–7, 58, 60, 62, 63, 66, 67, 68, 72, 75, 77, 78, 79, 82, 86, 89, 90, 96, 103, 107, 109, 111, 114, 115, 119, 124, 125, 126, 128, 130, 131, 133, 138, 139, 141, 142, 144, 146, 153, 154, 157, 159, 161, 162, 164, 165, 166, 167, 171; rise of, v–vi; merchants, 4 (*see also under* Tobacco merchants); education, 8; cultural activity 9; luxury trades, 10–11; merchant houses, 11; industry, 34–48; tobacco firms, 72–80; capital market, 92–8; debt owed, 111–15, 153–9; bankruptcies, 115–19; attitude to American War, 124; population, 166; building companies, 167.
Glasgow Arms Bank, 13, 82, 93, 95
— Bottleworks, 38, 83
Glasgow Chamber of Commerce, and Manufactures, 153, 158
— *Courier*, 166
— *Journal*, 104
— *Mercury*, 141
— Ropework Co., 37
— Tanwork Co., 35, 46, 83
— Town Council, 143, 153, 166
— Trades House, 42
— University, 8, 26, 27, 46
Glassford family, 26, 27, 39, 111
Glassford, Henry, 25, 26, 39, 40, 181
Glassford, John (1715–83), 4, 6, 7, 9, 13, 27–8, 29–30, 39, 40, 66, 74, 76, 93, 111, 164, 181, 187
Glassford, John and Co., 47, 59, 60, 62, 65, 66, 74, 109, 115, 125, 155, 187
Glassford, Gordon and Co., 74, 76, 108
Glassford, Ingram and Co., 10, 65
Glassworks, 37–8, 75
Glenbuck Iron Co., 41
Gordon, James, 36, 37, 40, 74, 181, 187, 188
Gordon, James and Co., 74
Gordon, John, 36
Gordon, William, 181
Government stock, 97–8, 119, 144
Graham, John, 181
Graham, Liddell and Co., linen merchants, 39
Grant, Adam, dyer, 40
Gray family, 65
Gray, Gabriel, coalmaster, 42–3
Gray, John and William and Co., 65, 73, 111
Gray, William, 181
Greenock, v, 11, 37, 65, 73, 108, 129, 132, 133, 134, 139, 140, 142, 146, 161, 163
— Banking Company, 13
— Bottlework Company, 38
— Ropework Company, 38
— Sugar House, 36
Grindlay, Alexander, 181
Grindlay, Alexander and Co., 111

Haarlem, Holland, 38
Haarlem Linen and Dye Manufactory, 39
Habbakuk, Prof. H. J., 19
Halifax County, Virginia, 84
Hamburg, 110, 131
Hamilton Farm Coal Co., 43
Hamilton, Alexander, factor, 155
Hamilton, Archibald, sen., 181
Hamilton, Archibald, jun., 181
Hamilton, Francis and Co., tanners, 35
Hamilton, Prof. Henry, 43
Hamilton, John, 181
Hampden and Sydney College, Virginia, 126
Hanover County, Virginia, 57
Harley, William and Sons, builders, 167
Harrison and Van Bibber, merchants, 130
Harvie, Alexander, 38
Hastie, Robert, 181, 187, 188
Hastie, Corbett and Co., 188

INDEX

Havre de Grace, 68
Hay, Francis, storekeeper, 85
Hay, John, 181, 188
Hay, Peter, 188
Hemp trade, 13
Henderson, McCall and Co., 70, 74, 76, 187
Henderson, Alexander, storekeeper, 59
Henderson, Archibald, 181, 187
Henderson, Archibald and Co., 74, 76
Henry, Patrick, 162
Heritable bonds, 98
Herries, Messrs., 83
Herries, Sir Robert, 90, 109
Herring fishery, 146
Highland regiments, 132
Hodge Podge Club, 9
Holland, v, 38, 64, 65, 67, 91, 110, 146, 164, 165
Holland Manufactory Co., 39
Hopkirk family, 7, 164
Hopkirk, James (1749–1836), 21, 22, 23, 24, 36, 37, 91, 181, 187, 188
Hopkirk, Thomas I, 181
Hopkirk, Thomas II, 37, 40, 72, 91, 181, 188
Houston family, 27, 42
Houston, Alexander, 21, 36, 42, 93, 134, 181, 188
Houston, Alexander and Co., 22, 141, 144, 145, 146, 187
Houston, Andrew, 38, 43
Houston, Burns and Co., cotton spinners, 45
Houston, George and Co., cotton spinners, 45
Hunter, Rev. Robert, 8–9
Hutchesons Hospital, 42

Indentures, 83–4
Industry, 34–51, 62–4
Ingram, Archibald (1699–1770), 9, 10, 181
Ingram, James, 181
Ingram, William, 187
Inkle Factory (for manufacture of linen tapes), 38
Insurance, 72, 143–4
Ireland, 65, 132, 140, 147
Irish Sea, 138, 142
Iron industry, 40–1, 75
Irvine, 147

Jack, Paterson and Co., 167
Jamaica, 73, 132, 140, 143
James river, 64, 68, 83, 108
Jamieson, James, 76, 181, 187, 188
Jamieson, James and Co., 188
Jamieson, John, 73, 181
Jamieson, Neil, 37, 47, 62, 125, 126, 187
Jamieson, Johnstone and Co., 116
Jay's Treaty, 159

Jefferson, Thomas, 155, 156, 162
Johnstone, Joshua and Co., linen merchants, 39
Jordanhill estate, 24
Justices of the Peace, 25

Kelvinside estate, 18
Kilbarchan, Renfrewshire, 11
Kilbarchan Bleachfield Co., 39
Kilmarnock, 11
King's Inch estate, 30
King St., Sugar House, 36
Kippen, George (1737–85), 13, 37, 181, 187
Kippen, George and Co., 74, 76, 115, 155, 187
Kippen, Glassford and Co., 73
Knightswood Coal Co., 40, 43
Knox, John, 20, 141

Lainshaw estate, 21, 28
Lanarkshire, 18, 19, 21, 23, 24, 25, 28
Lancashire, 14
Largs, 147
Laurie, Capt. James, 134
Lawson, Semple and Co., 63–4, 90, 96, 113
Lawson, James, 9, 90, 96–7, 113, 181
Lawson, Robert, 9, 75, 97, 188
Leather industry, 35
Lee, William, 60
Leitch and Smith, West India merchants, 45, 51
Leitch, Andrew, 97
Leitch, John, West India merchant, 36, 186
Leith Sugar House, 145
Leith Walk Iron Foundry, 41
Lewiston, 62
Letter of Marque, 132
Lindsay, John, 18, 188
Linen industry, 39–40, 62–3, 68, 75
Linwood Mill Co., 45
Liquidate penalties, 97
Lisbon, 13
Literary Society of Glasgow, 9
Little Govan Coalworks, 43
Liverpool, 63, 65, 67, 75, 87, 90, 157, 165
Logan, George, 41, 188
Logan, Walter, iron merchant, 41
Logan, Gilmour and Co., 115
London, vi, 7, 44, 55, 57, 62–3, 65, 66, 75, 78, 89, 90, 104, 108, 110, 112, 125, 132, 139, 144, 157, 159, 165
'Lords, Tobacco', *see under* Merchants
Low, Alexander (?–1790), 182, 187
Loyalists, 154
Loyalist Commission, 116
Luke family, 74
Lumber trade, 62
Lunenberg County, Virginia, 124

Mackay, Robert, 45, 182, 188

Mackenzie, John, 41, 118
Mackie, Alexander, 182
Mackintosh, George, 39
Madeira, 13
Managing partners, 77
Manchester, 63
Manson, William and James, merchants in Rotterdam, 97
Markets, *see under* Tobacco and Linen
Marseilles, 128
Marshall, William, 22
Maryland, 9, 46, 57, 59, 64, 66, 77, 78, 104, 105, 109, 112, 113, 114, 116, 124, 127, 129, 153, 156, 162
Maxwell, Sir John, 93
Mecklenburg County, Virginia, 126
Mediterranean, 62
Merchants: Number of, 4; origins of, 5–8; mobility of, 6–8, 26–7; education, 8–10, 26; culture, 9; wealth, 10–11; building, 11; inter-marriage, 12; and land, 18–30, 172; and agricultural 'improvement', 27–30; politics, 24–5, 166; industrial investment, 34–51, 166–7; leather industry, 35; sugar industry, 35–7; rope industry, 37; iron industry, 37–8, 40–1; glass industry, 38; textiles, 38–40, 43–6; coal-mining, 40–3; price-fixing, 61; American debts, 59–60; partnerships, 72–80; trading organisation, 72–87; bankruptcies, 7–8, 115–20; West Indies trade, 11–12, 62, 129–131, 165–6; and the American War, 103–167.
Merchants House of Glasgow, 34
Millar, William, superintending factor, 57
Miller, William, jun., 182
Milliken, James, 182
Milngavie Factory Co., 39
Milton Printworks, 39
Mingay, Prof. Gordon, 19
Mitchell, Henry, 188
Monkland Canal, 23, 42, 172
Monro, John, 182
Morson, Alexander, 14
Monteith, James and Co., cotton spinners, 45
Monteath, Walter, 7, 35, 187
Montgomery, Adam, 90
Mount Vernon estate, 18
Muirkirk Iron Co., 37, 40, 41, 47
Mull of Kintyre, 139
Munro, Alexander, 182
Munro, John Spens, 188
Munro, George, iron merchant, 41
Murdoch family, 4, 6, 45, 82, 93
Murdoch, Dreghorn and Co., 65, 82
Murdoch, Warrock and Co., 38
Murdoch, George (1715–95), 37, 182
Murdoch, John, 57, 82, 182, 187, 188

Murdoch, Peter (1734–1817), 8, 37, 38, 82, 93, 182, 187, 188
Murdoch, Peter and Sons, 188
Mushet, David, 41
McBrayne, Stenhouse and Co., linen merchants and bleachers, 39
McCall, Dennistoun and Co., 125
McCall, Elliot and Co., 65, 66, 76, 80
McCall, Smellie and Co., 76, 118
McCall family, 26, 65, 72
McCall, Alexander, 155, 156, 187
McCall, George, 7, 182, 199
McCall, George and Co., 75, 76, 118, 188
McCall, James (1726–1803), 91, 182
McCall, John I, 91, 93, 182
McCall, John II, 182, 188
McCall, John and Co., 188
McCall, Samuel (1681–1759), 7, 182
McCauslan, Cpt., 147
McColl, Neil, 125
McDowall family, 25, 27, 30
McDowall, James, 37, 181, 188
McDowall, John, 65, 182, 188
McDowall, John and Co., 126
McDowall, William, 36, 45, 93
McFie, Thomas, 182
McGregor, James and Co., linen merchants and bleachers, 39
Mackenzie, John, 182
McNair, James, 42–3
McNair, Robert, 182

Napier, John of Napierston, 13
Navigation Acts, 146, 161
Navy Board, 131
New Jersey, 128
New Lanark Company, 44, 51
New Smithills Coalwork, 43
New York, 120, 125, 128, 129, 130, 131, 140, 144
Newark Sugar Refinery, 36
Newbigging, A. and J., textile merchants, 39
Newcastle, 63
Newfoundland, 128
Nisbet, Patrick, 182
Non-exportation agreements, 103, 104, 107
Non-importation agreements, 127
Norfolk, Virginia, 126
North Carolina, 64, 65, 130, 162
North Channel, 140
Northumberland County, Virginia, 125
Norton, John and Sons, London tobacco merchants, 67
Norway, 65
Nova Scotia, 127, 128

Occoquam, Virginia, 59
Omoa Ironworks, 41
Orr, Matthew, 188

INDEX

Ostend, 131
Oswald family, 4, 6, 13, 25, 72, 110
Oswald, Alexander I (?–1786), 182
Oswald, Alexander II (1738–1813), 24, 36, 45, 182, 188
Oswald, George (1735–1819), 24, 30, 36, 182
Oswald, George and Co., 63–4, 65, 76, 111, 188
Oswald, James, 36, 45, 182, 188
Oswald, Richard, 13, 107, 154, 182
Oughton, Sir Adolphus, Commander-in-Chief, Scotland, 142

Pailjour, Robert, 188
Paisley, 6, 11, 43, 46
Paris, 154
Partnerships, 72–9, 187–8
Payne, Edward and Réné, 108, 125
Petersburg, Virginia, 26, 83, 164
Philadelphia, 125, 128, 138, 165
Planking, 13
Pollock, Lady, 13
Pollockshaws Printfield Co., 39, 46, 64, 83
Port Glasgow, v, 3, 11, 37, 65, 73, 108, 109, 110, 129, 133, 139, 140, 141, 142, 161, 162, 163, 164
— Ropework Co., 37
— Sugar House, 36, 83
Potash trade, 127
Potomac river, 56, 77, 83, 105
Press gang, 147
Prestonpans Vitriol Co., 39–40
Price, Bennet, storekeeper, 84–5
Price, Prof. Jacob M., vi, 64, 79, 92, 138
Privateering, 120, 132–4, 138–43
Provision trade, 62

Quebec, 127, 128

Ramsay, Andrew I (1688–1754), 183
Ramsay, Andrew II (1729–1775), 183
Ramsay, Monteath and Company, 65, 111
Rappahannock river, 68, 83
Register of Sasines, 18
Reid, Charles, 183
Reid, Robert, Glasgow historian, 115
Reid, Prof. Thomas, 9, 11
Reid, Thomas, factor, 125
Renfrew, John and Company, linen bleachers, 39
Renfrewshire, 19, 21, 23, 24, 25, 27, 29, 111
Renfrewshire Banking Company, 13
Reynolds, Monteath and Company, cotton-spinners, 45
Rice trade, 13
Richmond, Virginia, 70, 83, 126, 164
Riddell, Henry, 7, 9, 74, 183, 187
Riddell, John, 7, 155, 183, 188
Ritchie family, 4, 6, 18, 26, 27

Ritchie, Alexander, 187
Ritchie, Henry (?–1792), 29, 36, 37, 118, 183
Ritchie, James (1722–1799), 18, 24, 25, 37, 93, 128, 183
Ritchie, John, 18, 183
Ritchie, J. and H. and Co., 65, 125, 127, 128, 131, 155, 164
Robertson, Andrew, 45
Robertson, James, 45, 183
Robertson, John, 40, 45, 183, 188
Robertson, Robert, 94
Robertson, William, 188
Robinson, James, 82–7, 105, 187
Rockeyridge, Virginia, 84
Rodney, Admiral, 130
Rotterdam, 3, 68, 97, 110
Rowan, James (?–1754), 183, 188
Rowan, John, 183
Royal Bank of Scotland, 96
Royal Navy, 128, 130, 140, 143, 146
Rumney, John and Company, 41
Running ships, 145–6
Russell, David (1747–?), 36, 97, 183, 188
Russell, James, commissary clerk, 97
Russia, 62
Rutherglen Muir Coal Company, 43

Sacred Music Institution, Glasgow, 9
Saltcoats, 147
Sandyhill estate, 29
Sandyhill Coal Work, 43
Saratoga, battle of, 107
Scots Magazine, 104, 110, 142
Scotstoun estate, 24
Scott, Allan, 183
Scott, Joseph, 183, 187
Semple, John, 183
'Senex', (J. M. Reid), 116–117
Seven Years War, 139
Shaw, Sir John, 13
Shedden, Robert, merchant, 106
Shelbourne, Lord, 154
Ship Bank, 13, 93, 95
Shipbuilding, 62
Ships: *Albion*, 125, 128; *H.M.S. Arethusa*, 139; *Blandford*, 3, 68, 109; *Boyd*, 57; *Brittannia*, 145; *Castlesemple*, 141; *Catherine*, 140; *Charming Fanny*, 142; *Cochrane*, 68, 86, 133, 134; *Cunninghame*, 86; *Dolphin*, 140; *Elizabeth*, 134; *Endeavour*, 133; *Enterprise*, 133; *Hanover*, 145; *Hasard*, 134; *Janet Laurie*, 144; *Janett*, 86; *Juno*, 141; *Jupiter*, 141; *Katie*, 142; *London*, 140; *Margaret*, 86; *Neptune*, 86; *Ocean*, 86; *Reprisal*, 140; *Robert*, 141; *Sally*, 134, 140; *Satisfaction*, 139, 140; *Sharp*, 141; *H.M.S. Seaford*, 140; *Success*, 163; *Ulysses*, 142; *Venus*, 86, 140
Shortridge, William, 187

Shotts Iron Company, 23, 41
Shuttlefield Factory Company, 39
Silvercraigs Weaving Factory Company, 39
Simson, James, 8
Simson, James, merchant, 183
Simson, Robert, 8
Slave trade, 62
Slaves, 59
Smellie, Archibald, 22, 40, 118, 183, 188
Smellie, Richard, 118, 183, 188
Smith, Adam, 8, 9, 27
Smithfield Iron Co., 37, 41, 46
Smout, Prof. T. C., 19
Smuggling, vi
Snodgrass-McCall syndicate, 74, 188
Snodgrass, William (?–1815), 65, 183, 188
Soltow, J. H., vi, 87, 92
Somervell, James (?–1791), 8, 14, 37, 166, 183
South America, 61
South Carolina, 13, 156, 162
South Sugar House Co., 36
Spain, 62
Speirs family, 25, 30, 45
Speirs, Bowman and Co., 65, 73, 76, 92, 108, 110, 126, 187
Speirs, French and Co., 65, 73, 86, 77, 104, 110, 131, 133, 155, 187
Speirs, Alexander (1714–1782), 4, 6, 7, 10–11, 14, 21, 23, 26, 30, 35, 36, 37, 40, 74, 92–3, 111, 115, 164, 183, 187
Speirs, Archibald, 13, 23, 40, 183
Speirs, Peter, 8, 26, 183
Speirs, Martha, 92
Spinningdale Cotton Co., 45
Spreull, Somervell and Co., linen merchants, 39
Spreull, James (1699–1769), 183
Sproule, Andrew, 106
St. Andrews Church-by-the Green, 25
St. Croix, 130, 144
St. Eustatius, 130, 131
St. Kitts, 39, 144
St. Thomas 130
St. George's Channel 140
Stamp act 103, 111
Stewart, George, Glasgow historian, 115
Stirling, Alexander, 183
Stirling, Andrew, 42
Stirling, John, 39
Stirling, Walter, 39, 183, 188
Stirling, William and Sons, printers and bleachers, 39
Stirling's library, Glasgow, 11
Stirlingshire, 18, 19, 21, 23, 26, 111
Stockholm, 90
Store system, 55–9, 66–7, 108, 112
Storekeepers, 75, 77, 83–5, 165
Sugarhouses. 35–7

Sugar House Co. of Port Glasgow, 36
Sugar industry, 35–7, 75
Sugar trade, 13, 143, 165
Sun Fire Office, 44
Supercargoes, 56
Supreme Court of the United States, 155, 159
Sydney, Viscount, 158
Sym, Andrew, 183

Team Ironworks, Newcastle, 41
Thistle Bank, Glasgow, 13, 93, 95
Thomson, Alexander, 183
Thomson, Andrew, 183, 188
Thomson, John, 184
Thomson, Snodgrass and Co., 76, 188
Timber trade, 127
Tobacco: Scottish imports, v, 73; types, 64, 110; prices, 109–111, 127; source of imports, 129, 161; markets, vi, 64–8,107, 110–11, 129–30; glut, 107; see also under Merchants and Tobacco Trade.
Tobacco merchants, see under Merchants
Tobacco trade: costs, 3–4, 59, 60, 89, 107, 108, 111; expansion, v–vi, 6; profits, 10–11; unprofitability, 11–13; industrial supply for, 46, 61–64; and Scottish industrial development, 34–48, 165–6; customs duties, 3, 15; early trading methods in, 56–7; debts, 59–60, 111–5, 153–9; competition, 60–1; price-fixing, 6–11; Scottish advantages in, 66–8; companies, 172–80, 82–8; concentration in, 73–7; sources of capital, 89–98, 108; bankruptcies, 7–8, 115–20; during the American War, 124–47; after the American War, 161–6; from Charlestown, 128; from New York, 128; from Philadelphia, 128; from West Indies, 130–1; See also under Consignment system, Store system, Merchants and Tobacco.
Transport Service, 131–2
Treaty of Paris, 156, 159
Treaty of Union of 1707, v, 35, 62
Turner, John, storekeeper, 84
Turpentine trade, 13

United States of America, 62, 156, 161, 162, 164, 165

Verreville Glass Manufactory, 38
Virginia, vi, 3, 7, 9, 10, 13, 21, 39, 46, 56, 57, 59, 60, 61, 64, 65, 68, 72–3, 74, 78, 82–3, 94, 103, 104, 107, 109, 112, 114, 115, 124, 126, 127, 129, 138, 153, 155, 156, 158, 162, 164
Virginia Assembly, 126, 157
Virginia Convention. 124

Virginia Council, 153
Virginia State Loan Office, 157
Walker, David, storekeeper, 77
Wallace, Hugh, 184
Wallace, John, 24
Wallace, Thomas (?–1760), 36, 184
Wallace, William, 184
Wardrop, James (?–1799), 184, 188
Wardrop, John, 184
Washington, George, 107
West Florida, 127
West Indies, 13, 18, 62, 120, 130, 133, 134, 138, 140, 143–4, 144, 145, 147, 155, 165
Wester Sugar House, 36
Western Fencibles, 142
Wheat trade, 13, 62
Whithaven, v, 67, 75, 157, 173
Whitehill estate, 24
Wight, Andrew, 29–30

Williamsburg, Virginia, 60
Wilson, John, iron merchant, 41
Wilson, John I (1693–1763), 184
Wilson, John II, 184
Wilson, Robert, iron merchant, 41
Wilson, William, iron merchant, 41
Wilson Brown and Company, 115–6
Wilsontown Ironworks, 41
Wine trade, 13, 62
Wylie and Mackenzie and Company, 116
Wylie, Hugh (?–1782), 7, 35, 116, 118, 139, 140, 184

Yoker and Blawarthill estate, 23
York Buildings Company, 20
Yorktown, Virginia, 58
Young and Trotter, calico printers, 64
Yuille, George, 184